The
Great Escape
Manual

The Great Escape Manual

A Spirituality of Liberation

Edward Hays

Forest of Peace
Publishing
Leavenworth, KS

Other Books by the Author:
(available through Forest of Peace Publishing or your favorite bookstore)

Prayers and Rituals

Psalms for Zero Gravity
Prayers for a Planetary Pilgrim
Prayers for the Domestic Church
Prayers for the Servants of God

Parables and Stories

Little Orphan Angela
The Gospel of Gabriel
The Quest for the Flaming Pearl
St. George and the Dragon
The Magic Lantern
The Ethiopian Tattoo Shop
Twelve and One-Half Keys
Sundancer
The Christmas Eve Storyteller

Contemporary Spirituality

The Ladder
The Old Hermit's Almanac
The Lenten Labyrinth
A Lenten Hobo Honeymoon
Holy Fools & Mad Hatters
A Pilgrim's Almanac
Pray All Ways
Secular Sanctity
In Pursuit of the Great White Rabbit
The Ascent of the Mountain of God
Feathers on the Wind

The Great Escape Manual

copyright © 2001, by Edward M. Hays

Library of Congress Cataloging-in-Publication Data

Hays, Edward M.
    The great escape manual : a spirituality of liberation / Edward Hays.
       p. cm.
    Includes bibliographical references.
    ISBN 0-939516-56-X (pbk.)
    1. Spiritual life—Christianity. I. Title.
  BV4501.3 .H395 2001
  248—dc21   2001053211

published by
Forest of Peace Publishing, Inc.
PO Box 269
Leavenworth, KS 66048-0269   USA
1-800-659-3227
www.forestofpeace.com

printed by
Hall Commercial Printing
Topeka, KS 66608-0007

1st printing: September 2001

This book is dedicated
in the memory of

Gerald Hanus

March 14, 1946 – April 12, 1994

Before cancer prematurely ended his life,
this good friend lived each day daringly,
at top velocity, with a vibrant enjoyment and zestfulness,
in a lifestyle of freedom.

Author's Acknowledgment of Gratitude

I wish to thank my two editors for their efforts toward publishing this book in the spirit of liberty.

My longtime manuscript-editor Thomas Skorupa had the difficult task of ironing out my Haysian English so the text would flow smoothly, as well as extending to me the freedom to express my different theological opinions. A good editor is often like a vegetarian skillfully grilling to perfection a large steak for a non-vegetarian friend. I've often wondered if the editors and publishers of some books bearing their names wish to include the disclaimer frequently heard at the conclusion of radio talk shows: "The opinions and views expressed are not those of this radio station or its sponsors."

I especially thank my editor-publisher Thomas Turkle for his gift of the Freedom of the Press. He gave me complete liberty to express my theological ideas about the Revolutionary Liberator Jesus, an incarnational spirituality and the cosmically expansive Reign of God. In addition, since the author takes an almost sinful delight in being a non-E-mail hermit-recluse, his publisher is left with the task of responding to the feedback of readers.

I also thank Darren Henson, who was instrumental in the creation of this book. In his excellent theology paper, *Christological Issues Involved in the Christian Idea and Doctrine of God,* he aptly dealt with Jesus as liberator, and it encouraged me to undertake the writing of this book.

Finally, I am extravagantly grateful to the Spirit of God for being the source of any personal creativity, and especially for guiding me into the significant ministry of being a prison chaplain. Struggling to proclaim the Good News to those "inside the walls," I realized the overwhelming implications of Jesus' words that his work was to "set the prisoners free." This reality, united to the fact that only a microscopic percentage of the world's prisoners are *literally* behind prison walls, inspired the writing of *The Great Escape Manual.*

Table of Contents

The Crime of Kidnapping

Kidnapping is a shameful deed. It is my ardent wish to be free of the criminal act of plagiarism. Plagiarism is the crime of stealing another's ideas and words and using them as your own. The term comes from *plagiarius*, Latin for "kidnapping." Original ideas and concepts belong to creative persons as their thought-children. Those inspiring thoughts that we frequently quote in conversation or correspondence become our adopted children. This is especially true of those thoughts that mirror our personal hopes and ideals. With time the names of their parents are easily forgotten.

In this book I will attempt to give credit to those authors whose major ideas and words have influenced this book. I ask you the reader not to view my desire to give credit merely as a clever ploy for the pretentiousness of name-dropping.

I acknowledge with gratitude those authors and teachers whose thoughts and insights have influenced and inspired me throughout my life. However, after seven decades of instruction, the original sources of large portions of my knowledge are all too often forgotten. So, I also wish to thank all the unacknowledged parents of my adopted thought-children who appear in this book.

End of Chapter Inventory of Escape Tools and Unshackling Reflections

Liberation should be a reality, not simply a longing or an intellectual ideal. To assist you in becoming free of the various forms of incarceration addressed in this book, you will find at the end of each chapter a section called the Inventory of Escape Tools and Unshackling Reflections. This section contains various aids, tools and techniques for the art and spirituality of escaping, including quotations dealing with the theme of the chapter, diverse freeing devices and exercises, prayers for escapees, questions for pondering, parables and stories.

The Option of a Personal Index

Since each of the chapters of this book deals with specific issues, such as anger, fear, old age and death, a detailed alphabetical index is not included in this book.

However, whenever reading a book, one often finds significant passages or memorable ideas that one would like to return to later. The publisher has, therefore, intentionally left the last few pages of this book blank so that the individual reader might list subjects and page numbers of passages that are personally meaningful.

Naked and alone we came into exile. In her dark womb we did not know our mother's face; from the prison of her flesh have we come into the unspeakable and incommunicable prison of this earth. Which of us has not remained forever prison-pent?
— Thomas Wolfe, *Look Homeward Angel*

The Beginning

Are You Free?

As you begin to read the first page of this book, assess whether you feel imprisoned, trapped or held in bondage by something. If so, then it's only natural to want to find a way to escape from that bondage. The first thing you might want to free yourself from is the habitual restraint of feeling you have to read a book from the front to the back. The author gives you permission to skip over the beginning chapters and turn right now to the section that deals with whatever is most imprisoning you at this time. Perhaps it is anger, fear, your job or that most popular prison — the clock. These and other possible imprisoning conditions are listed in the table of contents. Be at liberty to return to this book's listing of chapters found on page 7.

TWO MILLION PLUS IMPRISONED

Do you feel imprisoned? If you do, don't feel ashamed. Today, over two million people are incarcerated in the United States, a greater proportion of imprisoned persons than in any other nation in the world!

However, that staggeringly large prison population is only a small percentage of the actual uncounted millions who are imprisoned! Of these many millions of prisoners, some are serving short sentences, others have been imprisoned for several years, and still others are serving life sentences in:

> the Prison of Poverty
> the Prison of a Poor Education
> the Prison of Racial, Ethnic and Sexual Prejudice
> the Prison of an Unhappy Marriage
> the Prison of a Meaningless, Boring Job
> the Prison of Fear and Loneliness
> the Prison of Anger and Revenge
> the Prison of Frustration and Despair
> the Prison of Religion
> the Prison of Aging and the Fear of Dying

At one point or another, those who are oppressed naturally yearn for a liberator to come and set them free. The Israelites enslaved in ancient Egypt symbolize all of us who feel overwhelmed by the power and might of oppressors and who feel powerless to escape by ourselves. The songs and prayers of oppressed peoples throughout history give poignant voice to our corporate longing for a liberator.

Welcome news! Your liberator has come! For you and everyone yearning to escape from the hundreds of millions of prisons with invisible walls, Jesus the Liberator announces his good news: "My work is to set the prisoners free."[1]

THE GREAT LIBERATOR

Jesus of Galilee stunned his family by those words. They and their neighbors were shocked when right in their village synagogue he applied the words of Isaiah directly to himself, "The Spirit of the Lord is upon me to bring good news to the poor...to proclaim liberty to captives...and to set the prisoners free."[1] His stunned listeners recovered from their initial shock and responded to him with resentful rejection. The vast majority of those in today's Western world, however, respond to his offer of liberty not with angry rejection, but with a yawn. They feel his offer for liberation is not addressed to them. "We are not prisoners in some penitentiary! He's not speaking to me."

This announcement of liberation in Jesus' inaugural address that echoed the words of Isaiah should raise at least two questions. The first is: Am I a prisoner? If the answer is yes, then you might next ask yourself: What is my prison or, perhaps, my prisons? The natural response of those of us with a religious upbringing is to believe Jesus is simply talking about setting us free from sin. Indeed, sin can imprison us, but the prisons that incarcerate hundreds of millions are not just a result of original sin or our unoriginal violations of the Ten Commandments.

Jesus the Liberator holds out no magical key to unlock your cell door. He promises no miracle angel to lead you out an easy escape tunnel. Yet Jesus does offer us an escape route: "Come, follow me."[2] Those three words of invitation by history's greatest escaped prisoner are without doubt his most challenging. Many of us eager for instant release from our imprisonment quickly arise to follow him when he says, "Come to me, all you who labor and are heavy burdened, and I will give you rest."[3] However, we need to hear the rest of his message: If you're really going to follow me, then deny your very self,[4] take up all your burdens — and transform them. Don't follow me as your liberator unless you are willing to embrace the hard labor of escaping.

Resist the ancient temptation of waiting for some liberator to arrive or something miraculous to come your way and suddenly set you free. No quick fix, no winning lottery ticket, no accident of fate is going to break the chains of your captivity. You must take personal responsibility for your own life and your actions. Since this is a fundamental reality of life, how then does the Great Liberator set us free?

Jesus is our Savior. All Christians agree on that. However, Jesus is more than a savior in the traditional sense. Years of religious development have conditioned us to equate being saved exclusively with getting to heaven. Yet the original Hebrew Old Testament word for salvation was used in a very different sense. It meant freedom: the well-being or security gained by the removal of some constriction or confinement. Isaiah used the term *salvation* to refer to liberation from any evil, personal or communal. Scripture scholar John McKenzie says that while the Scriptural use of salvation is synonymous with liberation, it also includes the broader vista of a new revelation about the nature of God. As such, it implies entering a new world.[5] Those two broader implications of salvation — a new image of God and a new world — are contained within the message of the Great Liberator, Jesus.

Time Out!

If you are feeling restless and are finding it difficult to stay engaged while reading this material, the reason could be that you are a prisoner of the clock. Don't be ashamed. Most of us in this hectic, hurried world lack leisure time for reading. Being inmates of Timelock Prison, (which is the subject of Chapter Three, pages 32-54), we are eager to get to the bottom line, the heart of the matter, the essence of the information, as quickly as possible.

Aware that many readers are eager to deal with those things that hold them hostage, I have summarized the first two chapters. I have moved the complete text of these two chapters to the appendix of this book. These chapters comprise the foundation of this book. The first chapter gives a theological and Scriptural understanding of Jesus of Galilee as Liberator. The second chapter contains a definition of spirituality, toward an understanding of a liberation spirituality and reflections on holiness and various types of prayer.

If you now have the freedom and time to read these first two chapters, you will find the complete version in the appendixes of this book. For you who lack that leisure, the following two chapter summaries will provide a helpful framework for reading the rest of this book. If you choose this approach, you can read the important information included in the whole text of these first two chapters when you do have the time.

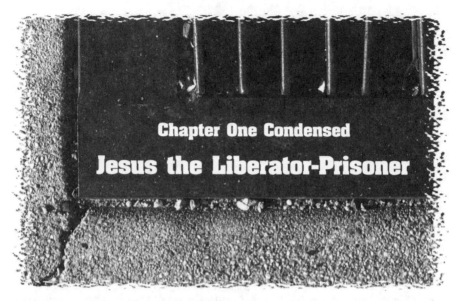

Chapter One Condensed
Jesus the Liberator-Prisoner

For Jesus, redemption was a lifestyle; it was fully part of the fabric of his life. His whole life was redeeming, and not just his death. We are thus redeemed by Jesus' parable stories, by his new code of morality defined by the primacy of love over law, by his association with outcasts and sinners, by his challenging of the religious rituals of his day. Viewing redemption in this way liberates the reality of redemption, exploding it outward beyond those last three hours of dying on the cross. The entire daily lifestyle of Jesus of Galilee is an invitation to live a redemptive-freeing life. That pattern of living was marked not only by his loving, sacrificial death but by all of his life and his whole humanity.

At the same time, St. Paul tells us that Jesus was like us in all things but sin,[1] which, then, implies he was a prisoner. In fact, his imprisonment was essential for the saving-liberating work of God. For how can you show others the way to escape unless you yourself have been a prisoner?

From his birth onward Jesus was imprisoned by hundreds of religious laws and ritual requirements of his Jewish religion. He would have been incarcerated by his cultural conditioning about the proper place and role of women in Galilean society and by legions of social restrictions and ancient taboos.

The Gospels are stories of the man from Nazareth escaping from prison after prison — and calling others to follow him. His life is a heroic story of an escapee who was able to break out of the innumerable prisons in which society raised him until his final great liberation by God from the most secure of all earth's prisons — death and the tomb.

Indeed, Jesus' message was radical and life-changing right from the start. After his baptism Jesus ended years of silence and began to proclaim the Gospel of God. The theme of his teaching was, "This is the time of fulfillment. The Kingdom of God is at hand. Repent, and believe the good news."[2]

THE KINGDOM

"Kingdom" is a restraining, if not extinct, term. In this twenty-first century very few kingdoms still exist other than in fairy tales. Yet the Kingdom of God is an expression whose meaning is rarely ever revised in a language of today's world. Perhaps we could consider experimenting with reinterpreting the Kingdom of God as "The New Era" or "The New Time Zone of God." It's not only a new day — a whole new way of being has arrived. It's a zone in which all clocks have moved ahead to God's New Time, a time both radically real and different.

To give a razor sharp edge to the "Kingdom of God," we might place in front of it the adjective *united*. The United Kingdom of God would suggest the inclusive implications of the New Era announced by Jesus. Traditional religions are often exclusive, whereas God is inclusive. "God's United Kingdom" would express the inclusive attitude and lifestyle of the Redeemer of Nazareth.

American priest-theologian Robert Barron uses another intriguing name for the Kingdom of God: "the Enchanted Universe."[3] This concept expands the Mystery beyond the confines of earth and out into the rest of creation, into the whole cosmos. For Barron, God's United Enchanted Universe is not a mythical construct, it's at the heart of reality.

Living in the Enchanted United Cosmos is joyful, jubilant and exhilarating. Sadly, most of us live our daily existence in another place, as inmates in the Prison of Unreality: We dwell in a fractured, divided world and, unfortunately, in a fragmented church. To escape imprisonment from an estranged and disunited existence in order to cross over and reside in the United Enchanted Universe requires, as

Jesus said, two actions: repenting and believing. The first half of the Great Liberator's equation implies the necessity for escaping. This need "to repent" can be simply expressed in a single statement: Before you can get in, you have to get out. You must get out of the old divided world before you can enter the new united world, must abandon the old you before you can become a new you. Each of us needs to "repent," to undergo a change of heart and mind.

THE GOSPEL OF LIBERATION

Embracing as your lifestyle the liberating lifestyle of Jesus is an evolutionary step forward. He is, indeed, an evolutionary Emmanuel. At around thirty years old, a very mature age for his day, Jesus began actively living out the Gospel of God in his human flesh. One great step for Jesus produced the next great evolutionary step for humanity. His announcement that the time of fulfillment had arrived proclaimed that it was time to grow up! The evolution of humanity required following his example of becoming a fully mature human being. In the process, Jesus showed us how to escape the prison of merely being human to become Godlike.

That very same Gospel of God, which Jesus enfleshed and went about proclaiming, is seeded in your flesh and body! Follow him, and so dare to live as fully as you can God's enfleshment in you. This is truly good news for those daring enough to live out a spirituality of liberation.

Chapter One Inventory of Escape Tools and Unshackling Reflections

FOLLOW THE LEADER

Jesus said, "Come, follow me."[4] This quotation from the Great Escape Manual of the Gospels gives us the greatest encouragement, for our Liberator has fully walked the path of freedom. Yet as attractive as Jesus' invitation is, it is also the greatest challenge. A Spanish proverb captures the danger of such a walk: "It's not the same to talk about the bulls as it is to be in the bull ring."

The Army teaches its young combat lieutenants who are to be the leaders of their troops to give the toughest of all commands: "Follow me." Similarly, Henry Kissinger identified the role of real leadership when he said, "The task of the leader is to get his people from where they are to where they have not been." Jesus is always ready to take us along the next unexpected stretch of our road to liberation.

ARE YOU A PRISONER?

Do not skip this important beginning exercise.

Take a few minutes to explore the landscape of your life. What is holding you imprisoned: a negative habit, some addiction, fear, emotion or attitude, some resentment, prejudice or religious constraint? Is it a past event or an ongoing situation?

This is an extremely important examination since being aware that you are a prisoner is absolutely essential to escaping. Only prisoners seek to escape. While rejoicing in your liberty as a citizen of a free country, be honest as you carefully examine your life for what may be imprisoning you.

You may be in more than one prison. Don't worry or feel ashamed if you find you're in several; it's very common. If you are, it's wise not to attempt one grand exodus-escape. Rather, begin by selecting one form of confinement from which you wish to be freed and proceed with patience. You may find that a little early success creates a domino effect so that one prison after another falls in the momentum.

ESCAPE TOOL #1 — BLOW UP YOUR PRISON

One strategy for escaping your prison is playfully exaggerating whatever holds you captive. Make it bigger than life. If, for example, you're a prisoner in Nicotine Prison, you might see yourself imprisoned inside the tall white tower of a giant cigarette smokestack that's belching stinking gray smoke. Now playfully begin to plot your escape from captivity through the chimney.

ESCAPE TOOL #2 — THE "BE POSITIVE" CROWBAR

Never be negative. In your efforts to become free, avoid the use of negatives like, "I want to stop smoking cigarettes" or "I will not eat chocolate." The mind loves pictures and will seize upon the visual image of you smoking a cigarette or eating a piece of chocolate. Using both the name of your prison and a mental image of it will only serve to reinforce the addiction. Want to escape? Try expressing your desire for freedom and for clear lungs by saying, "I wish to be free to breathe in only fresh air"; in the process, visualize yourself inhaling refreshing springtime air. Find similar positive images and verbal reinforcement for other addictions and bad habits.

A BRIEF DAILY PRAYER TO ENCOURAGE LIBERATION

O Jesus, my Liberator,
help me to seek today
to live in the glorious freedom
of the children of God.

A CRUCIFIX PRAYER

I look upon you, my Savior-Liberator,
not as crucified to your ugly cross,
but as hanging on for dear love.

May love nail me firmly alongside you,

securing me in loving loyalty,
regardless of the pain.

From all merely human boundaries
set me free to love without conditions
to the very end.

A Meditation Reflection on
the Canticle of Zechariah

Zechariah's hope-saturated song is prayed each morning as part of the church's official morning prayer. Because Zechariah doubted the Archangel Gabriel's news that he and his wife Elizabeth, being senior citizens, would conceive and give birth to a child, his tongue was imprisoned in silence. At the moment during the circumcision when the child was named John, Zechariah's tongue was paroled and he sang prophetically about the dawn of a Holy Independence Day of Liberation.

More than our tongues are immobilized by our doubts; our hearts are just as easily paralyzed. We become oppressed peoples dressed in hopelessness when we fail to believe in news too good to be true. Zechariah's song is concentrated energy for all those imprisoned by impotent imaginations and by the narrow horizons of their present circumstances. Greeting each sunrise with his Fourth of July prayer can feed your longing for freedom and can inspire you to escape from whatever imprisons you. Here is a contemporary form of Zechariah's prayer at the dawning of a New Time Zone:

A New Millennium Canticle of Zechariah

Blessed be God who visits us today
to set us free from our enemies:
hate, war, prejudice and greed,
from our bondage to work,
from our slavery to success
and from always having to be right.

May this new day see the fulfillment
of God's eternal promise of liberty,
a promise given again and again
from generation to generation
and fulfilled by those
brave enough to believe it.

This dawn banishes the darkness
of dungeon fears and apathy
and the gloom of self-doubts,
and calls us to live this day
in the glorious freedom
of the children of God.

A new day has dawned on all the imprisoned,
God's sunrise of liberating love,
by which we may escape our sins,
our human mistakes and failings.

THE GOSPEL OF FREEDOM

Joseph Cardinal Ratzinger's *Instruction On Certain Aspects of the "Theology of Liberation,"* the 1984 instruction from the Congregation for the Doctrine of the Faith, contains these words of hope:

The Gospel of Jesus Christ is a message of freedom and a force for liberation. In recent years this essential truth has become the object of reflection for theologians with a new kind of attention which is itself full of promise....[5]

The following quotes from that instruction are also worthy of reflection:

"The powerful and almost irresistible aspiration that people have for liberation constitutes one of the principle signs of the times which the church has to examine and interpret in the light of the Gospels" (from the Second Vatican Council's document *Gaudium et Spes).*

The aspiration for liberation, as the term suggests, repeats a theme which is fundamental to the Old and New Testaments. In itself, the expression "theology of liberation" is a thoroughly valid term. It designates a theological reflection centered on the biblical theme of liberation and freedom, and on the urgency of its practical realization....

Christ, our liberator, has freed us from sin and from slavery to the law....

God is recognized as the liberator....[6]

Chapter Two Condensed

A Spirituality of Liberation

Spirituality is usually defined in terms of exercises for nourishment of the soul: prayer, meditation, acts of asceticism, devotions and religious reading. However, I'd like to propose a definition that liberates and expands that one-dimensional understanding: A spirituality is a lifestyle flowing out of your beliefs.

Everyone has a spirituality or lifestyle that revolves around some core belief. What's yours? Do you desire a truly transforming, liberating spirituality that will inject zest and happiness into your life, one that will enrich you today and create vital, abundant tomorrows into infinity? If you do, consider a lifestyle, a spirituality, of liberation with this core-organizing belief:

> I believe God is enfleshed in my body
> and is revealed by my every action.
> I believe I live in the midst of
> the unfolding Reign of God,
> which envelops me and all creation.

Prayer was critical in the lifestyle of Jesus, and so it should have a central place in the daily life of anyone who seeks to follow him. In his prayer life he frequently "excommunicated" himself, going off in solitude to be in intimate prayer. Especially in our hectic, noisy world, we need to follow his example. Yet we don't need a desert; to quote Belden Lane, we only need "to stay in one place and be still."[1]

Prayer is not an optional exercise for those longing to be free. Indeed, praying daily is critical for our liberation. The command of our Savior-Liberator, "Watch and pray,"[2] is imperative for recognizing escape routes from what imprisons us. As St. Paul added, we are never to cease using the great escape tool of prayer if we wish to enjoy the "glorious freedom of the children of God."[3]

Besides being ceaseless, the prayer of a liberating spirituality is lifelong. Life is a continual process of maturing and growing toward the glorious freedom of the people of God. A frequently recycled heresy says that salvation-liberation can be achieved by a single act, whether accepting Jesus as one's savior or receiving baptism. As significant as those initial experiences are, they only begin the process. Salvation-liberation, like your finger- and toe-nails, grows continuously. Unlike your fingernails, however, it does not grow effortlessly. Liberation requires focused attention and personal work to mature. It's a lifelong process of escaping until you break out of the wrinkled prisons of declining aging and finally from the dungeon of death.

Whenever we are open-eyed to God's presence, we are praying. So practice being open-eyed, faithful to the Liberator's call, "Watch and pray." This watching is looking for and acknowledging the presence of the Divine Mystery cleverly camouflaged as the common. Such ceaseless praying is a constant act of consecration since it makes every aspect of life holy.

HOLINESS

A saint is another name for an escaped prisoner. Multimillionaires and billionaires are products of a lifestyle revolving around the core belief that money is the most important thing in life. When lived with passion and dedication, that belief often produces a very wealthy person. A saint is the product of a lifestyle lived with passion around a core belief in the Enchanted United Kingdom of God.

Saint is one of those words that sticks in our throats. Most people would be too embarrassed to designate sainthood as their destination in life. Yet Leon Bloy, a French author of the twentieth century, said,

"The greatest sadness is not to become a saint."[4] The purpose of any spirituality is to create a saint, a Godlike person, one who is holy. As with prayer, becoming a saint is not an option. Indeed, God, in the book of Leviticus, commands us to be holy as God is holy.[5]

Holiness involves living and acting in a Godlike way, and so that high attainment to which each of us is called may sound totally out of reach — or at least a long and difficult process. As a result, few of us seriously consider striving for such a seemingly inaccessible goal. Holiness, we conclude, is an elite state reserved for a select few, best left to the religious aristocracy, while simply getting to heaven is the goal for common folk.

Yet God says to everyone, "Be holy as I your God am holy," and that command is neither impossible nor optional. The Holy was embodied in the full humanity of Jesus to show to us what is expected in each of us and what is possible with enough grace and desire. Holiness does not require separation from the world but, rather, to act like God and be fully engaged in this world. If part of our core belief is that God is enfleshed in our body and our whole world, then we understand that the widest path to holiness is located in our daily duties and the ordinary activities of our lives.

The fourteenth century German mystic Meister Eckhart gave a simple prescription for becoming holy: "Do the next thing you have to do with your whole heart and find delight in doing it."[6] This way is easy to remember but extremely difficult to practice. Yet following the mystic Eckhart's simple formula is another way to pray ceaselessly. Doing everything with all our heart and soul and enjoying it as much as we can is an effective way for the desire for holiness to saturate the very fabric of our lives.

Saints are those who open themselves fully to the Divine Reality and then fill every task with all of themselves. Saints strive to enjoy — to have fun — doing everything. Saints do everything with passion. Ultimately, saints are escaped prisoners freed from a whole range of vain and shallow pursuits, from greed, gluttony, self-preoccupation, idle chatter, busyness and even the need to be useful. Saints are freed to live the abundant, fruitful, enchanting life of the Kingdom of God.

Perhaps a lifestyle of liberation requires only the courage to organize our daily life around the belief that the Time of God has arrived at our doorstep. A liberation spirituality not only promotes an attitude of ceaseless prayer, it may also carefully cultivate organized times and forms of prayer till they become more and more frequent, if not ceaseless. By such daily structured times of prayer and spiritual nourishment, we can evolve into holiness; we can grow naturally toward a fully developed prayer life. In any case, holiness is not a supernatural state, it is but the original natural and liberated state God designed for everyone.

Chapter Two Inventory of Escape Tools and Unshackling Reflections

MORNING EYE OPENER PRAYER

O Loving God,
    may everything I do this day
    be done with all my heart and soul,
    and with great delight
    and so be filled with you.

A HOG-SAINT REFLECTION

Saints are few and far between. The reason is found in the old expression, "Hogs and saints are only honored after they are dead."

HOLY AND UNHOLY COMMUNION

Question yourself about how inclusive your prayers are. When you pray, "forgive us our sins," whom does the "us" include? Do you link yourself with convicts, child abusers and corporate exploiters of third world laborers, or does "us" mean only those other nice people who share the same church pew with you?

When you pray, "Holy Mary, Mother of God, pray for us sinners now and at the hour of our death," with whom are you joined in sinful wicked communion? While we feel graced to be included in the Communion of Holy Saints, do we feel just as elevated by our incorporation in the Communion of Despicable Sinners — the ones to whom our Liberating Savior came to rescue from slavery?

Pray over these questions. Then whenever you pray these two cornerstones of Catholic Christian prayer, by being inclusive, you can make them truly catholic, universal and all-embracing.

Out of Touch Prayer

Recently I heard an advertisement for a mobile phone with new headsets. The lightweight earphone and microphone were made to be used while driving an automobile. The ad stated, "You can enjoy *hours* (emphasis mine) of comfortable hands-free use while safely driving your car or working at home."

A sign of the times: "hours of talking" on the telephone! New technology has helped us address — and has sometimes created — the need to stay in contact with family and friends. As marvelous a communication convenience as they can be, cell phones and pagers can also hold us hostage by our always having to be in touch. In the process we easily become out of touch with ourselves and the tangible mystery about us. Do you enjoy being out of touch? Even if you don't, it's healthy to practice short periods of being totally unavailable to others. Escape by solitude. Practice periodic fasting from your pager and cell phone, and you may find that, being an untouchable, you are far more in touch with life.

Blessed are the untouchables who are touched by God.

Be still and be in touch with the pulse of life at the heart of all things.

A Meditation-Reflection on a Sunrise Spirituality

The prophet Isaiah recorded these words of God: "Remember not the events of the past.... See, I am doing something new. Now it springs forth. Do you not perceive it?"[7] Each dawn begins an ever new Independence Day, fertile with God's ancient promise of fresh life and liberation for those impatient to be free and disposed to work on achieving their liberation. This new millennium requires extending our present limited horizons of mind, heart and imagination, as well as expanding our social and religious boundaries. To live with new horizons means constantly stretching our hopes and hearts as far as possible — and then gradually and progressively taking them even beyond those limits.

The shadow of death is cast over yesterday's old horizons, so life makes it essential to seek the dawn of new horizons. Those who fear to change and dread moving on to new possibilities prefer yesterdays and sunsets to new sunrises. The "things of long ago" that God told the people of Isaiah's time to "consider not" were God's own marvelous deeds of freeing Israel from slavery in Egypt. Yet even those greatest deeds of the peoples' history were dwarfed in the light of what God was doing in that new day. At the same time, those good old days are most important because they are the stuff for the creation of new tomorrows. Our own yesterdays are like barns overflowing with the harvest of the riches of tradition. Let us rejoice in yesterday's harvest and be grateful for the past. Then let us fill our pockets with the seeds of all those yesterdays and sow them in the fertile fields of our todays so we can reach out for the new harvest of our tomorrows.

A Story-Parable

The freedom fighter Jesus gave a one-line sunrise parable to explorers of new horizons: "Everyone instructed in the Kingdom of Heaven," he said, "is like a householder who brings out of his or her storeroom both the new and the old."[8]

Storerooms, of course, usually hold only old things, for who stores away what is brand new? Do our personal storerooms of mind and memory contain both the old and new? If we understand this parable and are learned in the wisdom of God's Enchanted Universe, then we might wonder why newness is so novel in religion. As you chew on that riddle, ask yourself a question: If you desire today to expand your horizons for yourself and for the world, what old treasures should you employ in doing so?

A Prayer to Live Out God's Enfleshment

O Jesus, my Liberator,
may the Holy Wind of Liberty
that blows wherever it wishes
and that ever inspired you
come to me this day
so that, like you,
I can boldly live out
God's enfleshment in me.

Holy Spirit of Freedom,
inspire me, as you did Jesus,
to be truly myself,
instead of the person
others want me to be.

The Prayer of Realizing

Do you realize you are in God's Enchanted Time Zone? To realize that fact doesn't simply mean being intellectually conscious of it. We realize something when we make it "real," when we make it tangible — a living reality — by our words and by how we live our lives. Be busy today with real-izing, making real, God's New Time Zone in which you live.

ESCAPE TOOL #3 – ESCAPING FROM PRIVATE PRAYER

To realize — to make real — the catholic or universal dimension of all your prayers, consider the following prayer as a possible conclusion to your private worship times.

> May my prayers reach you, O God,
>> through the Living Mystery of the Risen One
>> in unity with all the prayers of the Church
>> and of all Christians.
> May my prayers be one with all those who pray this day
>> in synagogues, mosques, pagodas and temples.
> May my prayer be united with the prayers of all believers
>> and all unbelievers,
>> one with all praying creation within the cosmos,
>> so that my prayer and my very person
>> might be fully united with you, my God,
>> who is one with all.

THE LIBERATION OF ALL

Any valid spirituality of liberation must include the work of justice for all. While previous spiritualities have separated love and justice, personal reform and social reform, that cannot be the case with a spirituality of liberation. God is love; God is justice. God's love embraces all humanity with an equality of social and religious rights, natural resources, food, housing, suitable working conditions and appropriate living wages. Within the web of God's love, the oppression of any individual or group restricts the freedom of every person. An incarnational prayer of equality means working to ensure the liberation of all who are enslaved politically by active assistance and by solidarity with the poor and oppressed.

A good spirituality is handcrafted — a personal spirituality. By its very nature it is thus constantly in danger of becoming a selfish spirituality. The comfortable bourgeois often have the leisure for spiritual exercises, retreats and pious activities, but these activities so easily can insulate them from the poor and oppressed. Every personal spirituality of liberation should, therefore, be married to a tangible social justice. If one's love of God and neighbor fails to find tactile expression in a lifestyle of justice, then it is not real love.

In his book *Theology and the Church,* which defends Liberation Theology from attacks by the Vatican, Juan Segundo writes that Liberation Theology unites praying and working. "Faced with evils that can and should be corrected in history, it [Liberation Theology] does not question the importance of prayer nor substitute enthusiasm for social change for the experience of divine transcendence."[9] He concludes this book with a prayer by Cardinal Henri de Lubac:

> If I lack love and justice,
>> I separate myself completely from you, God,
>> and my adoration is nothing more than idolatry.
> To believe in you,
>> I must believe in love and in justice,
>> and to believe these things
>> is worth a thousand times more
>> than saying your Name."[10]

Contemporary Reflection on Cardinal de Lubac's Prayer

The end of the twentieth century saw a regression among Catholic Christians to the medieval devotion of Adoration of the Blessed Sacrament. I say *regression* since it is contrary to a contemporary, biblically based theology of the Eucharist. The invitation of Jesus is to "take and eat,"[11] not bow before and adore. A true adoration (from *ad-ora*, which means "pray before") of Christ present in the Eucharist leads to seeing Christ present in the Living Eucharist of humanity and creation. If adoration before Christ in the Host is an eye-opener to Christ in the poor and homeless, in prostitutes and convicts, then it is a devotion of value. If not, it, like many devotions, borders on "idolatry." Those who promote this devotion would be well served to begin their hour of adoration with the above prayer by Cardinal de Lubac.

Chapter Three

Timelock Prison

Having explored the framework of a liberation spirituality, now it's time to get serious about escaping! The Great Liberator didn't just reform religion, he started something entirely new, and he began his revolutionary work by speaking about time. "This is the time of fulfillment! The Reign of God is at hand."[1] He invited those who wished to follow him to enter into a new time zone. He invited us to a new global neighborhood, where people live according to God's Time. We are familiar with time zones, like Eastern, Central, Mountain, Pacific and the others that divide the world. Those who move across time zones adjust their watches and activities to the new zone in which they are now living. Jesus invites us to live simultaneously in two time zones: God's Time Zone and the conventional time zone to which our clocks are set. To enter God's Time Zone is to live in a world where everything — while looking the same as it did in the Eastern or Central Time Zones — has become enchanted space.

ONE OF THE GREATEST ESCAPES
OF THE TWENTY-FIRST CENTURY

A vast majority of people in the Western World live in poverty. To people who live in the Third World, it may seem like those fortunate enough to be citizens of developed nations are free from the curse of being poor. But, in fact, the opposite is true. The majority of people in our high-tech Western World suffer from a great impoverishment — they are subject to a dire privation of time. Indeed, one of the greatest escapes of the twenty-first century may be from the prison of the clock.

Back in the good old days of the last century, a 1975 survey reported that a majority of Americans said they had enough time to do all the things they desired. Many studies and articles in those years dealt with the anticipated problem of what citizens in the future would do with all their leisure time. However, when that same time survey was taken twenty years later, in the mid 1990s, 85 to 95% of Americans said they had no leisure time! This condition, now so familiar to those of us in the twenty-first century who can't squeeze another minute out of our crowded agendas, was given a graphic name by Ralph Keyes: "Timelock." It echoes back to the notion of *gridlock*, the name for those times when traffic is so logjammed in large metropolitan areas like New York City that nothing can move. Prisoners in Timelock Prison are those with no free time they can spare. This form of incarceration has sinister implications for our soul-bodies.

When we suffer from a poverty of time, we are forced to hurry. When we are in a hurry, we usually throw overboard whatever's not considered important. Yet the first things we often abandon when racing the clock are actually among the most important: play and prayer. These two essential twins, prayer and play, are the first to be discarded because they are activities formerly reserved for leisure time. Prime time is almost always given to work. The constantly hurrying timelocked also find they are destitute of sufficient time for making love in all its countless forms. As a result, timelocked people may not live below the poverty level, but they almost certainly live below the pleasure level and the meaning level. They suffer from a scarcity of enjoyment and purpose in life. Ever hungry for more time, they cannibalize prayer times to have more time for work.

TRADITIONAL SPIRITUALITIES AND THE CLOCK

Jesus never used a clock. In fact, the classic spiritualities of the world's great religions are all B.C.: Before the Clock. The sun and the stars were the timepieces of the great spiritual masters, who were free from the pressures of the deadlines conceived by clocks and calendars. Clocks first became a reality for common people in the twelfth and thirteenth centuries. They were mounted in church steeples to help the faithful get to church on time. These timepieces were handless: Instead of visual cues, a bell struck at the top of each hour to announce the time. In fact, our word *clock* comes from the French *cloche*, which means "bell." When the dial first appeared on a clock, it had just one hand, which marked the hour; the minute hand only appeared a hundred years before the American Revolution. Clocks gradually moved from church towers into private homes of the wealthy as large household objects. In the evolution of timekeeping machines, portable clocks only appeared in the eighteenth and nineteenth centuries. Yet not only were these portable time-measuring devices so expensive that just the nobility and the wealthy could own them, they were also large and cumbersome by our standards. Their wealthy owners typically employed special servants just to carry their clocks for them. The clock carrier, upon request, would inform the owner of the correct hour of the day.

Our world suffers from a population explosion of clocks. They are everywhere. Their faces stare out at us from the walls of our rooms and our desks, from our television sets and VCRs, from numerous household appliances and the dashboards of our cars. Their faces even smile up at us from our wrists. One of childhood's first lessons is to learn how to read the sign-language of their hands, which are endlessly sending silent messages. Some watches are like those two-hundred-year-old time-servants of the wealthy, they report the hour aloud, only without being asked. Yet regardless of the style and abilities of your watches or clocks, the face on them is always the same: It is the face of a prison warden!

As instant communication, E-mail and other technical advances multiply, we echo General Napoleon's sentiments: "Ask me for anything but time." In his marvelous little book, *Holiness,* Donald Nicholl tells how in the revolution of 1871 young rebels went about Paris shooting the hands off the city's public clocks, denouncing them as "agents of enslavement."[2] Just as true today as then, the hands of our clocks are indeed agents of our bondage. However, this imprisonment is a unique kind of "doing time": It's a sentence of having no time.

Handcuffed by Time

One day when I was having lunch at an Applebee's Restaurant, I noticed that my waitress was wearing a watch on each wrist. Curious, I asked her why she had two watches. She pointed to the wristwatch on her right hand and said, "This watch tells me the correct time." Then, pointing to the one on her left wrist, she added, "And this watch tells me Applebee's time. I set my Applebee's watch ahead fifteen to twenty minutes so I won't be late to work."

While the very first wristwatch was made in Geneva in 1790, this so-called "bracelet watch" remained unnoticed until the late 1880s. When displayed at a 1914 Swiss exhibition, the first wristwatches were regarded as a "passing fancy" or simply an item for wealthy women. Then First World War aviators put them to practical use. Pilots wearing heavy flight suits in those early open-cockpit planes, found the "masculine" pocketwatch too awkward to use, and they began wearing bracelet watches. Today they are not only practical timepieces but are considered a piece of jewelry.

The two bracelet watches of my Applebee's waitress reminded me of the double bracelet handcuffs worn by arrested criminals. Even a single wristwatch can easily act as a handcuff: a restraining device used for prisoners in custody. The time that our watches keep, keeps us. They hold us in the bondage of deadlines — which, interestingly, is a prison term that originated during the American Civil War. The Confederate prison camp of Andersonville was a crowded encampment without walls or high fences. So a boundary line was drawn in the ground around the compound, and any prisoner who stepped on that line was shot by the guards. While deadlines can be helpful for accomplishing certain projects, they can also very easily become deadly to life.

Escaping from Timelock Prison

Yet there's a hidden blessing for those who are arrested. A Spirituality of Liberation should include a new beatitude: "Blessed are those who are truly arrested in the name of time, for they shall experience God." This beatitude is not a temptation to break the civil law but an enticement to freedom from the grips of the clock. For, paradoxically, being arrested is one of the fastest ways to escape from

Timelock Prison. Long before mechanical clocks were invented, King David, the great Hebrew Psalmist, gave voice to divine wisdom: "Be arrested, and know that I am God."[3] While that psalm is usually translated, "Be *still*, and know that I am God," the dictionary's first definition given for *arrest* is, "to stop, to prevent forward motion."

Be arrested, stop and be still. In your time-deprived life, spending a few minutes each day simply stopping in prayer is one of the most effective ways to tunnel your way out of Timelock Prison. You need no shovel to escape, only the willingness to sit and do nothing. This breakout exercise can be inserted frequently into your daily prayer. The opportunities to be arrested are numerous. For example, when you're required to wait for an appointment, rather than reading old magazines or fidgeting, you might try closing your eyes and stilling your body and mind. Upon opening your eyes, seek to see the world before you as intimately woven together in the Enchanted Universe of God. Such stillpoints can be productively incorporated into your day when your forward progress has been halted, when timelock becomes gridlock or any time that empty moments appear. Even when "dead spaces" are forced upon you, such times are opportunities to work on your escape tunnel.

The Spirit of God longs to arrest you. The Spirit is eager to still your restless heart, just as that same Spirit arrested Jesus and led him off to deserted places. Unstilled, we are stifled; life is suffocated and repressed.

JESUS OF NAZARETH IS ARRESTED

The lifestyle of Jesus our Savior-Liberator was punctuated with repeated arrests by the Holy Spirit. It wasn't just in the Garden of Gethsemane that Jesus was arrested. It happened frequently in the midst of his work. In the Gospels he often heard the Spirit's siren call, "Jesus, you're too busy! Get away; take time to feed your spirit by being alone with your Beloved." He found his survival quiet time when he escaped from the noisy, crowded conditions of his Palestinian village to isolated places. With a little creativity and a determined desire, you can find your own desert close at hand in your world. Whenever you are stifled, suffocating or lacking time for yourself, blow the whistle and call a personal *time out*.

Those caught in a lifestyle of hurrying are easily recognized. Speeders in life wear invisible dark glasses. The lenses of these glasses are black except for small, round openings in each lens, in the middle of which is a hairlike cross. People in a hurry unconsciously wear the bombardier glasses which are focused only on their next target, their next project or meeting. Yet living life on the run, rushing from one event to another, effectively blinds us to everything other than our next task. Frequently this targeted objective must be accomplished before quitting time, before our next meeting or even before dinner time. Always accelerating, we fail to see the needs of those we work with or meet on the street — even the needs of our children and spouses. This blindness created by the speed of life makes us oblivious to the omnipresence of God embodied in people and the world around us. We need to be still, to be arrested so we can see God, so we can recognize the divine presence in the fabric of our lives.

FREEDOM FROM THE CURSE OF HURRYING

Constantly rushing weaves an evil spell that condemns us to a prison workhouse. Indeed, hurrying is epidemic. It would be nice to wear plastic gloves when around those who are perpetually on the go. Because hurrying is not only contagious but also addictive, the spiritual exercise of slowing down requires perpetual self-discipline. As Meister Eckhart said, holiness only requires doing the next thing on your agenda with all your heart. The mind cannot simultaneously think two thoughts. Similarly, the heart cannot hold two concerns at the same time. While we applaud those who are able to juggle two, three or more things at once, blessed are the singlehearted, for they shall see God, as Jesus said.[4] "Single" in that verse is also translated as "clean," but either way, it doesn't mean sexually pure in the sense of celibate. Being single of heart allows us to devote our loving attention in a full and undivided way. The singlehearted are blessed to have learned how to train their hearts to attend to one thing at a time.

Discipline yourself to fully engage in whatever activity involves you. At first this may be painful. Being eternally short of time, you will attempt to save time by doing several things at once. Resist the urge. Take the necessary time to complete with loving investment each single task at hand. Refuse — as if it were the plague — to be imprisoned by deadlines, except in rare or unavoidable occasions. This exercise of purposefully slowing down your life may seem quaint and old-fashioned in our Hurry-Up-I-Want-It-Right-Now Age. But ask yourself if you agree with the following statement: To respond to all the demands of our high-tech, electronic world without being in a hurry is impossible. If you agree, then know without a doubt that you're serving a life sentence in Timelock Prison!

The Gift of Technology

Liberation is found in the fact that creation did not end at sunset on the sixth day. The Sacred Spirit never stops creating. Today's technology is a wonderful gift born of the Creative Spirit intended to make our lives easier and more comfortable. Timesaving machines greatly enhance the quality of our lives, and few would want to return to an era before their invention. Anyone who fondly longs for those "good old days" is likely suffering from Romantic Alzheimers! Consider having to go back to ironing every shirt and dress or having to obtain a block of ice to keep your food from spoiling in the summer or having to shovel coal into your furnace to heat your home — to mention only a few activities of the good old days.

Electrical Death

Lord, save us from Electrical Death. Deliver us not from the electric chair, but from the silent dark death of a power outage. When our ever present electrical power is suddenly taken away by a power outage caused by a storm, most of contemporary life and work comes to a dead stop. De-electrified, we are instantly catapulted back into the early twentieth century as our computers, fax machines, E-mail and other electrical forms of communication cease functioning. Electrical power failures in our homes catapult us back to log cabin days as our lighting, cooking, heating, air-conditioning, television and other electrical servants suddenly become impotent. Thank God, they are not really dead but only on a brief vacation.

Yes, God bless electrical power. Electricity first became a reality for the majority of Americans by the early twentieth century. It has been a great transformer of life, making our work easier and our lives richer. Yet that electricity which provides evening illumination has also made it possible to work late into the night, even all night long. In past eras the disappearance of sunlight signaled the end of the workday, providing a natural rhythm of work and creative, restful activities.

THE ELECTRIC PENITENTIARY

Unfortunately, when we lose that delicate balance, we are cast into the Electric Penitentiary, a cousin to Timelock Prison. Have you been made OOT by the two-handed god of technology? Hypnotized by the infinite possibilities of technology, we soon discover we are OOT, *Out Of Time*. At the same time as technology gives wonderful time- and labor-saving gifts, with the other hand it steals time from us. This is mostly true because these machines require more work time to pay for them as well as time to care for them. Another dark side of technology's gifts is that they provide endlessly expanding possibilities to do more and more in the "unexpanding" amount of time contained in a single day. No one has yet invented a time-increasing machine. Time forever remains a constant, even as the possibilities for how to spend it increase at the speed of light.

LIFE ON THE DOUBLE

Has our electric age got you doing double time? "On the double" and "double time" are army expressions for moving faster. Double-timers is a term that would fit most citizens of the twenty-first century. Ever-advancing technology, which allows us to do more and more, is coupled with the domestic reality of working husbands and wives trying to attend to the increasing demands of child rearing and increased calls for volunteer work from church and civil associations. The result is that the majority of us are living "on the double."

Life on the double translates into galloping to work and through your lunch or stampeding through traffic to arrive a couple of minutes early. Life on the double makes family life a track event. Family members behave like a relay team, running at full tilt and passing the baton of love from one racer to another. Life on the double means taking cell phones and pagers to plays, concerts and even to worship so we can constantly keep ahead in the madness marathon. Eastern temples and Moslem mosques require worshipers to remove their shoes or sandals when they enter. In our culture it's not shoes but cell phones and pagers that should be left at the door of every sacred place, unless we're expecting a call from God. Living on the double is not only exhausting, it estranges us from our sources of vitality and meaning.

One of the more painful aspects of any prison life is estrangement. Prison involves separation from one's family, friends, work and other essential elements of normal daily life. When we are *doing time* as inmates of Electric Prison, strapped by tentacles of technology to our work, we experience an estrangement from life and from core parts of ourselves. Along with self-constraint, consider making the prayer of recollection part of your daily life. This prayer's nickname is catch-up time.

CATCH-UP TIME

Jet-lag is a relatively new affliction. This traveler's curse, which is endemic to our electronic age, appeared as recently as the second half of the last century. Jet-lag is the psychophysical disorientation created by traveling at jet-speed across several time zones. Within the escalating tempo of daily life — as we attempt to keep pace with instant global communications, cell phones, E-mail, the internet, fax messages and the jangle of telephones — we can easily suffer from *soul-lag*. This common collective curse causes an unhealthy estrangement from ourselves and others. May the following story about soul-lag assist you in understanding this now-expanding affliction.

A group of Americans began their African safari by flying a two-engine plane into a small airstrip near an African village. There, waiting trucks were loaded with supplies accompanied by local porters. For about three hours the trucks drove deeper into the jungle to a place where the safari was to commence on foot. As soon as the supplies had been unloaded, the hired native porters all sat down on the ground. The American leader of the safari gave orders for the porters to stand up and begin their trek. They refused, however, to move from their seated position. The Americans became angry: They had not even begun the safari, and now, they thought, they were being blackmailed for *baksheesh*, for more money. But the English-speaking villager who was foreman of the porters explained, "Men do not want more money. They refuse to move — until their souls catch up with them!" At first the Americans were stunned, and then they found the situation humorous:

They had driven only three hours at not more than forty or fifty miles an hour!

Unlike the Americans on the safari, the African porters' sensitivity to their souls had not yet been deadened by living in a hectic, mechanized society. Like those Americans, we might find the foreman's explanation to be quaint or even humorous. Before lightly dismissing it, however, pause and rethink this story, for it is worthy of serious reflection.

Dog kennels are common sights at state prisons. These special kennels are not intended to house pets of the inmates or guards. Rather, they are for prison bloodhounds trained to follow the scent of escaped prisoners. The bloodhounds are given a sniff of an article of clothing belonging to an escaped prisoner. Then they are released to track the fleeing inmate. The bloodhounds' noses sniff along the trail of invisible flakes of body skin left behind by an escaping prisoner. Our human bodies are constantly shedding these naked-to-the-eye flakes of skin. Wherever we go, we leave behind a tiny stream of unique skin flakes with their own distinctive scent.

SOUL-LAG

Is Soul-Lag a reality? Just as jet-lag causes physical and mental disorientation, living at great speed causes a spiritual, soulful disorientation. Perhaps someday science will confirm that we leave behind us a trail of soul flakes as well as skin flakes. The prayer of recollection is the act of gathering up these pieces of our inner-selves that we leave behind as we hurry through our day from one event to the next.

The more emotionally intense an experience, the more of one's soul or inner-self that is left behind. If holiness involves striving to do everything with a fullness of attention, then it logically requires pouring our souls, our very inner-selves, into each work and event. If you've been fortunate enough to encounter a person whom you felt has been fully present to you — heart and soul — have you not continued to feel that person's presence after you've parted? After being with a person who gifted you with the totality of his or her attention and love, is not what's left behind more than just a memory of the occasion? Is this lingering presence not part of the profound mystery of the gift of a person's soul? Soul gifts are more intimate than body gifts. Just as the intimacy of making love leaves a potent, lingering and happily haunting imprint, so it is with intimate gifts of soul.

Recollection prayer, or catch-up time, could also be called inventory prayer since it's an act of reviewing how we've responded in the various situations of our day. This special period of prayer is set aside to examine our thoughts and emotions, particularly the ones we may have neglected as we experienced them. For a variety of reasons we tend to suppress certain emotions and intuitions that spontaneously arise within us. Failure to attend to them makes us deaf to messages from our inner-teacher and soul-guide who speaks to us through intuitions.

Like working a jigsaw puzzle, recollection prayer carefully recollects and reassembles the soul pieces of our feelings, thoughts, words and actions. Catch-up time also provides an opportunity to examine our behavior for those unintended, accidental acts of blindness caused by being too self-absorbed or in too much of a hurry. Souls grow larger and more mature by daily examinations of life. Soulful recollection is the necessary self-maintenance required to convert negative behavior into positive patterns. Also, whenever necessary they propel us to correct a past failure with apologies and an act of reconciliation.

A New Liberating Asceticism

We're all familiar with the old penitential act of fasting on bread and water. Perhaps a new asceticism for the twenty-first century would be the self-inflicted penance of hurrying only in emergencies. It would take great restraint, for example, to avoid driving over, or even at, the speed limit and, instead, to stay slightly below the posted rate. When you walk to and from a destination, you might experiment with moving at a leisurely pace. I assure you such small speed-restricting penances will itch worse than any hairshirt.

To practice the living prayer of a slowing-down asceticism will put you under the curse of Eisenhower's dilemma. When General Eisenhower became president, he wanted to operate the White House as he had run the army. He let his chain of command know that as president he would personally deal only with urgent or important matters. Eisenhower later revealed how he soon discovered that most everything fell into these two categories! You will likely also be snagged in President Eisenhower's dilemma of what is important. Both at work and at home, life is filled with what seem to be urgent and important issues. To be able seriously to embrace a slowing-down asceticism requires that we constantly answer a single question: Is this issue truly important and urgent? Be forewarned that it will not be easy to discern whether a particular matter is truly as urgent as it seems or if other people are only trying to make it so. Moreover, the instant accessibility of E-mail and the telephone creates an artificial urgency for immediate replies.

Sooner than we imagine, E-mail Time and Instant Fax Time will be escalated by new even-quicker-than-lightning machines and computers. They will enable us to be instantly and everywhere in direct contact with others. However, the shadowy side of such advances is the unspoken demand for instant responses. If we leave a recorded message on someone's telephone answering machine, we are usually disturbed if after two or three days we've not received a response. We can ask ourselves: Did the person receive my message, and if so, why hasn't my call been returned? We also expect E-mail messages to be returned at the same speed with which they were sent. We don't need to watch the clock to see how quickly time is moving, we only have to look at our lives: Time is shrinking into smaller and smaller bites and accelerating in ever-faster computer bytes. It's become an accepted reality that the shortest measurement of time isn't a microsecond, it's a honk-a-second. That's the space of time from a traffic light turning green till the person behind you honks.

A Naughty, Impolite Asceticism

Consider also practicing a "naughty asceticism." Along with the new liberating penance of not hurrying, you might add another freeing discipline. This spiritual austerity will likely prove even more painful than slowing down. It's the ascetical practice of frequently saying "No!" Adding this innocent-seeming two-letter word to your daily vocabulary will be as offensive as any of the famous four-letter words that are forbidden on television and in polite society. Yet without thoughtful and frequent use of the "naughty no," liberation from Timelock Prison will prove to be impossible.

If we are to survive in this technological era — if we are to sustain the vitality of our souls and spirits in the midst of our time crunch — we must first learn to say "No" firmly to ourselves. You will be the most difficult person to whom you will have to say *no*. But if you start with the most difficult person, the rest will be easier. Reform, as well as charity, begins at home. To enjoy in this world the "glorious freedom of the children of God"[5] requires prioritizing and organizing our lifestyles around what is truly important and necessary. The primary purpose of saying *no* is so that we can say a wholehearted *yes* to those significant activities like prayer, play, reflection, love and friendship. *No* is a twenty-first century survival word. This new millennium and century is one of perpetually increasing demands on our prehistorically limited amount of time. While technology has endlessly expanded the possible uses of our time, the actual time we have available remains the same as it has for the past fifteen millennia.

Besides being a survival word, *no* is a saint's word. It not only marks a refusal to sin, to engage in selfish indulgence and negative emotions, but a saint also says that naughty word to many good causes. Only by your gentle but firm *no* to countless requests made by your church, civic organizations and volunteer groups will you have any time to say *yes* to the most meaningful of these appeals. Moreover, only by this ascetical practice will you truly be able to say *yes* to your family and your God. Only by saying *no* to countless good activities will you be able to say *yes* to the times and activities that nourish your soul and mature your spirit. It takes time to do things that feed the best in you — and to do them with all your heart and soul, and with great delight.

GUILTVILLE JAIL

Your *No* Penance, however, must be bulletproof. If your fortitude is not steel-reinforced when you are asked to do something, you'll likely respond with a halfhearted *yes*. So be prepared, for unlike any other word, little *no* opens prison gates of stinging guilt.

Life and business contain many "shoulds" — including weddings, funerals, parties and dinners. Whenever you say, "I should do...," realize that you are speaking like a prisoner. If you do anything because you "should," it usually implies doing it with half a heart and out of a sense of guilt. Any choices made with less than a full heart incarcerate us in Guiltville Jail. When we really don't want to attend an event or don't truly wish to serve on a committee, lukewarm acceptances take us hostage.

Many of life's social obligations are unavoidable; they are the natural result of being communal persons. So, getting out of Guiltville Jail requires creativity. Whenever you are faced with an obligation-bound commitment, before agreeing to it, take time to creatively consider how you might make it something valuable and even fun. Then send your positive RSVP with a resolution that you will not attend the event as a prisoner. Remember, *saint* is only another name for an escaped prisoner. Recall too, as Meister Eckhart suggests, that being a saint only requires striving to do everything with as much heart and soul — and delight — as possible.

THE CORRECT TIME

"What is the correct time?" That is an often asked question in our watch-full age that runs on precise time. The real answer to this question is, *"This is the time of fulfillment.* The Reign of God, the Time of God, is here now."[1] If we truly knew the correct time, then the face on every clock and watch would be a round reminder for us to wake up and live according to God's Time, which is also to live and act ahead of our time. Each period in history is actually behind the times. It is tardy in terms of evolutionary maturity. One sign of this evolutionary retardation is when the majority practice discrimination and refuse to treat all persons with equal respect and dignity regardless of race, religion, sexuality, sexual orientation or ethnic origin. War, violence, vengeance, exploitation of workers and the poor are further signs of evolutionary retardation.

Those who know the correct time are engaged in escaping from the prison of time. Those who are *on time* according to the clocks of God's Time Zone, are paradoxically living years or even centuries beyond their time. Their watches are synchronized to Prophet's Time, that future clock where justice and peace are a reality for everyone. God asks, "Why wait till the future? Hasten tomorrow into today." Anticipating the future age now, however, is lonely work. Fear, insecurity, a loss of limited power and a host of other prehistoric reasons keep most of humanity snailing its way toward the radically new time announced long ago.

PROPHETIC TIME

The Galilean named "God-liberates" knew the correct time. In an age when women were regarded as property, Jesus treated them as persons, as equals. Divine Time is always equality time. Those who live according to Prophetic Time treat others with equal respect and dignity regardless of their religion, race, gender or sexual orientation. Those who march according to Prophetic Time find life continually fresh and invigorating. As we might expect, they are also people of hope and acceptance. While it is a time of justice for all, this is especially true for the poor and those on the outer fringes of society and religion.

Loyal disciples of the Prophet are themselves prophets. Jesus avoided the title of Messiah, or Christ, the anointed one. Yet he was called prophet several times, and he actually used it for himself.[6] His disciples are anointed as prophets at baptism and so are expected to live out that dangerous vocation. Like the Applebee's Restaurant waitress, loyal disciples of the Prophet of Galilee should also wear two wristwatches. One watch would be set to the present time zone so they can be "on time" for appointments and work. The watch on their other wrist would tell them Prophet Time so they can act toward others as if the future had already arrived. Living simultaneously in these two time zones requires gymnastic balance and inventive creativity. Our Liberator-Redeemer modeled such a double lifestyle — as well as the cost of this double life. Indeed, the crime for which he was crucified was being too far ahead of his time.

CONCLUSION

After visiting Guiltville Jail, Timelock Prison and the Electric Penitentiary, in the next chapter we'll be ready to tour the really Big House, the global prison in which everyone in the world is incarcerated. As we do, it is apparent for you personally and for all of us that one of the great challenges of the twenty-first century will be escaping from the imprisonment of time.

Chapter Three Inventory of Escape Tools and Unshackling Reflections

A NATIVE AMERICAN STORY: THE MINK THAT STOLE TIME

The Salish Native American Tribes of the Northwest coastal area tell of a time long ago when the People had no light. Because their world was dark and cold, Mink felt compassion for the People. He had heard that on the other side of the world there existed something called the Sun, so Mink decided to steal it for the People. It was, indeed, a difficult feat. But Mink was up to the challenge, being a great thief, and in time he was able to steal the Sun. He set it in the sky in such a way that it shown equally for the People on both sides of the world. The People were overjoyed and praised Mink. Meanwhile, Mink, growing proud of himself, thought, "What other good thing could I steal for the People?"

Mink searched and searched but was unable to find anything worth stealing. Then the Europeans came to the land of the People, and these visitors had great power. After much thought about what gave them power, Mink said, "These New People possess something they call Time, and that is what gives them great power." So Mink the Thief waited until dark and then sneaked into the house of the New People where they kept Time on a shelf in a shiny box that made little noises. The face of Time had two little moving arrows, one small and the other large, and Mink could tell it was very powerful. Mink stole the box with the face and its two ever-circling arrows.

The People praised Mink and rejoiced, for now they had the great power of Time with the face and two moving arrows. But Mink and the People soon found it was not easy to live with Time. They found they were always watching those two little arrows on that shiny box to see what time it was. They also had to wind up the box every day, so now poor Mink and the People had no time. This was a great puzzle to them. While they now had Time, they didn't have time to do the things they once enjoyed doing, like fishing and hunting. Now they had to get up at a certain hour and go to bed at a certain hour; they had to go to meetings whenever the hands of Time told them it was time.

Mink and the People were no longer free. Now Time owned them, and sadly it has been that way ever since.

Soul Flakes and Soul Kisses

The Eskimos, the name Europeans gave to the Inuit Native Americans of Northwestern Canada and Alaska, know that souls can be left behind. Their meal prayers acknowledge with gratitude the gift of the souls present in the food they are about to eat. They prayerfully thank the spirits of the seals and fish for sharing with them the gift of their souls.

After a meal or time together at which some deep sharing has taken place with a friend, consider saying a prayer of gratitude that your friend has shared with you the precious gift of his or her soul. Upon leaving your spouse or a dear friend, consciously breathe out a part of your soul as if it was a spiritual kiss. This holy kiss at parting says, "May God go with you — and part of my soul as well."

People in a Hurry Are "Fat"

People in a hurry have too much on their plates, and trying to clean their plates makes them "fat." Good advice for those of us who wish to keep our weight down is to use smaller plates and never let others put food on our plates. Indeed, large plates heaped with too much of a good thing cause dangerous weight gain.

Technology has given us the largest plates known in history. Large plates create the craving to fill them. Our bosses echo our mothers: "Now clean your plate, or no desert!" Today's Technology Buffet offers up countless possibilities, and our eyes become larger than our limited time. The only way to clean our plates is to hurry up. The more we pile on our business plates, the more we need to sprint to accomplish all the tasks.

Those whose lifestyle has become one of perpetual hurry may appear to have physically trim waistlines, but their soul stomachs are bloated with the business they are trying to accomplish. Perhaps we need a new Weight Watchers for the soul, to coach us in the art of restraint, to teach us to insist on small plates of technology — and always to serve ourselves.

Question: Is your agenda for this day served on a big or small plate?

ESCAPE TOOL #4 — USE TIME TO DELAY

When someone makes a request that you are not inclined to accept, don't give an immediate answer. Buy some time by using your Time-Delay escape tool. Avoid the trap of giving a direct answer by saying, "I'll have to check my calendar, and I'll get back to you," or "Let me check with my husband/wife." Such a time-delayed answer will allow you either to find a polite excuse for not accepting or a good reason for accepting without being taken hostage.

ESCAPE TOOL #5 — THE PRAYERCRASTINATOR

When asked to serve on a committee or give a presentation, consider saying, "I'm honored by your invitation, but let me pray about it before I give you my decision." This is not procrastination, but prayercrastination. Praying about important commitments is an excellent way to make all serious decisions that involve your work and time.

> Blessed are the prayercrastinators,
>   for the Spirit of God shall lead them.

Be Cautious Not to Boxcar Your Daily Life

Timelock Prisoners usually boxcar commitments and projects one after another, as close together as freight trains, in order to get as much done as possible in a limited amount of time. Such a tightly interlocked agenda requires a smooth day with no interruptions, unexpected crises or delays. Yet such flawless days come around once in a blue moon. Unrealistic schedules that boxcar appointments create an ideal environment for the sins of irritability and resentment.

To avoid such minor yet harmful emotions, leave a safe space between projects in your day to allow for unexpected interruptions and delays. Breathing space between our agenda events also provides opportunities to respond to surprise visitations of God. When efficiency demands that you link together activities, try to make those links out of latex so they will be as flexible as possible. Live in a way that prepares you to stop, look and listen whenever your hidden God becomes visible.

Escape Prayer of Slowing Down

Practice slowing down frequently, whether you are walking or driving, eating or working. This is an exercise in learning how to live more fully in the present moment. Slowing Down Prayer has amazing awakening powers and thus is a practice well worth cultivating.

A perfect set of symbols to help us awaken our mindfulness, our wonder and our gratitude can be found in our home away from home, our automobiles. Our cars have a special gauge called a speedometer, which indicates the vehicle's speed, and an odometer, which records the number of miles traveled. These and other gauges are located on a panel under the windshield that we call the dashboard.

The dashboard is a very symbolic name. Perhaps it originated when automobiles dashed along the road at the then hair-raising speed of twenty to thirty miles an hour. I suspect automobile manufacturers borrowed the word from the sport of track. A dash is a foot race less than a quarter mile long that's run at top speed. If only our dashing about was limited to areas of less than a quarter of a mile! Today we constantly dash at top speed from event to event beginning the moment we reach our morning's starting line. So the next time you drive your car, take a careful look at the gauges on your dashboard and practice a slowing down prayer. And the next time you find yourself dashing through life, remember to gauge your speed so you can live more fully and more freely.

SPEED KILLS

"Speed kills" say the highway signs. We believe that message, yet we continue speeding through life, racing through our working, loving, eating and praying. Speed is both a dangerous illegal chemical drug and an attitude of life that is addictive. One of the ways speed kills is by anesthetizing us. The word comes from the Greek *anaisthetos,* meaning "without feeling." The anesthesia of speed deadens sensations in both body and soul. Those perpetually in a hurry find it difficult to feel the subtle messages from their soul-body. Anesthetized souls and spirits are sedated, unable to propel and energize us to greatness.

SCOTCH WISDOM

Spirits both in and out of the bottle take time to mature. Consider adapting the label from the single malt scotch whiskey from Scotland's famous Glenlivet distillery, making it your personal motto: "Unhurried since 1824."

A PRAYER FOR CLOCK WATCHERS

O God who lives beyond time
   and yet is immersed in time,
    whose very timelessness tingles in my flesh,

may your ageless Spirit
 inspire me this day
 to realize that I'm a millionaire.
Help me rejoice in my Clock-Bank fortune,
 my vast riches of minutes and hours.
Help me be aware that I own
 all the time in the world.

Holy Spirit of Wisdom,
 guide me to use prudently
 my precious ticking fortune.
Slow me down.
Slow my pace down,
 from double time to single time
 by limiting my activities to one at a time.
May I be silently attentive to you.

Inspire me to arrest myself,
 to stop and be still, so as to see
 the divine face everywhere.
Lead me into the temptation
 of escaping from Timelock Prison.
And tempt me again whenever I'm recaptured.

And though I'm rich with time,
 may the face of every clock and watch tell me
 I'm living on borrowed time.
May I behold my clock's hands
 as hourly holding out to me
 precious gifts of time-on-loan.

O God, with delight and gratitude
 may I extravagantly spend
 my fabulous fortune of time
 until you wink and
 wind all my clocks centuries back
 to time's beginning,
 till all my personal time
 runs out.

Then you and I
  will once again be one
  in the fullness of time.

ESCAPE TOOL #6 – AN ESCAPE PARTY

Celebrate your escapes — great or small. Becoming free of some addiction, habit or self-limiting condition demands to be celebrated. Throw a party for yourself whenever you successfully escape from any form of imprisonment. You might invite significant friends or guests, or it can be a private party. If it's private, buy yourself a gift — perhaps a new article of clothing — or treat yourself in whatever way best symbolizes the gift of your new freedom. You might even name such a gift "my liberation shoes" or "my freedom coat" or "my emancipation meal." Whenever you wear your new shoes or shirt, let that gift be a reminder of your personal victory. The following prayer of thanksgiving to the Holy Spirit of Freedom, who was a co-conspirator in your escape, is intended for use at such escape parties.

I thank you, Holy Spirit of God, for my new freedom,
  and for your assistance in my escape from _____.
O ever-conspiring Spirit of Freedom,
  come to my assistance again
  and help me to be liberated
  from my bondage of_____.

This Holy Spirit prayer is three-sided. First, the prayer gratefully acknowledges God's hand in your newfound liberty. Second, it is a prayer of confirmation and affirmation that you have the ability to escape from other forms of imprisonment since you've already escaped from this one. Third, it's a prisoner's prayer challenging you to continue to seek freedom from whatever conditions or attitudes still keep you in bondage.

Go to Jail

As we prepare to leave this first of the prisons on our tour, Timelock Prison, we take a brief detour to a place of incarceration that can capture us at almost any time. Monopoly games have that surprise card "Go to Jail," which briefly takes us out of the game. Jails or *hoosegows* — the cowboy slang for jail, which comes from the Spanish *juzgado* for "courtroom" — are usually places of short incarceration for minor offenses.

The next time you find yourself hoosegowed, make a resolution never to land in there again. It's easy to react and say the wrong things when you are caught up in a heated discussion or argument. Even the most prudent mind can be taken prisoner by the siege mentality of an argument. It can happen in an instant, like a trap springing shut when you react instinctively to protect your ideas or self-image. The Hoosegow of Regret is both a jail and a courtroom where your heart is the judge and jury. Since we seldom act prudently in an argument, the heart-court judges you guilty of the inappropriate words you now regret.

Don't attempt to get a quick release from this state of regret. Instead, sit in your conscience-cell and trace the path that led to your arrest. Did you land in this jail of "I-Wish-I-Haden't-Said-That" because you discussed subjects you knew from previous experience were explosive, but you went ahead anyway? Did it begin innocently with an exchange about your in-laws, money, disciplining the children, church, politics, or even the dog? Become aware of your trail to jail. With such knowledge, determine to avoid traveling down it again. If it becomes necessary to discuss those subjects again, do so as if you were walking through a mine field or opening a letter-bomb. Whenever potentially explosive subjects arise again, remember your brief, regretful jail experience and simply try to listen reflectively, offering no suggestions or comments that might fuel the fire. Those who speak little seldom go to the hoosegow.

Chapter Four
The Great Primal Prison

The oldest prison in the world is estimated to be at least 200,000 years old. This Great Primal Prison was unconsciously created by *Homo sapiens,* the thinking human. The precise prehistoric date when our ancestors' brains had enlarged enough so they could think as we do today is unknown. On that day, however, humans took a great evolutionary step forward — and they also stepped into prison. Buddha and Jesus both spoke of the need to be unshackled from the captive powers of the mind. They along with other holy liberators continue to call their disciples to escape from the rigorous tyranny of their thoughts.

Human evolution took a great jump forward some two million years ago with the appearance of *Homo erectus*, our upright-walking ancestors. Then another enormous evolutionary leap forward was taken when our upright-walking ancestors became Homo sapiens, thinking-humans. These conscious creatures now had the capacity for self-reflection — something no other creature possessed. They could also calculate the correct distance for throwing a rock at an enemy, and they could figure out how to harness fire, wind, water and other forces of nature. They could think thoughts of making art and weapons, of making love and war, and they could endeavor to make meaning out of the great mysteries of existence. As they pondered the mysteries of birth, life, death and the Great Beyond — to which their beloved dead had departed — they created the first spiritualities. This evolutionary breakthrough of spirituality witnessed humans making ritual and prayer as well as fire some 70,000 years ago — millenniums before the first religions appeared at the time of the agricultural revolution.[1]

Anne Foerst points to our ancient heritage when she suggests how "from evolutionary biology we know that we share 98% of our genes with chimpanzees."[2] Yet the development of the human brain allowed us to leap light-years ahead of our cousins in creation in terms of what we could create and accomplish. Indeed, the marvel of the human brain is mind-boggling. It would take a twenty-first century super-computer to perform the tasks of a single human neuron, a nerve cell in the human nervous system connected to the brain. And each of us has several billion neurons! From this miracle of the human mind comes all the contemporary marvels of technology, science, literature, poetry, the arts and medicine, and also the most common form of imprisonment.

IMITATE GOD — MAKE A WORLD

"With our thoughts we make our world," said the Buddha. "Think evil thoughts, and evil will follow you as surely as the cart follows the ox. Think good thoughts, and goodness shall follow you all the days of your life."[3] The Buddha's profound truth suggests that we have the capacity to create our personal worlds, the heaven or hell in which we daily live. This is critical information for those seeking happiness and peace. While the thoughts we think are essential to our happiness, or lack of it, the majority of us go about life seemingly unaware of what we are thinking. The expression "Humans do not think, they are thought" captures how the human mind tends to operate on automatic pilot, seemingly self-regulating. Our minds like to think what they want when they want to. Yet the great liberators Buddha and Jesus were evolutionists. They continue to call their Homo sapiens disciples to grow up, to take the next essential evolutionary step forward: to become *thinking humans who choose their thoughts*.

Did the early Homo erectus have to practice standing up? Two million years ago, how many of those first creatures resisted the process of learning to stand up straight? Perhaps many complained, "It's too painful, too difficult and unnatural." Yet we walk about erect today because heroic pioneers long ago endured the pain of growing up by standing up straight. Likewise, training our minds what to think and what not to think will require the same evolutionary determination. The labor of liberty is always hard work.

HEART OR MIND

Jesus never spoke about the mind — at least not in the way we understand it. In most ancient cultures the heart rather than the brain was considered the source of thoughts as well as human emotions. For example, when embalming bodies, the Egyptian mummy-maker priests carefully removed the deceased's heart, liver and various other organs, which were separately embalmed. After removing the brain from the skull, however, unaware of its function, they threw it away because they thought it unessential for the afterlife.

In Biblical language the chief human organ is the heart. Its functions of pumping blood and circulating oxygen throughout the body were unknown to the authors of Scripture. For Jesus and the prophets the heart was the internal pumping station not for blood but for emotions, desires and beliefs. Moreover, the functions normally attributed to the mind were commonly associated with the heart. Scripture speaks of "discerning the thoughts and intentions of the heart"[4] and describes the heart as cheerful, sad, firm and courageous as well as calling it the fountain of all thoughts, desires and deeds. "Change your hearts," cried Israel's prophets. "Let the finger of God write upon them a new covenant." The early disciples of the Risen One reflected this common belief when they proclaimed that the Holy Spirit is sent into our hearts, affirming that God pours love into our hearts.

The common Scriptural idiom, "to say in the heart,"[5] particularly as it was used by St. Paul, essentially means to think. And Jesus gave us some striking images about thoughts that come from the heart. He surprised his listeners by proposing a revolutionary law when commenting on the Jewish dietary laws that forbade eating certain unclean foods. He said, "It's not what goes into your mouth that makes you unclean; rather, it is what comes out of your hearts: evil thoughts, unchaste acts, theft, murder, adultery, greed...." He concluded by saying, "All these evils come from within, and they, not certain foods, defile a person."[6] It was truly a novel teaching that one's thoughts and not pork — or the natural flowing of blood in childbirth or the menstrual period — make one unclean, unfit for worship and prayer. Jesus may not have broken with tradition regarding the heart being the center of human thought, yet he was certainly revolutionary regarding the relationship of thought to holiness.

THE EVOLUTION FROM THE DEED TO THE THOUGHT

God has always forbidden murder and adultery. Millenniums ago God's decree to Moses banned them along with eight other forbidden actions. Two millenniums ago Jesus extended that ban even to *thoughts* about deeds of murder and adultery. The Liberator of Galilee decreed that if anyone has angry thoughts about another, that person is guilty of murder. He ruled that even harboring violent attitudes in the form of name-calling is spiritually lethal. "Call another a fool or an imbecile," he said, "and you will be liable to punishment."[7]

Is this Jesus the poet or Jesus the liberator speaking? Are his words merely a form of Palestinian poetry, typical Jewish exaggeration intended to emphasize an ideal ethical action? Or is he not, rather, prophetically announcing the next essential step in our evolution? Thoughts are the blueprints of the brain. More than benign designs, however, thoughts are forms of measurable electric energy that hold the power to heal, to vitalize the immune system and to illuminate life with joy and happiness. As patterns of real energy, thoughts hold lethal powers to injure the people toward whom they are directed, as well as those who think them.

Our thoughts can make us holy. Our thoughts can make us saints. Think thoughts of peace, harmony, love, unity, acceptance, serenity, compassion, contentment, gratitude, joy and delight, and you will make yourself and the world more lovable and Godlike. Or our thoughts can condemn us. Our hateful and angry thoughts make us sick and contribute to the pestilence of hate in the world. If your mind is full of fearful thoughts, you'll live in an anxiety-filled world. Think thoughts of malice, revenge and hatred, and your world will be at war. Whatever you want the world to become, become that yourself — and realize that you become who you are, to a large degree, by choosing the thoughts you entertain.

Teilhard de Chardin, the prophetic Jesuit visionary of the last century, asked, "What are humans becoming?" We should, of course, be becoming more Godlike by struggling to become responsible for our thoughts. We cannot escape our accountability for our thoughts any more than we can for our actions. By controlling and creating our thoughts, we shape their powerful energy into a force field that determines the quality and potency of our actions. By choosing our thoughts wisely, we evolve, becoming daily more humanly divine. We enable God, who is embodied in our flesh, to become more visible and active in our lives.

TOILET TRAINING FOR THE MIND

"Ever Upward" is the evolutionary call. The next imperative stage for us humans involves growing up, becoming mature persons who can exercise wise control over our thoughts. Along with a few prehistoric creatures like the turtle, we still live with the prehistoric mind. It retains the ancient survival programing to respond instinctively, since our primal survival required being able to react spontaneously without thought. However, the Spirit of Ongoing Creation says, "Do not react, but act! Those who react are not free; only actors are. The time of fulfillment is here — grow up." This choosing to act instead of react is an evolutionary emancipation.

God is continuously creating the world, and so also are you. Each of us is invited to be a co-creator with God in shaping our world by our thoughts. Yet disciplined, creative practice of controlling our thoughts is no easy matter. Awake or asleep, the mind is constantly busy: It is estimated that the average person has over 66,000 thoughts a day. These myriad visitors come and go as they please. Some are significant, while most are of little consequence. The more passionate and emotionally powerful the thoughts, the more they can accomplish, and the more they can imprison us. The mind can become an all-powerful dictator doing whatever it wishes and making us feel helpless to revolt against its tyranny. It can seem like we need to develop superhumanly strong brain muscles to throw out unwanted thoughts and to prevent them from returning to power.

Yet the control that is required can be achieved in a natural, if not effortless, way. Our mind needs to be trained in a way similar to our bowels. Toddlers are taught to control their bowel muscles in that essential process called toilet training. Parents must be patient yet diligent throughout this process until the proper time when children can begin to be self-responsible for this training. Thus, as small children we naturally yet progressively learn to control our bodily processes of elimination, which once were spontaneous. Toilet training makes it possible for us to live in a clean and healthy world.

Unfortunately for most of us, as well as for society at large, our thought training is surprisingly neglected in comparison. Although our parents, religion and society taught that certain thoughts were wrong or even sinful, we received precious little training in how to control such thoughts. While we are liberated by toilet training, lacking mind training has condemned many of us to a life sentence in the prison of the mind. Most children become self-responsible for toilet training around the age of three and move out of diapers. Are you now at an age where you feel responsible enough to learn how to control your thoughts? As toilet training made our daily lives and homes clean, beautiful and sanitary, so prayerful thought training will transform our minds and our world into homes for the Kindom of God.

CONCLUSION

The Great Primal Prison of the Mind is actually a large complex of prisons and jails. Inside the perimeters of the Primal Penitentiary are a variety of other prisons, including those named Anger, Fear, Revenge, Prejudice, Resentment, Anxiety and Impatience. In the following chapters we will tour some of these places where so many are incarcerated. If you should inhabit any of these, find hope in the words of our Savior-Liberator, "The Spirit has anointed me to set the prisoners free."[8]

Chapter Four Inventory of Escape Tools and Unshackling Reflections

BUILD YOUR OWN PRISON

If you ever pass through Yuma, Arizona, I encourage you to visit what the guidebooks describe as "the most notorious and fascinating tourist sight in town" — the Yuma Territorial Prison. Constructed in 1876, it operated till 1909, when it outgrew it usefulness. Because of its location on a hill beside the Colorado River, further expansion was impossible and the prison was closed. When you tour this abandoned prison, you can go inside the small, narrow cells, each of which held six inmates, often in temperatures that reached 115 degrees.

The Yuma Territorial Prison was built by the prisoners themselves. In fact, most prisons of the nineteenth century — including famous penitentiaries like Leavenworth — were put up by the forced labor of inmates. That build-your-own-prison tradition continues today, as countless millions build theirs stone by stone. If tourists could visit your present prison, like the one at Yuma, what would they see? Would they find yours to be fascinating or terrifying? While the inmates at Yuma's prison were forced to build theirs, did anyone force you to construct yours?

Make your present prison — whether it is fashioned out of anger, impatience, resentment, fear or any other building material — like the one in Yuma: not a tourist attraction, but an abandoned prison!

A Blindman's Prison Tour

Taking this tourist trip through your prison has no admittance charge and doesn't even require leaving your home. Just close your eyes, sit for five minutes and do nothing. Be patient, and after a short time you will become aware of a continuous stream of uncontrolled thoughts passing through your mind. Do not attempt to control them, but, like a tourist, simply observe them.

Daily visiting the prison of your mind can make you more aware of your thoughts, and the sooner you are conscious of what you are thinking, the quicker you can escape the incarceration of negative thoughts. Moreover, this blindman's prison tour can be a form of prayer. The use of a prayer word or phrase can be helpful to focus your mind and transform your thoughts. Lovingly and prayerfully attending to prayer words like *peace*, *freedom*, *love* or *Christ, my Liberator* is a form of liberating thought training. With practice you may be surprised to learn that you can control your thoughts as effectively as you control your bowels. Furthermore, saturating the fabric of your thought process with your prayer word can transform your prison into a holy temple.

THOUGHTS AS JUDGE OR OBSERVER

Jesus taught that those who do not judge others will not be judged themselves. This is truly good news since by not judging we have a sure ticket to heaven. On the other hand, it's bad news because the mind seems obsessed with judging most everything. Perhaps this tendency has prehistoric roots from the time when early humans had to determine in microseconds if some noise behind them was coming from a predator or simply the wind moving a branch. Our conscious minds, it appears, are pre-wired for judging, even when evidence to support a conclusion is lacking.

Fortunately, minds can be re-wired. This process is best initiated by soliciting the services of the Master Electrician, the Spirit of the Liberator from Galilee. It also begins with the belief that thought training is possible, that we can control our thoughts as well as our bowels. When you become aware you're having a judgmental thought, the first step is resisting the urge to judge it. Then gently replace the judgment with an observation. The thought in a judge's robe says, "John is egotistical and self-centered." Ask the judge thought to step aside and invite a neutral-observer thought to view John. It might say, "I observe that John often talks about himself and seems to put his needs ahead of others."

Each time a thought appears in your consciousness attired as a magistrate, make it remove its robe so it can become an observer. You may be surprised at the freedom this exercise can bring you.

POSITIVE OR NEGATIVE: THE FRAME IS YOUR CHOICE

Everything can be viewed in more than one way. You can view a set of circumstances through a suspicious, defeatist, negative frame, or you can look at it through a trusting, hopeful, positive frame. From one perspective, a situation may appear to be a clear defeat, but with another light on it, it may be recognized as an adventure or an opportunity. Samuel Goldwyn, the movie giant, was notorious for his habit of twisting logic. When you are faced with a difficulty, meditate on one of his famous remarks: "It's an impossible situation, but it has possibilities."

THE PRAYER OF MEDITATION

All the great religious traditions have their methods of mental prayer or meditation, which is the classic method for gaining control over your thoughts. In light of the chapter on Timelock, most people today find it difficult to create time for meditation as an integral part of their prayer life. Yet meditation can expand the quality of time and can effect an escape from both the Primal Prison of the Mind and Timelock Prison. Meditation methods are many as are the resources to learn how to do it. More important than learning a particular form of meditation, however, is the willingness to dedicate twenty minutes daily to practice it.

LIVING MEDITATION

Are you among the 99%? I'm referring to the great majority who have the desire for inner peace but are realistic enough to know that the discipline of daily meditation is not possible for them. Do not abandon your desire for inner-peace, however. Instead, mull over the idea of cultivating a living meditation. If you keep in mind Meister Eckhart's simple rule for holiness, "Do the next thing you have to do with all your heart," and practice that as best you can, you will be engaged in living meditation. When your heart, soul, mind and attention are all fully focused on whatever task is before you, you truly are meditating. Living meditatively does not require sitting still and concentrating on a *mantra* or a prayer image or your breath. Instead, it happens when your mind is engrossed in folding the laundry, drying a dish, or being fully attentive to someone, listening like a sponge.

ESCAPE TOOL #7 – LAUNDRY MEDITATION

If you attempt to be fully present to the present moment, you'll almost certainly be distracted. Whether you are practicing classic centering prayer, meditation, contemplation or a living meditation, you will be tempted to think other thoughts. When this happens, for example, while you're literally doing your laundry, gently bring your attention back to carefully folding your clothes. Fold each article with loving care, feel the texture of the fabric, smell the freshly laundered aroma of the clothing, and you will immerse yourself in meditation. With each returning of your mind to what you are doing, you are practicing thought training. Each time you "launder" your thoughts from preoccupation on anything other than the present moment, you are engaged in escaping from the prison of the mind.

THE LIFESTYLE OF THE ENLIGHTENED

A Zen story tells about a monk who before he learned how to meditate carried water in a bucket from the stream, prepared tea and chopped wood. After he was enlightened and became a master of meditation, he carried water in a bucket from the stream, prepared tea and chopped wood. And, we might add, did his laundry.

THE ENVIRONMENTAL PRAYER

Silence, by itself, has meditative, exploratory, revealing and healing qualities. Cultivating silence requires no training by a guru, no books or tapes, not even the need to attend a workshop. A good place to start the practice of silence is with an environmental prayer.

Simply strive to make your living space quiet. Turn the TV off regularly, share silent moments with friends or family members and minimize even the "white noise" of clutter. When your environment is silent, your soul more naturally falls into prayerful silence.

> Silence will illuminate you in God...
> and deliver you from phantoms of ignorance.
> Silence will unite you to God....
> In the beginning we have to force ourselves
> to be silent. But then from our very silence
> is born something that draws us into deeper silence.
>
> —Isaac of Nineveh, seventh century Syrian monk

> Imprison yourself in silence.
> Resist trying to escape.
> Let silence suck you
> into deeper silence,
> saturated silence;
> then you will
> escape.

A KISSINGER LESSON

Once when Henry Kissinger was Secretary of State, he was given a report to read. The next day he called the person responsible for the report into his office. Handing it back, he asked, "Is this the best you can do?" The person took the report, rewrote it, and then returned it to Kissinger. The next day Kissinger again handed it back with the same question, "Is this the best you can do?" Two more times he rejected the report, then when he repeated his question a fourth time, the staff person answered, "Yes, damn it, that's the best I can do." Kissinger smiled and said, "Good, then I'll read it."

Doing something with all your heart and soul — fully investing yourself to make whatever you're engaged in the "best" it can be — is perhaps the best way to practice the ancient liberating art of meditation.

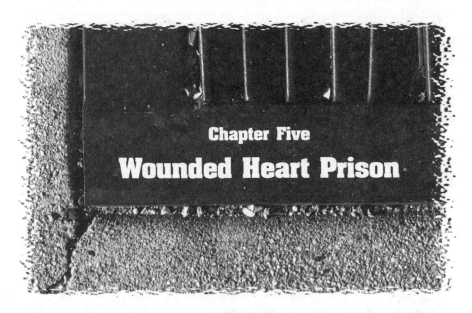

Chapter Five
Wounded Heart Prison

There are many kinds of injuries that can cast us into Wounded Heart Prison, from physical or sexual abuse to rejection or unrequited love, to abandonment or betrayal. Moreover, Wounded Heart can be a jail where we're only confined for a few days, or when we're deeply wounded it can be a prison where we are incarcerated for years, or even for life. Regardless of the nature of our wounds or whether it's a jail or prison, we are still prisoners. Medieval prisons and political concentration camps of our day are famous for torturing their prisoners. Similarly, Wounded Heart Prison inflicts on its inmates the painful torture of an anguished or broken heart.

STICKS AND STONES

"Sticks and stones may break my bones, but words will never hurt me" is a false childhood taunt! Indeed, words do hurt. While verbal wounds may not be as serious as spouse battering, rape or other violent crimes, they are at the root of other expressions of violence. And because being the target of hurtful words is a form of wounding with which we are all familiar, it will be the focus of our exploration of Wounded Heart Prison.

Rare are those of us who are unaffected by unkind and angry

words. Harsh words can injure as easily, and often more seriously, than sticks and stones! Words of disdain, criticism and ridicule puncture deeply, especially when they are unexpected. Pearl Harbor-style verbal attacks do greater damage because they catch us "off guard." This term implies a defensive position of being "on guard." And we usually don't employ such protective postures with lovers, spouses, friends and family. Verbal attacks are particularly painful when they are in response to some unintended offense — to a time when we have touched a sore spot of which we were unaware. We can also feel battered when we're the subject of a barrage of real or perceived offenses that have been stockpiled over time.

Words also imprison. When we are the target of thoughtless or intended verbal anger, we are incarcerated in several ways. Firstly, we can be imprisoned behind self-pity's barbed wire. We can feel sorry for ourselves at having been the victim of a verbal attack, especially when it is undeserved. The suffering of these wounds also separates us from the usual enjoyment of life. The savoring of our usual joys is spoiled by the bitter taste in our mouths and hearts. We are also held captive by a sense of loss that springs from the temporary or total termination of a close relationship. The anger and hostility behind a verbal assault is often lethal to a once mutual friendship or love.

First Aid

A word wound, like any tearing or piercing injury, requires treatment as soon as possible to prevent infection. Gangrene of the soul is a real and deadly danger following untreated verbal wounds. Because these neglected wounds can quickly fill with the pus of rejection or revenge, first aid should be given as soon as possible. Begin the healing by medicating the wound with prayer, which is a powerful triple treatment that cleanses, heals and liberates. Indeed, prayer both cures the wound and is a way of escaping from Wounded Heart Prison back to our normal life.

Perhaps the first form of prayer to administer to the wound is the healing salve of silence. Simply resting in God's restorative presence can release powerful antibodies against the infection and take the sting out of the wound.

Jesus the Healer-Liberator gives the injured this further, and challenging, prayer prescription: "Pray for those who wound you."[1] Pray for what? Earnestly petition God that the attacker's verbal violence will not boomerang back upon him or her. Verbal anger and abuse are acts of violence. Every venting of violence begins as a thought-seed. The longer the thought-seed is soaked in brooding indignation, the more explosive will be the anger. This, in turn, creates a greater harvest of evil to be reaped by the sower. The Liberator Buddha warned his disciples in the clearest and strongest of words about the consequences of even spoken violence.

> Never speak harsh words
> For they will rebound upon you.
> Angry words hurt
> And the hurt rebounds....
>
> He who harms the harmless
> Or hurts the innocent,
> ten times shall he fall —
>
> Into torment or infirmity,
> Injury or disease or madness,
> Persecution or fearful accusation,
> Loss of family, loss of fortune.
> Fire from heaven shall strike his house.[2]

We always reap what we plant. Plant evil, and you'll reap evil. Plant hostility, and you'll reap upon yourself a harvest of outrage. So pray that the one who caused you pain be spared the fruits of his or her wounding, angry words. Ask God to make sterile that person's seeds of animosity. And because every thought is a seed, plant wisely your return thoughts. Happy are those who sow only good seeds.

ANTISEPTIC PRAYER

Praying for the good of the offender is truly a cleansing antiseptic. This antiseptic is essential before complete healing can take place. Like any flesh wound, even after proper treatment the wound will continue to bring you pain. So do not expect prayer and forgiveness to instantly remove the pain caused by the offense. The most ancient therapeutic knowledge affirms, however, that time heals.

As a patient, be patient. Frequently throughout the first days, cleanse the wound with antiseptic prayer for your attacker. Then, take care in the days after your word-injury not to disturb your wound by mentally going over the offense again and again. This has the effect of picking at a scab before it's had a chance to heal. When tempted to do so, remind yourself that you are a prisoner in the infirmary of Wounded Heart Prison. Repeatedly taking offense at the original act of violence only hurls you deeper into the dungeon of the prison. Continue, rather, to re-escape from the injury whenever your mind returns to mulling it over. When tempted to probe the wound by thinking about it, remember that the mind can only think about one thing at a time. With gentle discipline turn your mind to something else. Turn your attention back to prayer or to some project or work. Each time you discover you are back in prison because you are again feeling sorry for yourself, escape once more in the same way. Especially in the days right after the attack, remain diligent in the process of escaping from Wound Heart Prison. If you continue to prayerfully cleanse your heart wound, opening to God's grace and praying for the good of the offender, you will find that each night of sleep will reduce the shock and pain of the injury.

IN PAIN, BE GRATEFUL

Gratitude heals. Your word wound will heal more quickly if you also frequently apply the maximum strength antibiotic cream of gratefulness. The will of God, as Paul of Tarsus says, is "…in all circumstances to give thanks."[3] "All circumstances," of course, includes that painful one which has imprisoned you in Wounded Heart Prison. Naturally, the use of antibiotic gratefulness will require being creative as you explore ways for giving thanks in the midst of your pain. But as you pray for the offender, one thing you can be grateful for is that you have an opportunity to personally practice one of the great acts of heroism required of his disciples by the Savior-Rescuer. As we will see in more depth in chapter ten of this book, gratitude is also a most magical source of liberation.

SOULS CAN GROW BY DISORDER

When we are emotionally troubled, we are *disturbed*, a word that originally meant being thrown into disorder. Grace, however, is hidden everywhere. Examine carefully the action that caused you pain for the special grace it may contain for you. The poet Maya Angelou once asked a friend about an unsettling experience, "Did it disturb your soul and call you to grow?"[4] When something disturbing happens to us, we are aroused out of our routines. The normal, often unconscious, order of daily life is shaken or even thrown into chaos. Yet this kind of pain can be awakening. The soul can be stirred into growth, or it can shrink. The suffering that disturbs us can enlarge our spirit and strengthen us, or it can cause our will toward life to shrivel.

Soul-growth occurs when we do not probe the wound but carefully examine it with sterile, surgical question marks. With gentleness ask yourself what made this attack so painful? Which word-weapons caused the most pain? Were the arrows of accusations valid? In all of this what can I learn about myself? about the other person? Has my pain awakened me to ways that I may have caused pain to others?

PACIFISTS MAKE THE BEST LOVERS

The healing process and praying for the offender are both acts of liberation. Praying for the offender cuts through the chains of resentment and revenge that so readily incarcerate us. Whenever we are attacked, either verbally or physically, we're in danger of being captured by the prehistoric passion to strike back in self-defense. Weapons for this reactive assault are not in short supply: A stockpile of word weapons and other military tactics are at our disposal to inflict pain on the perpetrator. In our hidden underground arsenals is ample ammunition fueled by our as-yet-unexpressed resentment, which can at any moment be launched in a retaliatory attack. To truly be nonviolent in thought, word and deed requires perpetual vigilance along with constant inspection of our underground arsenals to disarm any old wound-memories. The memories will remain rusting away if we don't engage them, but their warheads are so dangerous and resilient that usually more than one defusing is required.

THE IGLOO PRISON

Resentment, especially when the verbal attack is judged as unjustified, can confine us behind walls of solid ice. When injured, we sometimes insulate ourselves against the offender by retreating into a personal igloo. However, icy indifference, the cold shoulder or a South

Pole silence are not only signals that we have been injured, they also can be used to punish the guilty party. Sadly, we may even enjoy the ice-alation of being indifferently cold when punishing those who have offended us. Yet when we retaliate, we hurl ourselves into the pit of Igloo Prison. In Dante's Divine Comedy the lowest level of hell was not a place of unquenchable flames but of frozen ice.

The good news, however, is that prayer is an ice pick, a tool to escape from igloo prison — that is, if we desire to break loose. Often before the icy walls can begin to melt, some psychological or physical distance is required. It is, therefore, wise to declare a mutual Silence-Zone to create psychological space into which each can retreat for whatever time is required to quiet the angry turmoil within. Paradoxically, we must often cool down in order to defrost. Yet if we make our retreat into a zone of prayer, the space between us not only becomes a neutral zone — a buffer in the midst of a battle or a time of cease-fire — it can also be the fertile ground out of which reconciliation emerges.

Of course, it also takes heat to melt ice. Prayerful physical distance can act like the sun and can hasten the melting process. And the warmth of genuine prayerful concern for the other can further help defrost our igloo anger. While it's often difficult to generate enough heat on our own, through our prayer we may access the fiery love of God's Spirit that can melt even the most formidable iceberg. Even more, our prayer can prime the fiery passion to be free.

THE TIME FOR RECONCILIATION

Once our ice has melted, the next stage in the process involves reconciliation. True reconciliation seeks to heal and unite, never to harm. When the offender offers reconciliation, extreme care is required by the one injured. We need to be alert to the danger of using this divine occasion as an excuse for diabolic revenge. As swords were once hidden inside innocent-appearing walking canes, so revenge can be a disguised weapon. While accepting the apology from the offender, we can be tempted to seek leverage by expounding on the depths of our wounds. Reconciliation that's a true and liberating sacrament of peace requires both parties to discard all weapons. To escape permanently — rather than just temporarily — from Wounded Heart Prison requires that we forgive and then forget. Pray for the gift of holy Alzheimers, the grace of a special forgetting. This grace uses the mind's natural erasing abilities, which have the capacity to delete recollection files of ugly, painful memories (see Escape Tool #8 on page 75). Be patient, however, for the deeper the wound, the more deeply buried are the tangled roots of a memory. Be patient and disciplined as, again and again, you dig up the roots of old, dark memories until they die from lack of support. Forgiving-forgetting is a Godlike feat, which at times seems impossible without divine assistance. Yet it is possible for mature evolving humans, otherwise we would never have been challenged to practice holy reconciliation. In fact, St. Paul tells us that in the process of "God reconciling the world to himself" God has given us the "ministry of reconciliation."[5] The world is indeed wounded and continues to suffer from ancient memories, the roots of which grow evil thistles of ethnic and national wars, the killing of others in the name of God and other ghastly inhuman horrors. As Gandhi said, "We must be the change we wish to see in the world." For the wounded world to heal, we must be ministers of reconciliation in our individual worlds. And to do that, we must allow our own wounds to heal.

OLD UNHEALED WOUNDS

Wounds heal and wounds fester. Most verbal wounds heal in time and linger only as painless, memory scars. Yet past word-of-mouth wounds that never heal completely imprison us. Rather than painless scars, they can leave scabs that continue to ulcerate and blister. While the actual injury may have happened many years ago, the inflammation can cause us continual distress or, if less serious, may only occasionally flare up.

The inventory of possible old wounds is long, and those listed here are but a few:

THE LITANY OF OLD WOUNDS

A betrayal by a good friend,
A spouse's rejection by divorce,
Not being loved enough by a parent,
Childhood jealousy and envy,
Early teenage ridicule,
Institutional abuses,

Rejection or correction by an authority figure,
Being subjected to religious shame,
A major life failure,
Racial, ethnic, sexual or religious prejudice,
A psychological illness,
Personal sexual mistakes,
Being a victim of physical or sexual abuse,
Being falsely accused....

Old, unhealed wounds imprison. Unhealed injuries to the soul are like bruises that cause pain when they are touched. Unhealed wound-memories can awaken without warning. For example, people in authority, simply by their presence, may rub up against a scab of an old wound caused by a parent or other authority figure. Similarly, a wholesome sexual exchange, or even an innocent gesture of affection may trigger the memory of a past sexual exploitation or impropriety!

The Great Liberator was deeply wounded. He was flogged, crowned with thorns and pierced in his hands and feet at his crucifixion. Yet the incisions that cut more deeply were his being betrayed and abandoned by his companions and close friends — and, even more, his experience of being abandoned by God. Ponder the image of the risen Christ: After being raised up from the tomb he goes at once to visit those who pierced him by their unfaithfulness. The accounts of his post-Resurrection appearances contain an intriguing fact: He still has his wounds in his hands, feet and side! These nail wounds, however, are not oozing blood, and they do not cause pain. Now they are glorious. Jesus' wounds are more than a means for his disciples to identify him. They are victor's trophies and heirlooms of holiness.

The unpierced disciples have their wounds too. They are wounded by their guilt and shame and are fearful of being confronted with their betrayal. Instead, Jesus greets them with the healing gifts of peace and forgiveness. Dying on the cross, their Savior-friend had cried out, "Forgive them Father — not just the Temple priests, the Roman soldiers, Pontius Pilate and the mob of people crying out for this crucifixion — forgive my disloyal disciples too. For none of them know what they are doing; they have temporarily lost their minds."[6] Now with his wounds made glorious, Jesus gives his disciples the fruit of that forgiveness.

Making Glorious What Is Ugly

Forgiving those who wound us in any way does more than heal our wounds. It can make those wounds glorious. When granting pardon to those who have caused us great pain seems beyond our reach, we can pray as did Jesus on the cross: "O God, forgive them, for they have acted without thinking, unaware of the damage they are doing." In that pattern, our glorious wounds can become beautiful scars, our most valuable trophies. By contrast, our unhealed, ugly, unforgiven, non-glorious wounds are orphans. They separate us from ourselves, from those who have wounded us and from the suffering family of the Body of our Liberator Christ. "If one member suffers," as St. Paul wrote to the early disciples in Corinth, "all the members suffer."[7] This is the reality of the United Kindom, in which all are members of one body, one holy family.

Our orphaned wounds are not conscious of belonging to those of our Redeemer-Liberator on his cross. These unhealed and life-draining old wounds imprison us in the past and prevent our liberty in the present. When they are rubbed against, we tend to react. Yet when they are awakened to their intimate connection to the wounds of Christ, we can begin to act, to act in forgiveness, compassion and love. And when we begin to forgive, we are able to rejoice that we have been gifted with the opportunity to share in the sufferings of Christ.[8] Uniting our pain to his gives us a share in his redemptive liberation and healing of the world.

Mystical Math

Forgiveness that is freeing must be repeated again and again. When Simon Peter asked, "How often must I forgive my neighbor? As many as seven times?" Jesus answered, "Not seven times, but seventy times seven times."[9] "Forgive seventy times a day,"[10] echoes the sacred wisdom of Islam. Indeed, this is practical wisdom for how to make all our wounds glorious. The greatest generosity is giving forgiveness, and the good news is that each of us has the resources of a billionaire. Your forgiveness bank account is unlimited, so be unsparing in your generosity, aware that the more generous you are in such gifts, the larger your soul becomes and the more you are at liberty. Go about your day being extravagantly generous, giving pardon seventy times seven a day — to drivers who cut into your lane, to co-workers or customers or store clerks who are rude to you, to friends or family who rain on your parade by disappointing you, even to those who talk behind your back or falsely accuse you.

It's not only charity — forgiveness also begins at home. Forgive yourself seventy times seventy times for your dumb mistakes, your faults, your wrong choices, your injuries to others. Self-absolution makes it easier to forgive others. Just as love of neighbor begins with love of self, so forgiveness of neighbor begins with forgiveness of self.

Practice giving conscious absolution to those who offend you in person and even to those you see on the news who have murdered, raped or inflicted any violence. Practice retarded absolution — a backwards forgiveness toward those guilty of causing you pain in the past. Finally, there is no copyright on the priestly ritual of absolution. Whenever possible, grant pardon and absolution for another's sins by tracing the sign of the cross over the person, saying, "I forgive you in the name of the Father, and of the Son and of the Holy Spirit."

Chapter Five Inventory of Escape Tools and Unshackling Reflections

ESCAPE TOOL #8 — I CAN'T REMEMBER

In order to remember, we need to forget; and when we forget, we re-member. The mind's function of memory is marvelously well-suited to daily life. Each time we remember something important we must forget something. Imagine how difficult grocery shopping would be if you never forgot your previous grocery lists. To remember where you parked your car at the crowded shopping mall requires that you forget where you parked it the last time. According to Dr. Neil Macrae, a psychologist at England's University of Bristol, this automatic, unconscious process called *temporary forgetting* is essential for remembering life's daily details.

This unconscious, automatic mental ability can become conscious and intentional when we prayerfully *intend* to forget in order to forgive. When we are engaged in such holy forgetting, we re-member the body of Christ; through reconciliation we rejoin two members of the Body that had been separated. Yet even in this intentional prayer of forgiveness, let nature take its course: Choose to remember what is important today, in the process letting past personal injuries and offenses become unimportant. In time these less and less significant wounds will disappear.

ESCAPE TOOL #9 — CATCH YOUR BREATH

Having the wind knocked out of us hurts. This is the pain we feel when we are a casualty of angry, spiteful words. Without wind, our sails and our souls become depressed. And having been walloped windless makes us spiritless, so it becomes prime time for prayer.

Pray to the Wind and for some wind. Entreat the Spirit-Wind to fill your sails and soul with vitality. Let the main body of your prayer be inhaling, breathing in deeply. Again and again, fill your lungs and your heart with mystic breeze. As you breathe in, you might pray these words: "Wind of the Spirit, fill me with your Holy Breath."

Repeat this prayer, or one of your own creation, as you spend several minutes in deep breathing. Then, pray for the person who knocked the wind out of you.

ESCAPE TOOL #10 — BITTERSWEET REMEMBRANCE

Among your possessions you might have some things that were given to you by the person who has caused you affliction. The very sight of these items will likely increase your sense of loss and agony. But do not remove them from sight or throw them away. Instead, use them as bittersweet remembrances inviting you to give thanks for the good times and love they represent. "Giving thanks in all situations"[3] is the golden rule for disciples of the Liberator, and this includes being grateful in painful times. This bittersweet attitude, indeed, leads to a prayer of gratitude: being grateful for happier times while we are suffering. The pain we are experiencing has been caused by the very one who once gave us happiness. And the sense of communion and peace that we are experiencing has been indirectly caused by the very one who brought us pain. Within this circle of God's grace, gratitude is good medicine. It holds a healing balm and the key to liberation.

PARDON PRAYER FOR WORDS OF WOUNDING

Not rough sticks and hard stones
　　but sharp, piercing, angry words
　　have battered and pierced my heart,
　　causing me great pain
　　and plunging me into Wounded Heart Prison.

O Holy Healer, ease my heartache
　　and salve my stinging wounds.
Even more, help me to pray for my offender.
Move my heart
　　and endow me with a priestly tongue,
　　that I might speak those pardoning words,
　　"I forgive you. Go in peace."

O God, you who are a Perpetual Pardoner,
　　form my heart according to yours
　　that I might earnestly pray
　　that you spare my transgressor
　　the harvest of his/her harmful seeds
　　born of angry words and deeds.
Genetically alter the DNA of those unholy seeds,
　　refashioning them forever into
　　seeds of blessing and grace.

Alzheimer my unerasable memories
　　of all my past injuries and hurts

till I am free of their ensnaring roots.
For only by my loving pardon
will I, and my wounded world, find the boost
to take another giant step of growth
away from violence and war
and toward the kingdom of life.

ESCAPE TOOL #11 – PAPER AND PEN ESCAPE: THE ANGRY REPORT

Anger can be a whirlpool of various emotions. To keep from drowning by being sucked into this swirling vortex of feelings, take a pen and explore on paper the cause of your anger. This descriptive diary can be very intimate and detailed, encouraging you to record your most hostile feelings and the reasons for them. All during this reporting, try to zero in on the source of your anger.

A cousin method would be to list all the reasons for your anger toward the responsible person in a narrow column down one side of a single page of paper. Then on the other side of the page write a column itemizing all the reasons why you like the person. Then compare the two lists. In the process, hopefully, you may put your anger in perspective.

A third form of paper and pen exercise involves assuming the position of a neutral observer making out an anger-accident report. Be as impartial and detached as possible. Simply record what happened and the various reactions and emotions that were expressed, concluding with your nonpartisan evaluation of the situation.

Chapter Six
Angerville Prison

This chapter tours two of humanity's more familiar places of incarceration. Anger is one of the seven deadly sins. It was placed in the heart of the list by St. Gregory the Great (540-604 A.D.), right between envy and melancholy. His Deadly Seven were: pride, envy, anger, melancholy, avarice, gluttony and lust. That list was adjusted by Thomas Aquinas and other medieval theologians into two groups, spiritual and carnal. Spiritual sins were pride, anger, envy, covetousness and sloth; while the carnal sins were lust and gluttony. Anger, *iracudus*, was counted a vice by the Latin poet Horace (65-8 B.C.), was denounced by Buddha four hundred years prior to that and was included among the deadly sins by the desert father Evagrios of Pontus. Yet, despite this strong tradition, the contemporary concept is that anger is only an unavoidable aspect of human behavior in any stressful, overworked society. In fact, to speak of sin today is perhaps the only sin — and certainly one that is sure to raise the ire of many people.

Yet, regardless of how you categorize it, there's no denying that anger cages the angry. Those incarcerated in Angerville Prison can be sentenced there for brief periods of time, perhaps only a few minutes at a time, or they can be forced to serve life sentences. Escape is impossible, and will not even be attempted, until we are aware of our incarceration. When anger is morally judged simply as an unavoidable passion for those living in a hectic, imperfect world, it is often justified and even made righteous. Such an attitude obscures the reality that the angry are held captive. So the first requirement of any liberation from anger is an honest acknowledgment of being restricted by chains and constricted inside a cage.

KNOW THE FACE OF YOUR JAILER

As there are seven deadly sins, so there are seven deadly angers. Anger's seven henchmen are: Indignation, Rage, Fury, Madness, Ire, Wrath and Scorn.

Indignation is an expression of anger arising out of some injustice, ingratitude, mean behavior or affront to our self-image. It is often justified and described as *righteous*.

Rage is violent, uncontrolled anger, as in a raving fury. Paradoxically, it can also mean a craze or fad, as in the expression, "It's all the rage." In our times, rage has become "the rage." *Rabid,* a cousin to rage, is an expression of unreasonable or even fanatically zealous anger in our beliefs. It's also related to rabies, an infectious disease transmitted by the bite of a dog or some other animal — or of a religious zealot.

Fury: Being furious implies an intense expression of rage, as in a fierce storm or violent whirlwind, in which a person approaches a state of frenzy.

Mad: one of the more common terms for anger. It more properly means being insane or mentally ill. The more colloquial meaning, however, is a frenzied state of anger. The fact that anger is associated with insanity reveals how this emotion can capture the rational mind and judgment.

Ire carries the sense of irritability, the condition of being easily annoyed. Like a low-grade infection, ire is lingering anger. It has more intense expression in those who are hot-tempered, who quickly fly off the handle as well as those who tend to be cranky, touchy or overly sensitive.

Wrath is another name for passionate anger or fury. It is often attributed to the punishing anger of God or the vengeance of humans.

Scorn is an angry and extreme contempt for someone or something. It is an anger born out of hatred.

Naming the Terrible Seven and being aware of their presence is a way of being freed of their diabolic possession.

THE NATURE OF ANGER

The very word anger denotes imprisonment since its root meaning involves being squeezed or confined to a narrow place. Humans share anger with animals, which tells us it is a primal emotion, a primordial relic of our evolution. Animals respond with anger when they are threatened by humans or another animal, when something imperils their offspring or food or attempts to take over their territory. Among humans anger can also be an unconscious reaction to some threat against our pride or self-image. While a primitive part of our personality, anger can be good. It is high-octane aboriginal energy that can be used to fight or flee. And when directed by a higher consciousness, it can be a force that helps us overcome monumental obstacles. It can help us express what needs to be said, as in outrage against a moral or spiritual injustice.

Sentencing children to prison is barbaric. Yet, countless children even in civilized societies are incarcerated in Angerville by various forms of abuse inflicted by a parent or other adults in authority. Since a child's anger cannot normally be expressed because of a lack of status as a responsible person, that anger is forced to go underground. Unexpressed and unresolved, anger becomes liquid and flows deep beneath the surface of consciousness. These subterranean rivers can unexpectedly and volcanically erupt to the surface as fountains of indignation and spurting springs of hostility, often over minor issues. During teenage years anger can be unexpressed rage of resentment toward fate or God at having been shortchanged in gifts of personality, intelligence or physical beauty. It might seethe in a low-grade rage toward authority or erupt in a sporting event or a disagreement with peers. Anger can also become a continuous cellar source of irritability in adult life: a dissatisfaction with one's job or marriage, one's social or financial status. The underground rivers can also erupt in adult life on a regular basis like Yellowstone's Old Faithful, like a geyser of steaming anger over some personal affront or ideological injustice.

Anger can be focused or unfocused. Anger can be active or passive. It can be denied or disguised. Yet regardless of its forms, both Jesus and

Buddha were uncompromising in their teaching: Angry thoughts are dangerous and can be lethal, even the more socially acceptable varieties.

INDIGNATION

Indignation was at the top of the Seven Deadly list and appropriately so because it merits special consideration. Again, indignation is an angry reaction to an affront to our dignity or self-worth, to meanness, ingratitude or injustice. Indignation is often equated with righteous anger. We too easily convince ourselves that our anger is righteous indignation and so is guiltless. Neither Jesus nor Buddha, however, granted dispensations for justified anger. Paul Jordan-Smith writes, "The problem of righteous anger lies not in the anger *per se,* but in the contamination of the self, so that it becomes *self-righteous,* and it is seldom that we see a truly righteous anger."[1]

In the normal course of daily events, it's much safer for our souls simply to acknowledge that anger is anger — and not try to justify it. Moreover, Jesus taught that even thoughts of hate and violent anger counted the same as physical acts of murder: "Whoever is angry with his brother (or sister) will be liable to fiery Gehenna (to the judgment of murder)."[2] And again, Buddha taught that those who think evil and angry thoughts create their own world of encompassing evil and violence. These two holy Liberators knew that our thoughts are energized magnets attracting either good or evil — and angry thoughts create a hellish world.

We too often see how angry social and moral prophets, outraged (in-a-rage) at injustices and oppression, set in motion a downward spiral of vicious hate. Deceived by a false sense of it being guiltlessly righteous rage, they earn themselves a place in Angerville Penitentiary, if not fiery Gehenna. If you feel the flames of such fury because of the oppression of women, because of injustices done to migrant workers or because of racial, sexual or some other discrimination, do not put out the fire. Rather, convert these prophetic fires fanned by moral injustices into the revolutionary energy of laboring for reform. Unconverted justified anger is deceptive and destructive. Angry reformers are not true reformers. While the social changes they long to accomplish may be very valid, the verbal or physical violence toward those guilty of the injustices is far from valid, and because it is invalid it is impotent. Only love reforms. True reformers are those who love that which they seek to change.

The moment your inner warning light indicates that you are becoming indignant, take the advice of Psalm 37: "Calm your anger, forget your rage."[3] Quickly switch on your converter and begin to transform your anger-energy into a positive propellant for good. Perform some work — something constructive to correct the injustice — regardless of how small or insignificant it may seem. Hostility directed toward those who inflict political and social injustices on others is itself an unjust act of violence. Replace "righteous" hostility with love. Pray for, bless and love those who engineer exploitation of the poor, who are the architects and enforcers of social oppression.

DIVINE ANGER

Reject the temptation to be Godlike! In the preceding pages holiness has often been equated with being Godlike. Yet for the disciples of Jesus, being holy absolutely requires that you *not* be Godlike — at least not in the sense of the wrathful God of the Old Testament. Divine wrath at sinners was expressed with fire and brimstone, lightning bolts out of the blue or life-destroying floods. Natural disasters, diseases and birth defects were acknowledged to be acts of divine wrath. That concept lingers with us today. The medical term "stroke" is used for a sudden attack of paralysis or a cerebral rupture. The term originated in a belief that the paralysis was caused by a blow — a stroke — by God! Scripture is crowded with expressions of an angry, wrathful God. We still summon up such a quick-to-anger God to visit vengeance upon sinners or our enemies. The theme of one of the most famous sermons of Jonathan Edwards, a Calvinist theologian of the eighteenth century, "Sinners in the Hands of an Angry God," is frequently recycled today by fiery preachers. Those endeavoring to baptize their anger as righteous, especially against what they perceive as being sinful, are quick to claim they are instruments of a wrathful God.

DON'T BE LIKE JESUS!

The anger of the gentle Good Shepherd is often piously honey-coated as righteous indignation. Yet consider the Sabbath when he was in the synagogue and was approached by a man with a withered hand. When Jesus asked the Pharisees present if it is lawful to do good, to save life, on the Sabbath, their only response was silence. Mark tells us that "Looking around at them *with anger,* he said to the afflicted man, 'Stretch out your hand.' He stretched it out, and his hand was made whole."[4] Because they were trying to bait him to violate the Sabbath law nothing less than a laser-like anger from the Master pierced the Pharisees' religious facade.

A more famous incident is his frenzied tirade in the temple, which has been sanitized by the title "the Cleansing of the Temple." The violence he used to drive the money-changers, sheep-sellers and dove-peddlers out of the temple area, (all of whom had a "legitimate right" to be there) kicking over their tables and seats, would fit the description of uncontrollable rage. His disciples must have been shaken by his actions since he had so passionately preached patience, peace and nonviolence. His behavior needs to be framed by his previous prophetic action. In Mark's Gospel the riot in the temple immediately follows the scene where Jesus curses a fruitless fig tree. On the way to Jerusalem from Bethany he notices the tree and goes over to it to see if it has any figs, but he finds only leaves. Disregarding the fact that it was not the season for figs, he curses the tree, "May no one ever eat of your fruit again!"[5] The fig tree is clearly symbolic, but cursing is a form of the violent speech he had forbidden along with being angry at others. Perhaps Walt Whitman spoke for Jesus when he said of himself, "Do I contradict myself? Very well then, I contradict myself. I am large, I contain multitudes."

At the Temple Jesus quotes Psalm 69: "Zeal for your house consumes me." Is this one of those rare occasions, in Paul Jordan-Smith's words, of "a truly righteous anger"? If so, Jesus models for us how infrequently in the context of his whole life such righteous rage erupts. Is it also possible that these are occasions where Jesus was ensnared by his emotions? If so, the wholesome good news is that he was fully human, capable of anger and then of escaping from it.

No one plans in advance to fly off the handle. What makes Angerville such an insidious prison is that the various forms of anger are usually involuntary, so we feel powerless to prevent them. Yet as with fire prevention, we can practice some anti-anger safeguards. Perhaps the best prevention begins with thought-watch. Flare-ups commonly begin with seething thoughts. We need to be vigilant in removing these seed thoughts — or at least ensuring that they get no air to breathe. Ask yourself that great exploratory question: Why do I bristle and then blow up over this or that? Why does having my flight canceled or being the victim of someone's inefficiency make me angry? Such questions are easier answered when we remember the trio of anger-triggers, the famous SCS trinity: Self-image, Control and Security. When any of these is threatened, we are likely to react. We can react indignantly to some perceived violation of our rights, or when circumstances or the actions of others cause us to feel out of control, or when anything endangers our sense of security. Moreover, the source can also lie buried, so we need to be willing to trace back any angry adult flare-up to its corresponding childhood trauma or tantrum.

ROAD RAGE

Today's increasing incidents of road rage and airliner rage are essentially childhood-induced adult tantrums. The evolutionary call is to "…be free of anger."[6] The purpose of spirituality is to mature. Individually and collectively, we need to move beyond childish tantrums so as to be liberated. One of the places to start is to be aware that tantrums are self-destructive boomerangs. Throw a tantrum and it will come back at you with amazing speed and force. As our poverty of time, the abundance of demands on us and our cultural decline in politeness daily make social life more irritable and incline us toward tantrums, we need to make equally impelling evolutionary steps toward spiritual maturity if we are to find tranquility and peace.

The next time your radar indicates your mind is being visited by an impatient intruder thought, recall a piece of wisdom credited to Thomas Jefferson: "When angry, count to ten before your speak; if very angry, a hundred." And to keep your sense of humor, you might try Mark Twain's version: "When angry, count to a hundred, when very angry, swear."

As this chapter ends, it's comforting to know that God is patient even when we aren't. Aware that overcoming anger is a long, evolutionary process, God inspired the author of Ephesians to say, "Be angry and sin not: Let not the sun go down on your anger."[7] Interesting admonition: "Sin not." Many years ago I read a book by a spiritual writer whose name I do not remember. He compared anger to two types of fires. One type is caused by a flame igniting a pile of dry straw. Instantly the blaze flares up and almost as quickly disappears. These spontaneous, unconscious flare-ups of anger are not sinful. The second kind of anger-fire is built in a fireplace by constantly adding logs seasoned with reasons to be angry. These various logs are consciously, or sometimes unconsciously, fed into the fire to keep it ablaze. This brooding, nurtured anger is dangerous and sinful.

Moral for fire fighters: Keep your straw wet and your log pile low.

Chapter Six Inventory of Escape Tools and Unshackling Reflections

THE GRANDEST OF SPECTACLES

In the mid-1880s Thomas De Quincey wrote, "Call for the grandest of all earthly spectacles, what is that? It is the sun going to his rest. Call for the grandest of all human sentiments, what is that? It is that man should forget his anger before he lies down to sleep."

THE GOOD ANGER RULE

A thumbnail Mental Health Rule: Never allow yourself to become angry about anything over which you have no control. This only adds to frustration and is harmful to your health. It's especially in situations beyond our direct influence that the truth of this maxim reaches home. Anger does more harm to the vessel that holds it than it does to the one upon whom it is poured.

ESCAPE TOOL #12 – LOST AND FOUND DEPARTMENT

Playfulness is the Holy Spirit's charism of fun. Indeed, blessed are those who are full of fun. While playfulness is common in children and young pups, it is often sadly misplaced by adults. Lusting to be taken seriously, most of us have pawned our playfulness for trinkets of busyness. If your sense of play is pawned or missing, go to your inner Lost and Found Department and recover it as soon as you can.

Playfulness defuses anger. Just as the physical exercises of walking or jogging in place help to flush out the surge of adrenaline and other chemicals created by anger, so also does the play of self-humor. You might try to escape your growing anger by smiling — even if you don't feel like it. The purely physical act of looking happy has the power to create a rapid reduction in negative hormones and an increase in calming endorphins.

Be creative. Find something you can laugh at in the behavior or circumstance bothering you. Turn it upside down or inside out. Play with it instead of fighting it; see your situation as a playing field rather than a combat zone.

> A great person is one
> who does not lose
> a child's heart.
> —A Chinese proverb

ESCAPE TOOL #13 – AN ANGER ENEMA

Enemas can be messy. Yet blessed are the peacemakers who help to administer anger enemas. Liberating others is an essential part of being free yourself. When you encounter someone bloated with anger and eager to vent it, gently assist that person in flushing the toxin out of his or her system. But do be careful: This can be messy. Be prepared to get splattered in the cleansing process. Yet if you're going to be effective, you need to be a self-assured assistant who is convinced that healing can come with emptying. Giving advice, on the other hand, is an additive that often only muddies the waters and so is not good medicine when assisting someone having an enema.

Although the two processes may look alike, administering an enema is different from encouraging venting. Contrary to contemporary folk medicine, venting anger is not always healthy, and it often even increases anger. Venting does not solve the problem and at best is only a temporary release. Research has shown that those who engage in high levels of anger have increased coronary disease and hypertension, which increases their chances of a heart attack and other illnesses. An enema assistant knows that both the stressful irritant and the anger have to be flushed and so is patient with the patient: first by listening with real interest and concern and then by carefully asking the kind of questions that will help the anger-infected person explore his or her hostility. The best enemas are those that completely cleanse the patient, so a loving enema assistant will compassionately probe to make sure that all the resentment has been expressed and released.

While self-administered enemas are beneficial, the power of talking out your anger with another person — and with God in prayer — make assisted enemas much more effective.

BE A CONQUEROR

Buddha taught, "If one were to conquer in a battle a thousand times a thousand men, the one who conquers oneself is the greater warrior."[8] Self-control is a form of self-conquering that frees us from allowing events and circumstances to have dominion over us. This personal responsibility is recognized by all the world's great religions as essential on the road to true power. For example, we see this same admiration for self-control in Hinduism: "The one who restrains his rage from bolting within him is the true hero and charioteer, not the one who slays in battle many foes."[9]

Chinese Taoism echoes it again: "The one who overcomes others is strong. The one who overcomes oneself is mighty."[10]

The Ultimate Weapon Against Violence

Hate is never diminished by hatred;
Hate is only diminished by love
This is the eternal law.[11]

—the Buddha

Reflection

That eternal law spoken by the Buddha is denied whenever revenge is sought, even when it is disguised as justice. Buddha and Jesus called humanity to exercise the only way to diminish violence and evil, the way of love. Those who believe that they are making the world less violent by violently punishing criminals are ignorant of the eternal law. And in legal courts, ignorance of the law does not excuse us. Since childhood we have heard the eternal law, "Love your neighbor; do good to those who injure you; never return evil for evil."[12] Each act of refusal to live according to that eternal law is not only wrong, it contributes to global violence, hatred and evil. As Buddha and Jesus warned, those who return hate for hate and violence for violence must harvest what they plant.

Historical Parable of the Boomerang Theory

The British General Henry Shrapnel invented shrapnel, the antipersonnel bomb that sends lethal pieces of sharp metal flying outward in all directions when it explodes. Ironically, Henry Shrapnel was the first man wounded by his invention in a premature explosion at the 1793 evacuation of Dunkirk during the French Revolutionary Wars.

Making God Present

Where there is forgiveness there is God.[13]

—Sikhism

This teaching of the Sikh religion is ecumenical. For persons of every faith, every household act of pardon is like the Holy of Holies in the great Temple of Jerusalem, a tabernacle of the True Presence, a Mount Sinai, a Mecca, and every other sacred shrine of the Divine Presence. Forgiving another makes the place where reconciliation takes place "holy ground." The two parties involved should remove their shoes.

ANGER ESCAPE ADVICE

When you find yourself the target of another's anger or rudeness, avoid the tendency toward the primeval behavior of fight or flight. When attacked, you can strike back physically or verbally, or you can retreat into silence. Yet neither of these ways is helpful. Sam Horn, author of *Tongue Fu! How to Deflect, Disarm and Defuse Any Verbal Conflict,* proposes that as quickly as possible we attempt to trade places with the rude person. Ignore the urge to judge the rudeness as a personal attack.[14] The source of this rudeness may be the pressures of the work place, a problem at home, frustration with another person, a headache or a bad hair day. Yet regardless of the reason, ironclad your resistance not to judge the person or the person's behavior. Be compassionate. Smile, and try saying something like, "I'll bet this has been a hectic day for you."

BAD SILENCE

Silence is the most perfect expression of scorn.
—George Bernard Shaw

Escape Tool #14 — Belonging to the Bomb Squad

Angry blowups between spouses, partners and companions come in all shapes and sizes, ranging from firecrackers to one-ton bombs. Usually the hostile blast causes both parties to retreat in anger. Because of this normally hostile setting, reconciliation can be difficult and awkward without practice. Techniques for bridging the bomb crater caused by a blowup can include writing a note or letter expressing regrets — to which you might add a brief suspicion about the fuse that ignited the bomb. Another way to fill in the crater is to do something nice for the other person. Go out of your way to perform some small act of kindness that might have happened spontaneously before the blowup. This can serve as a nonverbal expression of reconciliation. However, since nonverbal messages can easily be decoded incorrectly, whenever possible accompany them with spoken regrets and at least a share in the blame for playing with matches. George Bernard Shaw said, "The test of a man (or woman's) breeding is how he (or she) behaves in a quarrel."[15]

Angry Prayers

'Twould ring the bells of heaven
The wildest peal for years,
If the Parson lost his senses
And people came to theirs,
And he and they together
Knelt down with angry prayers
for tamed and shabby tigers
And dancing dogs and bears,
And wretched, blind pit ponies,
and little hunted hares.[16]

—Ralph Hodgson, "The Bells of Heaven"

The Darkness of Anger

Anger has such a violent, cruel face.
It lies coiled beneath the surface,
in the dark, unlit recess of our being
striking out of unresolved hurt and pain.

It chokes the heart and sits
like a heavy, leaden beast within our breast,
leaving no room for the lightness
of compassion, understanding and love.

It finds its reason for being in
blame, false judgments and self-pity.
It slithers out from beneath the
rock of our needs and our inward lack.

Anger can lash out in angry looks
or words or come masked in humor.
The intent is still the same,
to vent hurts or fears upon another.

But anger cannot withstand
the light of truth and love.
It uncoils and relaxes its grip upon
the heart as we come to new understandings.

The heart unrestrained by resentment
and fear has the freedom to beat
with joy and acceptance for
each person and lesson along the Way.

— Diane Mitchell

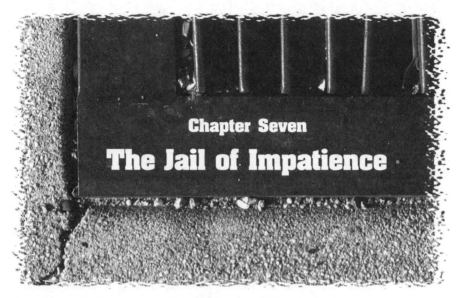

Chapter Seven
The Jail of Impatience

Impatience incarcerates. City and county jails are places of temporary detention. A victim of impatience is tossed temporarily into the "slammer" or "pokey." The term "slammer" seems to have come from the sound of the iron prison gates being slammed shut behind incoming criminals. It's an appropriate image for impatience, since those suffering from it are itching to release their pent-up anger by slamming doors, plates or people. This same urge is also contained in "pokey," whose name comes from the temptation to poke someone or something. Pokey originally came from the French word *poche,* for "a small enclosure," which well captures the cramped, cell-like feeling of those shanghaied by impatience.

While impatience can happen to us anywhere, surprisingly it is frequently a domestic, homegrown affliction. Parents with small children and teenagers know the feeling of being taken hostage by impatience. At the other end of life, caring for an aged family member can also cause us to lose our patience. We have learned to be polite when dealing with the public, fellow workers and strangers, and so expressions of impatience are usually muzzled in social situations. But we can easily be tossed in the "pokey," jailed by impatience, when we are in a hurry and find ourselves stalled in a traffic jam. That cramped, cell-like feeling can also seize us when we are forced to wait in a long checkout line or when we're placed on seemingly indefinite "hold" by some company's automatic telephone service. Impatience can take us hostage and be a source of irritation while we are shopping, traveling, at work or at home.

Impatience most often results from feeling "out of control." On the home front, it might happen when we're faced with the unending demands for attention by small children, the erratic behavior of teenagers and the constant complaints of aged people. Away from home, rush hour freeway gridlock, long waits at the doctor's office, slow service at a restaurant and failures of co-workers to do their assigned tasks are painful for anyone with a particular need to be "in charge" of life's events. A clear indicator of one's degree of both maturity and personal freedom is the ability to let go of having to control life and of scheming to make things happen. Free people, while they plan and organize, are able to let go of their day's agenda and can just let life happen. Those who are free can float with the unexpected and uncontrollable, and are even able to creatively find blessings hidden in such times.

LOSING YOUR PATIENCE

To lose anything implies ownership in the first place. That folk expression "losing your patience" presupposes that you are a patient person who only temporarily has misplaced this virtue. Patience is a learned ability that comes with maturity. Patience is absent in small children, and their lack of it often causes their parents to lose theirs. "When will we get there?" is the age-old car question repeatedly asked by traveling children who are unable to properly comprehend distance and time. Small children can't wait for Christmas and so go peeking in closets for gifts, or they shake already-wrapped presents in an attempt to find out what's inside. Teenagers, who are older children but not yet mature, are restless for adulthood and anticipate adult pleasures and behavior — usually with painful consequences.

Yet adults are not necessarily mature and can be retarded learners of this virtue. Lovers, for example, can be impatient, wanting to rush to the climax like children who want their dessert before the meal. Incidentally, climax is a wisely chosen word. It is Greek for "ladder." Impatient lovers are bad lovers. They want to race to the top of the ladder as quickly as possible. Patient lovers, on the other hand, climb the steps of the ladder slowly, and with great delight, the process being as much to the point of making love as the end result.

Old age often recycles childhood, and the elderly can once again find it difficult to wait calmly, even becoming irritable complainers. The infirm and sick can be impatient with their bodies, which no longer can do what they once did. Regardless of our age or state of life, we are challenged to keep learning the art of patience. And as Sir Thomas Browne suggests, we are continually confronted to measure up:

> There is another man within me,
> that's angry with me, rebukes,
> commands, and dastards me.

Browne, a seventeenth century English author and physician, has diagnosed well our human condition. This inner person he describes "dastards," which means to denounce one's behavior as cowardly and meanspirited. The higher self within us becomes angry because we refuse to grow up — to think, speak and behave in a mature way. Those who have not grown deaf to that inner-sage should feel rebuked when acting like an impatient child. That inner voice suggests there is one area where we should be impatient: with our passivity about our imperfections, particularly being little-spirited, if not meanspirited. We need the grace of the Holy Spirit to help us grow in spirit. We need to become as large-spirited as the Galilean Liberator when the Spirit of God anointed him.

JESUS THE IMPATIENT

The good news is that the enfleshment of God in Jesus meant he was fully human as well as fully divine. His humanity is easily eclipsed by that glowing halo that artists and preachers have placed around his head. Yet Jesus was impatient. At the Last Supper after three years of close association with Jesus, the disciple Philip said to him, "Master, show us the Father, and that will be enough for us." If we look beyond the text into the face of Jesus, we will see an edge of impatience, as he responds, "Philip, have I been with you for so long a time and you still do not know me? Whoever has seen me, my works and my love has seen the Father. Oh, Philip, how can you say, 'Show us the Father'?"[1]

He also loses his patience with the Rock, Simon Peter the Chosen, for his slowness to understand and stubborn refusal to embrace the necessity of Jesus' death on the cross. Directly after giving Peter the keys to the Kingdom of Heaven, Jesus predicted his approaching crucifixion and death. Peter took Jesus aside and rebuked him, saying, "God forbid such a thing should happen to you." Jesus lost his patience and snapped, "Get behind me, Satan!"[2] Again and again, his disciples seemed out to lunch, failing to comprehend his plainly worded references to his impending death. Indeed, Jesus needed to practice the large-spirited patience of his predecessor, Job. His followers wore that patience paper thin as he tried to explain that he was not the Messiah his disciples were expecting.

JESUS THE PATIENT

Moreover, our Emmanuel Emancipator demonstrated a great depth of calm endurance as God's mysterious plan slowly unfolded in his life. On the cross he exhibited not only heroic courage but infinitely patient suffering. He did not whimper as he embraced a painful and unjust crucifixion. Though "he *lost* his patience" with his disciples and the religious leaders of his day, a careful reading of his life reveals the possession of an abundance of God's patient endurance. Fittingly, the letters exchanged by the early churches are sprinkled with admonitions to be patient and long-suffering, enduring present trials with hopefulness.

Like any art, patience must be learned and practiced. As with many of life's great lessons, however, formal training is lacking. Perhaps the reason is that virtue requires suffering, which the word patience implies. It comes from the Latin *patiens* or *pati*, meaning to suffer, and is a cousin to the word "patient," a person who is sick and in need of a doctor. We avoid suffering whenever possible, which helps explain why so many of us are held in detention by our lack of capacity for calm endurance. Patience sometimes carries the connotation of passivity, which is unfortunate. It might be better to call the virtue "productive waiting," for that conveys activity and full engagement rather than a numbed, static acceptance. For, indeed, patience challenges us to a creative use of a given situation.

ESCAPE AN IRRITANT BY FRAMING IT

When you find yourself in some situation in which you feel moment by moment sucked more deeply into impatience, quickly attempt to frame the event. This creative act of framing takes only a few seconds, and the reward can be great, so be disciplined in its practice.

Find the largest frame possible. Then place it around whatever is irritating you. For example, if a small child or a teenager is the source of your impatience, you might imagine standing over a casket containing the embalmed body of your child who has just been killed in an accident. Such a frame will help reduce the source of irritation to its appropriate size. Or you might pretend you are attending the wake of an aged parent who at present is frequently causing you to lose your patience. Picture yourself standing beside your parent's casket free of regrets since you had calmly endured all those complaints. Such framing heals, and it puts things in perspective. Those circumstances that are sources of impatience between spouses and among those living in the same house are usually minor and insignificant. The molehills that are easily inflated into Mount Everests can readily be shrunk back to their proper proportion by practicing the art of framing.

Perform this framing technique when you find yourself in that uncontrollable situation of being stalled in a traffic jam. Place around this exasperating delay the frame of a classroom blackboard. Then, read the lesson written on the blackboard: "Control is an illusion." The actual number of things in this life over which we have any real control are few if not infinitesimal. We delude ourselves into thinking we are in control most of the time, for in an instant any number of powerful forces can take control over us. While waiting in stalled traffic, write the word "control" in the middle of your framed blackboard. Then, draw spoke-like lines out from the center, and at the end of each write down another word for control, like Domination, Supremacy, Clout, Mastery, Prestige and Power. Unless afflicted with the illusion of grandeur, few of us would consider applying such terms to ourselves. Yet framing control in this exaggerated way can help us understand our hidden reasons for demanding that we can exercise control over the events of our lives.

Pretend, to Gain Proper Perspective

Another device for escaping your irritation at being forced to wait is to pretend you are incognito royalty. When you're forced to wait, imagine yourself as a king or a queen who is cleverly disguised in commoner's dress. Then come back to reality. This playful reminder that you are not a monarch with absolute power can be an exercise in humor and humility that helps you embrace your predicament. Absolute sovereignty is an illusion of spoiled toddlers.

The Book of Ephesians offers a trinity of qualities that define the lifestyle to which we are called: "with all humility and gentleness, with patience, bearing with one another through love."[3] Patience follows directly after humility and meekness. Meekness is not sheepish docility but is the powerlessness that enables us to yield to and flow with the tides of life. Humble people are meek, elastically compliant toward both the positive and negative circumstances in which they find themselves. In a positive situation they rejoice and yet wisely refrain from attempting to control the pleasure by wanting to make it a permanent possession. When the circumstance is negative, they bend like a green tree in the wind as they explore their present condition for its hidden gifts. Remember that some of life's best gifts are presents in dark or disagreeable wrappings.

Indeed, impatient people make bad lovers. St. Paul told us that "love is first of all patient...." It's not our sexual abilities or romantic skills that make us good lovers first, but calm endurance. Paul continues, "Love does not insist on its own way (attempting to control others by insisting things be done our way); it is not irritable (does not get angry)."[4] Real lovers make love by earnestly making patience a priority as they respond to each other's little follies. Knowing how easily we lose patience with those who are closest to us, such patience requires sleepless vigilance.

Parents love their children and delight in giving them gifts. But forget going to the toy store. The greatest expression of affection a loving parent can give to an immature child is showing patience. In the process a parent becomes a teacher of an indispensable art. Such love-soaked patience, of course, continues with teenage and adult children, who by their lifestyles and behavior can frustrate their other-generation parents.

PLAY LIFE BY EAR

Be patient also with life itself. Those who love life are tolerant of its ups and downs, its reversals and leaps forward. Those who love life enjoy *playing it by ear,* engaging life without a printed score, simply flowing with its melody. By keeping our agendas flexible and minimizing our demands, life can be a melodic song. Whenever circumstances interrupt the normal rhythm of life, those who cultivate patience and inner freedom are able to improvise with a life situation like jazz musicians, making up music as they go along. The emphasis in *playing it by ear* is on playfulness. Those who use that gift of the Holy Spirit make their way gracefully through life.

GET A GRIP ON YOURSELF, NOT LIFE

When you feel you're losing your patience, pray to the Spirit. A liberation lifestyle calls us to "live by the Spirit," to be as free as the Spirit-Wind.[5] That Divine Energy is the Spirit of "love, joy, peace, patience, kindness, generosity, faithfulness, gentleness and self-control."[6] Whenever we are losing our ability to respond properly to life, we need to pray for that spirit-gift of self-control. In painful circumstances beyond our control, remember that the only thing we can control is our response to the situation. In this unmanageable world of unexpected accidents and stock market crashes, of the loss of employment and health care, of destructive tornadoes and hurricanes, of unpredictable terrorism and violence, the only thing over which we can exercise any control is ourselves. Each mature person has the power to control how he or she thinks, speaks and acts. We have the final say as to what we judge as good or evil and how we respond to life's unexpected situations.

As you pray, seek after patience using another of its names, "endurance," since God oozes with patient endurance.[7] God lovingly and faithfully hangs on with us regardless of our circumstances. The patient are truly Godlike. Petition God for that divine gift of tenacity and endless endurance by which you may take yourself beyond your present limits and boundaries, and ultimately become fully free.

Being personally responsible for your behavior means learning mature self-control. It is a key to opening the iron gates of countless prisons. As Jainism, an ascetical religion of India, teaches, "It is difficult to conquer one's self. But when that is conquered, everything is conquered."[8] Rejoice each time you overcome any temptation to be impatient, for you have taken another large step toward your ultimate liberation.

Chapter Seven Inventory of Escape Tools and Unshackling Reflections

ESCAPE TOOL #15 – THE JEFFERSONIAN COUNTER

Counting to ten or, as Jefferson advised for difficult occasions, to one hundred is an old tool for getting a grip on yourself and calming down. While aged, it's an excellent apparatus for escaping the pokey. As you count to ten — and, if necessary, beyond — be aware that it can be a true expression of love. Those we love should be able to "count on us" to count to ten or ten thousand before expressing our impatience with them.

A useful adaptation of this old instrument would be to account your love for the person who is stretching your patience: One — I love you, two — I love you, three — I love you, continuing until your love exceeds your impatience. If the source of your rising restlessness is a long delay in the checkout line or the dentist's office, adapt the exercise: One — I love life, two — I love life, three — I love life. While you may still be irritated at the delay, this system of mystic calculation can remind you that life — even when it's held up — is more enjoyable than the alternative.

ESCAPE TOOL #16 – HOW TO ESCAPE A MARATHON TALKER

We've all been temporarily held up — not by a robber, but by a one-way conversation with someone who talks endlessly. Such a holdup ignites impatience as we ask ourselves, "When will he stop talking? Will she ever give me a chance to say that I must be on my way?" Marathon talkers do not leave pauses in which one can politely conclude the conversation. Indeed, being trapped in a talkalong breeds impatience, frustration and low-grade anger. Sam Horn[9] suggests this escape mechanism: Interrupt the speaker by saying the person's name. This will usually stall the person long enough for you to be able to speak. Quickly summarize what the person has said, showing that you have been listening, and then end with a wrap-up statement putting the conversation in the past. Sam Horn suggests concluding with a firm, downward inflection in your voice, since a tentative tone tends to keep the door open for continuing the conversation.

THE JOY OF ANTICIPATION

A French luxury ocean liner company had the motto, "Half the fun is getting there." Our contemporary need for speed has short-circuited the enjoyment of being on the way to anything. In reaching the zenith of lovemaking or presenting a fine dinner, half the love is getting there. Children ideally should be taught the joys of anticipation, but adults also need to learn that ancient art. It involves not simply waiting, but tasting the joy as you progress toward its fullness. If we translate anticipation as "anteroom," waiting becomes a vestibule, and we already have one foot inside the door of delights. Each step along the way toward what is anticipated is sensually enjoyed: "Ah, this is so marvelous! Who could ask for more?" Yet there is always more to come.

How intoxicating it would be to approach every activity in such a way.

UPSIDE DOWN OR RIGHT SIDE UP SINS

If once a man indulges himself in murder,
very soon he comes to think little of robbing,
and from robbing hc comes next to drinking
and Sabbath-breaking, and from that to
incivility and procrastination.[10]

— Thomas De Quincey, 1827

REFLECTION

Do not simply dismiss De Quincey's quip as humorous and skip on to the next section. Read it again, perhaps this time aloud. De Quincey's inverted escalator of sins is a parable: What we consider minor indiscretions are, from this perspective, the serious failings. Most of us are not guilty of murder, robbery or drunkenness. It's, thus, not these sins that will keep us from being Godlike. But jam-packing every day of the week, and the Sabbath, with work and neglecting prayerful silence will. So will procrastination, which leads to holes in our time, ultimately forcing us to wait. Our impatience at waiting then leads to being rude and offensive, which is failing to be civil, civilized and mature.

HOW TO FIND A SPIRITUAL MASTER

Love yourself and watch,
Today, tomorrow and always.
To straighten the crooked
You must do a harder thing —
Straighten yourself.

You are your only master.
Who else?
Subdue yourself,
And discover your master.[11]

> — Words of the Buddha,
>   from the *Dhammapada*

Chapter Eight
Blue Dragon Dungeon

The Blue Dragon is not a Chinese prison! This place of detention is located "down in the dumps" and is a section of the Primal Prison called the Mind. Those imprisoned here have committed no crime; it is melancholy that has jailed them.

The Blue Dragon has no shortage of inmates, particularly in our contemporary culture. The twenty-first century world is full of expectations, and daily life always has more than its share of them. Technology promises much, and because so many of our expectations about life and the future can't be realized, disappointment is the usual result. Disappointment spirals downward into a state of sadness and sadness into depression. It's at this point that the Blue Dragon rears its ugly head.

Recall, from Chapter Six, St. Gregory the Great's list of the seven deadly sins, and that between *anger* and *avarice* he placed *melancholy*. Medieval spiritual masters labeled it *acedia* or the "noonday demon," a type of siesta-like inertia that produces spiritual sloth. *Acedia,* which effects a neglect of one's spiritual life, is more than dulled inactivity or laziness. It is a state of empty dryness and even sadness and dejection, the melancholy that springs from being self-preoccupied. While much of today's neglect of the inner life is due to the Dawn-to-Dusk Devil of our workaholic lifestyles, many of us are still beset by the Noonday Devil.

Melancholy is commonly defined as a gloominess, irritability and dejection that expresses itself in an abiding sense of sadness. While these emotions are not deadly sins, they can be deadly to the inner life and to our happiness. Melancholy is different from melancholia, a mental state of extreme depression that borders on psychosis and requires professional treatment. Those suffering from clinical depression will find relief in professional treatment, counseling and being faithful in taking their prescribed medications. Prayer and spiritual exercises, while always beneficial to soul and spirit, should not be seen as substitutes for sound therapeutic practices in addressing melancholia or severe depression. In the same way, this chapter is not intended for those who find themselves in a state of clinical depression. Rather it is meant for those who are depressed in the sense of being sunken below their surroundings. So we need to distinguish between depression as the blues and depression as the "purple pit of sadness," a cousin to the hellish "holes," the infamous prisons within prisons. When your address is "down in the dumps" for more than a few days or a week, when melancholy becomes an ongoing state of life, some form of professional help should be sought.

The Blue Dragon holds bound those suffering from "the blues," which can be caused by a complex cocktail of chemicals created within our brains. When these are mixed and shaken with various external events, they can cause severe emotional reactions. Some mornings we wake up in a bad mood and are incarcerated in the Blue Dragon even before we go off to work. And other days we can depart from home happy and return home in a bad mood. The exterior causes of these moods might be the breakup of a love relationship, an argument with the boss, a failure to achieve some goal or perhaps a physical illness. Sadness can also have a subterranean source — since "sad" is often an expression of "mad" turned inside out. Suppressed anger at something or someone has the power to recycle and seize us as a state of sadness. But regardless of how we get there, when we find ourselves detained in the dungeon of gloom, even when it is only a temporary mood incarceration, we should attempt to escape, and to do so it is helpful to know more about the sources of sadness.

The Secret Chemical Factory in the Attic

Illegal drugs are frequently concocted in laboratories hidden in innocent-looking basements and garages. Yet you and I are walking drug laboratories. The attic chemical factory of our brain is constantly creating chemicals such as serotonin, a mood stabilizing and balancing substance that helps us negotiate life's normal roller coaster ride, along with dopamine, norepine and a host of other neurotransmitters and stimulators. These chemicals are constantly being manufactured by our brains according to uniquely personal cycles. These chemical substances influence our outlook on life; they, in turn, are influenced by various drugs, foods and alcohol. Our daily moods and attitudes are the result of how these powerful mind-juices interact together, or whether they are either under- or over-produced by our hidden attic chemical factory. Those who are always sunny and optimistic have cause to be humble. A positive outlook and a pleasant disposition begin with, and are largely a result of, being gifted with good family genes and a mind capable of producing beneficial chemicals. Yet while a good genetic disposition is a great advantage, it must be accompanied by a disciplined lifestyle that includes a fruitful prayer life, the mastery of thoughts, good physical exercise and a proper diet.

If you should awaken to find yourself locked in the Blue Dragon, a wise first thing to do is to say a little prayer inviting God into your blue-tinted cell. Then you would do well to take a brief inventory of your life. Review material stored in your mental warehouse to search for some recent or past events that may have activated a chemical release. Sudden mood swings can be chaotic to experience and even frightening, since they imply a lack of self-control and can trigger uncertainty about what's going on inside us. A brief life inventory can be beneficial, firstly, because it gives the sense of taking some positive action. But beyond that, it can actually provide an escape route from our sadness. An example of how this process is liberating may be helpful. If you discover in your mental storehouse a recent memory of your boss, or some other significant person, frowning at you, that could be the generator of your low-grade depression. This seemingly minor event may have unconsciously hooked onto a painful unresolved childhood memory of your mother or father angrily frowning at you when you were naughty. Memories are potent chemical button pushers for both positive and negative moods. Positive memories can lift our spirits, and negative ones can imprison us or at least cast long shadows over our daily lives. Our negative memories need special attention, but they can be converted by reshaping them. Negative memories can be turned inside out so that the good present in them is on the outside, and the negative is hidden on the inside. Once we have reinforced the positive, the chemical factory in our mind again takes over to help keep us happy.

THE HAPPY DAY QUIZ

Often we get locked in Blue Dragon Dungeon because we have a misguided or distorted sense of what happiness is or what can make us happy. We're all familiar with the popular parting expression, "Have a good day." Logically, to have a good day it must be a happy day. The following is a two-part happiness examination to help you make your days "good."

Part One

Do you enjoy your work; does it make you happy?
Do you have a happy marriage or love relationship?
Do you experience being happy most of the time?

Part Two

Would you be happier if you had more money?
Would you be happier if you had a different body?
Would you be happier if you had better health?
Would you be happier if you were living somewhere else?
Would you be happier if you were driving a new car?
Would you be happier if you were free of your mortgage or other debt?
Would you be happier if you were given a promotion at work?
Would you be happier if you were famous?
Would you be happier if you purchased something new?
Would you be happier if you could live your life over again?

Most of us have been bewitched by advertising, when we believe the message that we won't be happy until we have (_fill in the blank_). We are soon cursed with perpetual discontent. Constantly trying to escape from discontent by buying more and more things is a form of greed, which is one of the seven deadly sins. Misinformed by the media, the lifestyle of a majority of us is based on the belief that all we need for happiness is more money, better physical health, a bigger house, a better paying job or a vacation in paradise. It should thus come as no surprise that the actual percentage of those living a happy and contented life is truly microscopic. If you question that statement, ask yourself how many really happy and contented people you know.

BE HAPPY — TOMORROW

Along with the captivating curse of the witchcraft of advertising, we are exposed to an opposite but just as pervasive cultural practice: delayed gratification. Pleasure postponement begins early in life. From grade school through high school through college into our early employment, we are told to delay enjoyment. We are taught to study and work intensely so we can be happy later — when we're married and successfully situated in our career. In the middle years of life, our happiness is usually postponed until our children are raised and have left home and the mortgage is paid. As mature adults, we are then encouraged to patiently wait until our harvest years of retirement to enjoy life. Yet, as with any muscle, if you don't use it you will lose it. If the enjoyment of life is delayed long enough, we awaken one morning to find our capacity for pleasure has become dormant. Crabby elderly people suffer from the effects of a lifetime habit of delayed enjoyment. Patterns of postponing enjoyment become habits, and these negative habits create bittersweet lifestyles where happiness only makes occasional surprise visits. Sometimes, for the fortunate, this human ability can be aroused even in retirement years. For others, sadly, the ability to enjoy life becomes embalmed some time before we even reach our fruit-bearing years.

HAPPINESS IS JUST AROUND THE BEND

With great expectations of enjoyment we eagerly purchase this or that desired object or move into a new home or we sacrifice our lives and family for a promotion, having fully bought into the fable that once we go around the next corner we'll discover complete happiness. Regardless of what prize we find around the bend, it soon loses its luster and fails to make us happy. So we again begin to itch to go around another turn in the road, and then another. Happiness, however, is not just around the next bend. Happiness happens on the road. Strive to daily walk it with enjoyment and enjoy the moment, even when it's raining. Aspire to walk the road of life daily with contentment and with gratitude. Most importantly, walk it awake.

Those who are not sleepwalkers know the real source of happiness is not something outside of them, it is created in their minds, hearts and spirits. To "have a good day" requires having good thoughts, which leads to having good attitudes, which is the basis for cultivating a good disposition. How we inwardly regard any situation has the enchanting power to transform it. Brooding over some negative remark creates a gloomy mood, which can cast dark shadows over us. We need to beware of fearful thoughts and anxious attitudes, for they are highway bandits that can steal away happiness.

Life is like sweet and sour Chinese chicken. It contains both good and bad times, uplifting and depressing events, disappointing and hopeful feelings. Understanding that balance, we need not be afraid of negative feelings and thoughts. Whenever we are angry, suspicious or frustrated, we can simply be conscious that we are thinking such thoughts. Being aware of our thoughts and attentive to our feelings, we can begin to search for their source.

WATCH AND LISTEN – WITH GOOD HYGIENE

Our contemporary world abounds with news reports of negative, fearful and stressful situations. Television and radio news programs continuously fill the air with their reports of rape, kidnapping, murder, robbery, violence, terrorism, crazed killers on shooting sprees, festering wars and revolutions. All these have a powerful influence on shaping our attitudes about the world in which we live. An increasing number of people are fasting from the daily news as a spiritual discipline. They find it poisons their view of life, creating paranoia and joylessness. In reality, for every disaster there are a thousand acts of kindness. While disasters and violent crimes make interesting news, they result in a lopsided view of people and life. Practice good hygiene after watching TV news. Instead of washing your hands, cleanse your heart.

THE LIBERATOR'S TOPSY-TURVY KINGDOM

The Enchanted Kingdom in which Jesus lived was an upside down world. For him, happiness was to be found where no one else would have guessed it possible. Living in God's topsy-turvy world, he found happiness on the bottom rather than on the top of life. In the Gospels of Matthew and Luke, Jesus provides us with an infallible guide to happiness. His Beatitudes give us a pattern for a happy life that isn't dependent on external riches or privileged position or even on having things go well for us.[1] The Beatitudes is a list of upside down attitudes of blessing, in which the poor, the powerless and the socially unfortunate are the happy ones. In Jesus' society, power purchased wealth, and wealth, in turn, bestowed honor — which is the opposite of our society, where wealth buys power, and power creates respect. But in both cases, the unfortunate poor are without honor and respect and are the helpless prey of the greedy and powerful. In Biblical terms, *the rich vs. the poor* had more the sense of *the greedy vs. the socially powerless*.[2] People were blessed by being honorable, for having honor was the authentic ancient source of happiness.

This translation of the Beatitudes into a twenty-first century terminology is intended to make them come alive for us with a liberating promise:

> Blessed are the poor — the politically and socially weak — for theirs is the Kingdom of God.
>
> Blessed are those who associate with the politically and socially weak, for theirs is membership in the Kindom, the family, of God.
>
> Blessed are those who weep — who cry out for justice — for they will be given justice.
>
> Blessed are those who speak out for justice toward the voiceless oppressed, the socially mute, for they enjoy living in God's Reign.
>
> Blessed are the meek — those powerless before the dominance of the Great Powers — for they shall reside in God's Reign.
>
> Blessed are those who join in solidarity with the poor whose benefits have been slashed by the government and with theologians who have been silenced by the church — and all those who are mistreated and oppressed for the sake of the Kindom — for they shall dwell in God.

The Beatitudes of Jesus, says Scripture scholar John McKenzie, is a list of explicit rewards synonymous with living in the Kingdom of Heaven. He says Jesus declares in them that, "…wealth, joy and fullness have nothing to do with one's true happiness, which is found only in the Kingdom of God."[3] Happiness, Jesus promised, was to be found in being faithful to daily living in his prophetic way. Jesus' Declaration of Happiness is also a Declaration of Independence from society's counterfeit promises about the rewards of wealth, fame, power and prestige. Faith — living with full trust in his promises, in the face of the blinding, neon-flashing, ear-deafening sales pitch of the corporate and clerical counterfeiters — is required for real beatitude to exist.

Don't run after fleeting happiness. The American Declaration of Independence speaks about the rights of "life, liberty and the *pursuit* of happiness." Yet faith in — loyalty to — Jesus' Declaration of Independence tells us to not chase after happiness, for those who attempt it never catch what they pursue. Happiness is a by-product. Forget yourself, Jesus says, and you find what you've lost. Give generously of yourself and your time to others, go out of your way to help someone in need and, to your surprise, you'll be happier. Help others celebrate a birthday, holiday or special occasion, and by so doing you'll find that you've been gifted with happiness in return.

Escaping the Blue Dragon

The Blue Dragon is like the devil, who hates humor and finds it intolerable to be treated as some kind of joke. In contrast, escape requires cultivating a lightness of being. Explore and enjoy self-comedy — laugh at yourself — when visited by blue moods, and you will find that the Blue Dragon, who hates laughter and being ridiculed will flee. Remember too that the chemical factory in your head operates both day and night. If the blues capture you, try to create good mood chemicals by recalling memories of love and good times, and also by engaging in some form of work or physical exercise. Endorphins, the good-mood chemicals, are created by these bodily activities. A healthy spirituality involves the body and includes a good diet and regular exercise, along with selfless service to others and times of intimate prayer. These practices also produce endorphins.

When gloom moves in, we should move out! Dr. Martin Groder, a psychiatrist from Chapel Hill, North Carolina, suggests an immediate change in environment. He encourages doing such simple things as rearranging the furniture or pictures in our home. Move out of doors, and allow yourself to be responsive to the vast world of creation so Dr. Nature can heal you. Groder also encourages spending time with the arts: listening to classical music, visiting an art gallery, even flipping through a book of beautiful paintings. Engage life creatively, not only by enjoying the art of others but also by creating your own: drawing and painting, playing a musical instrument or preparing a creative meal.

YOUR WILL BE DONE

Before this chapter concludes, it is essential to repeat the admonition expressed at its beginning. The exercises of this book are not intended for those suffering from clinical depression and other mental problems. These require the ministry of competent professionals, counseling and perhaps prescriptions for drugs to alter moods and correct any chemical imbalance. Unfortunately, some well-intentioned persons believe that prayer, exorcisms and religious exercises are the best approach to these illnesses, sometimes resulting in tragic consequences. As the body can be seriously afflicted, so also can the mind and our emotions. Just as there is no shame or disgrace associated with cancer, none should be linked to clinical depression. Those who suffer from cancer are prudent not to seek healing exclusively through alternative means, particularly not by attempts at prayer, fasting, retreats or religious exorcisms to drive out the demon of sickness. Rather, seeking professional medical help and embracing sickness in a healthy way is wise for anyone suffering from cancer or mental sickness.

Moreover, it would be theologically flawed to see cancer or clinical depression as God's will. Neither sickness nor any other misfortune is visited upon anyone by the will of God. God is certainly operative in the midst of these situations, but God never intends them. As with pursuing happiness, an indirect approach is more effective. Rather than seeking God's will, pursue gratitude instead. It is difficult to remain gloomy when you are filled with gratitude. Just as the mind can only think one thought at a time, when the heart is absorbed in gratitude it cannot dwell on gloomy tendencies and self-pity. But besides being a mood-changer, giving thanks in all circumstances brings healing and peace. As the Letter to the Philippians says, "Rejoice always...with thanksgiving, and the peace of God, which surpasses all understanding, will dwell in your heart."[4] Such constant thanksgiving is God's will. In describing the threefold practice for holiness, St. Paul tells us, "Give thanks at all times and for all things. Pray without ceasing and rejoice always...this is God's will for you."[5] That easily remembered threefold rule of life — which is potent and packed with enchanted powers — will be explored in the next chapter.

Chapter Eight Inventory of Escape Tools and Unshackling Reflections

ESCAPE TOOL #17 — BE CALM

The average detention in the Blue Dragon Dungeon is brief. So be calm and do not panic. If after using these various escape suggestions you find you are still "down-in-the-dumps," have confidence in the human body's natural cycles. We can mistakenly believe that a blue funk caused by a serious mistake, the loss of a lover or the undoing of something very important, will hold us prisoner endlessly.

The ancient rule is "What goes down must come up." Patiently trust in your body and mind's natural, continuous self-healing activity. With time, your mind will engage in an instinctive antigravity process, and you'll float up and out of the dumps. After being battered by the storm of some disappointment or series of disappointments, be patient as your mind creates new chemicals — and as the Spirit realigns your spirit — to correct your minor case of depression.

CHAIN REACTION

G.I. Gurjieff said, "Liberation leads to liberation." Once you have broken one set of chains enslaving you to some attitude, habit or addiction and you begin to taste freedom, you will want more. Each liberation will rally you to break another, then another set of chains. The first shackles from which you break free will intoxicate you with a sense of empowerment, confirm your capacity to be liberated and inflame your desire to slip out of other restraints. Each time you are liberated by the Liberator, you will be more apt to welcome yet another liberation.

ESCAPE TOOL #18 – IMAGE YOUR REWARD

A powerful device in achieving any life-change involves picturing yourself already enjoying the reward of accomplishing your goal. Eighty percent of learning is visual. In the process of reforming some undesirable behavior, frequently focus as vividly as possible on an image of yourself having reached your desired destination and enjoying its fruits. Especially when tempted to abandon any personal life-reform, focus again and again on the joys of your successful achievement.

ESCAPE TOOL #19 – MY DRUTHERS

Expectations in life are as dangerous as package bombs or land mines. They are so lethal because very often they cannot be realized, thus setting us up for deflation or even despair. So it's wise to replace expectations with defused desires — with preferences. Instead of saying, "My desire is…," try saying, "My preference would be…." A preference is different from an expectation or desire since it leaves room for an acceptable alternative. "My preference is chicken" is more freeing than "I want chicken." A preference liberates because it doesn't lock us into only one choice. In the 1800s, "druthers" — a whimsical folk form of saying, "I would rather" — was a common word for expressing a preference. Life is a Wheel of Fortune with both winners and losers: We don't always get what we want when we want it. The really happy winners are those who always spin the Wheel of Fortune with their druthers.

Keep Your Appointments, Not Your Disappointments

Life disappointments are one of the major factors responsible for creating the blues. Yet good appointments generally far outweigh dis- (short for dismal) appointments. A typical life is usually filled with 20% disappointments, due to failures and disapprovals, and 80% good appointments, which come with success, love, friendship and happy times. Surprisingly, we often tend to judge life by tipping the scales in favor of our disappointments and discounting the majority of good things in life. The antidote is to live in reality. Do not live in the illusion that life is not supposed to have its share of disappointments, frustrations and dissatisfactions. Remember the law of day-to-day gravity: What goes up must eventually come down. A wholesome life is one lived in light of that psychological, emotional and spiritual gravity. A wholesome life also knows the dexterity both to soar and decline gracefully. Those who embrace life's rhythms of highs and lows can come down from the high of some success and allow themselves to feel physically drained — and so don't have to sink all the way to mental depression.

The Secret of Prison Freedom

Stone walls do not a prison make,
Nor iron bars a cage;
Minds innocent and quiet take
That for a hermitage.
If I have freedom in my love,
And in my soul am free,
Angels alone that soar above
Enjoy such liberty.[6]

— Richard Lovelace, "To Althea: From Prison"

Prayerfully reflect on these poetic words of Richard Lovelace. What imprisons is so often beyond our direct control: an unpleasant circumstance, an unloving marriage, an unavoidable work situation, a disabling physical condition. Minds that are innocent can enjoy the soaring freedom of angels. When we are free in soul and in our loving, we can enjoy heavenly liberty. The next time you feel imprisoned by some delay or condition, rather than rattling your cell door in anger and rage, instead turn the cell holding you prisoner into your hermitage — a place of inner work. God's work is making good out of evil. God longs to be your cellmate and to work with you in transforming your affliction into affection, the grace of loving holiness.

ESCAPE TOOL #20 – BREAKING OUT OF SOLITARY CONFINEMENT

All cells in the Blue Dragon Dungeon are designed for solitary confinement. When blue moods isolate us from others, melancholy imprisons us in a dungeon of depression. Yet while we may not feel like associating with others, this is precisely the time to break out of solitary confinement. Leave home and do something kind for someone, visit an elderly friend in a nursing home, surprise a friend with a telephone call — but not to talk about your blues. Breaking out of isolation by seeking companionship with others — blended with compassionate concern for their needs — is both healing and liberating.

ESCAPE TOOL #21 – VISIT THE IMPRISONED

Whenever you discover that you are the prisoner of another person's bad mood, instead of attempting to escape try to be lovingly compassionate with the person in his or her suffering. Don't sing happy songs to the sad. Don't endeavor to look on the bright side of life or try to talk the person out of his or her depression. Instead, become the person's cellmate. Patiently and compassionately climb down into the pit the person is in and temporarily share the captivity. Don't give advice. Give two better gifts: empathy and love. If the person's state of depression continues for more than a few blue days and if it appears to be a serious anxiety, gently propose praying about the possibility of the person seeking professional psychological assistance. By your patient companionship and prayerful support become a living enfleshment of God's love in this time of suffering. As you do, remind yourself that by so doing you will be a companion and visitor to a gloomy Christ suffering in the dungeon of depression.

In Jesus' Final Judgment parable in chapter 25 of Matthew's Gospel, he rewards with paradise those who had visited him in prison. Surprised, they ask when they had visited *him* in prison, and he tells them, "Whenever you did this to the least of my brethren you did it to me."[7]

WHOSE FINGERPRINTS ARE ON THE SHOVEL?

Besides its definition as sadness or dejection, depression means a recessed area or hollow in the ground. That's fitting because the experience of depression is like being held captive in a gloomy cavity, the purple pit, a dispirited hole. We're likely to think that our worst enemy is responsible for digging this pit in which we're ensnared. Yet, rather than an enemy, or even fate, it's more probable that our own fingerprints are on the shovel that dug the depression. More often than not, the depression is a result of some choice we've made that has gone wrong or some situation in which we were freely involved. This awareness, however, can double the pain, and so it requires giving ourselves the gift of pardon for our lack of judgment. Surprisingly, the simple act of giving ourselves absolution for our involvement helps to liberate us from the black pit.

ADDICTION

Are you an addict? Addiction enslaves and creates unhappiness. The Latin mother word for addiction is very descriptive; *addictus* means "to hand over" or "give over." It suggests giving one's life over to a substance or behavior as a slave. *Addiction*, which looks a lot like the word *addition* is always a mathematical negative paradox. Something is added to our life which simultaneously, or ultimately, subtracts our freedom. The list of addiction's slave masters and mistresses is long; among them are alcohol, drugs, tobacco, sex, money, gambling, work, cleanliness and even love and religion. And because a large number of us is knowingly or unknowingly imprisoned as addicts, this brief reflection on addiction is included in this Inventory of Escape Tools.

Numerous books and programs have provided excellent lessons in liberation from these various forms of enslavement. As the best of these programs is quick to assert, freedom is only possible for addicts who have acknowledged their imprisonment. Nothing can free those who deny their imprisonment. Unfortunately, denial is a big part of addictive behavior. If something has the power to enslave us in addiction, it's because it has the power to engage our passions and our deepest desires. In such cases of passionate involvement it's not only difficult to disengage from the tentacles of what holds us bound, it's hard even to acknowledge that we're being held hostage. On the other hand, we're also likely to deny the addictions we don't see: we can be blind to behaviors that are hidden in our unconsciousness or in the shadows of our souls.

Hard and Soft Addictions

I'd like to suggest that this enslavement comes in two forms: hard and soft addictions. Hard addictions are those that are "hardwired" in our brains, where our whole lives are colored by and revolve around a particular activity. A good example of a hard addiction is heroin or another illegal drug. Once hooked, we'll do anything to get a fix — or the money we need for the drug — and so a host of other illegal activities can spring from the first. We can also see the hardwiring in addictions to gambling or alcohol, in which families are destroyed and fortunes squandered — both financial and spiritual — in order to support the habit. Even house payments are gambled away or wedding rings pawned to play the lottery. And life-dreams and the energy of life needed to make a relationship work are instead poured into a bottle before the booze is poured out. It's not so much what we're addicted to as how stuck we've become that makes something a hard addiction.

By contrast, a soft addiction is one that doesn't tend to capture our whole lives. It might be a compulsive behavior or compelling action like washing one's hands, keeping one's living quarters spotlessly clean or personal dogmatic duties like prayer, meditation and other spiritual or religious practices. Of course, each of these can be wholesome activities and disciplines that ensure the health of our soul-bodies. But any of them can also become self-limiting and ultimately self-destructive to our relationships to ourselves, others and God. And any addiction, soft or hard, has no place in an authentic lifestyle of liberation.

Often, we first get attracted to the positive effects of an activity: the endorphin rush of running or other physical workout, the psychological satisfaction of a job well done, the intellectual stimulation of study or research, the flood of emotional fullness from a loving relationship, the waves of ecstacy in enriching sex, the spiritual high from meditation or a transcendent experience. However, we can get hooked on the "high" of our exercise, work, study, love, sex or spiritual practice at the expense of significant responsibilities — like the need to care for our families or the demands of social justice. Or we can lose sight of the more significant aspects of relationship — the part of loving ourselves, others and God that causes us to mature.

At other times we can get hooked into dry, lifeless activities because they're something we "should" do. Once they become established patterns, we tend to christen them in order to justify our addictions, making it difficult to acknowledge and escape from our imprisonment. We would never baptize alcoholism as a virtue, yet compulsive cleanliness, thrift and efficiency are commonly converted to virturehood. Heroin addiction would never be baptized as virtuous, yet daily praying, attending church and meditating are viewed as virtuous without hesitation — even when we keep to them at the expense of responding to real needs around us.

Addiction is always compulsive. Those hooked cannot take it or leave it. The evidence for being convicted as an addict lies in one simple question: Am I free not to engage in it? Am I free not to perform a religious activity, free not to go jogging or free to walk away from my desk when it's piled Pike's Peak high in great disorder? A second significant set of self-examination questions can be asked: Is this activity that I'm so fully engaged in life-giving? Has it blinded me to larger life concerns: to poverty, homelessness, war, violence — or even to how my behavior might be causing others pain. Am I continuing to grow and mature — is my spiritual practice opening me to a greater capacity for love and compassion? Discipline is absolutely essential for spiritual growth and for making the activities of daily life enriching, rewarding and effective. Indeed, the tree of discipline bears healthy fruit. Yet all too easily what begins as a positive self-discipline can become an addiction. If upon examining the evidence of an action in our lifestyle, we find we're a prisoner of a positive addiction, we need to acknowledge our bondage and then plot our escape.

"POSITIVE" ADDICTION
AND THE AFTERMATH OF ADDICTION

As we've seen, there are any number of positive substances or activities that can become addictive: from work, sex and physical exercise to art, study and even love. Yet perhaps the only true positive addiction is to the freedom from being addicted. Anyone who has stopped smoking or drinking ultimately has remained free by being addicted to the joy of freedom. Yet not all post-escapee addicts are really free. Often only a militant, insistent and dogmatic determination never again to indulge in an addictive substance or activity ensures not becoming reincarcerated. Because of this, some ex-addicts become equally dogmatic after addiction. While those who have been released in joy are peaceful, nonviolent and non-evangelizing — not lapel-pulling others to join the cause — other liberated addicts, perhaps out of fear of being reimprisoned, lash out angrily at those presently enjoying whatever was once destructively addictive for them. Truly freed ex-addicts are able nonjudgmentally to enjoy the company of those under the sway of what once enslaved them. The fruit of positive addiction — the intoxicating happiness of freedom — is what truly "converts" others.

ESCAPE TOOL #22 — LAUNDERING AN ADDICTIVE DESIRE

Desire is one of the most effective tools for escaping. Exercise care, however, when expressing your desire to be liberated from some addiction, bad habit or behavior. Choose your words carefully, for the mind thinks in pictures. Refrain from using words that contain the object from which you wish to be freed. For example, the desire expressed in the statement "I am going to quit smoking" contains the vivid seed-image of yourself smoking. Even with a verbal negative in front of it, the mind will create a picture that reinforces the addiction. You can launder your desire by rephrasing it as a positive intention without naming whatever is enslaving you. Such a laundered desire to stop smoking might be, "I desire only to inhale clean air — delightfully fresh and revitalizing oxygen." While similar to Escape Tool #2 (see page 19), resurfacing this practice in the context of addictions can give it even more impetus. Using this freshly scrubbed laundering escape tool whenever expressing your desire to make any significant behavior change will not only free you from your addiction, it will free you to a fuller life.

Escape Tool #23 — A Pen and Paper Exorcism

As with compulsions and addictions, there is no shortage of worries and cares in contemporary culture. Besides being unwelcome hitchhikers riding in our mind, worries contribute to depression and sadness. When they become permanent residents of our minds, they cast sinister shadows and can be like demons that possess us. Insidious anxieties and worries imprison us, blocking our capacity for happiness and our enjoyment of the glorious freedom of the children of God. In attempting to be dispossessed of these cares, consider using a pen and paper exorcism. Write down any unwelcome concerns that seem to have taken possession of your mind. By putting them on paper, you make them conscious and concrete. The very act of naming your worry-demons gives you power over them, making it easier to be freed of them. There is an ancient belief that if one knows the name of the demon or dragon holding one prisoner, one can expel it simply by commanding it by name to depart.

This exorcism ritual can also be taken a step further. First, place the page upon which you have written your worries into a fireproof container. Say a prayer of deliverance from the shackles of your concerns. Then set a match to your list of dreary dragon worries, watching them go up in smoke.

ESCAPE TOOL #24 – RAS:
RETICULAR ACTIVATING SYSTEM

As we've seen, reforming ourselves is at the heart of Jesus' requirement for entering the reign of God. This reformation is not a once in a lifetime act. Rather, reform is a central and continuous activity in any good liberating spirituality. When desiring to make any changes in our life, we will more likely be successful if we write them down. As the title of Dr. Henriette Klauser's book, *Write It Down, Make it Happen,* suggests, it's not as effective simply to think about the changes we wish to make.[8]

The act of writing out our desired changes appears to stimulate a part of our brain called the Reticular Activating System, which filters pertinent information to the conscious part of our mind. In the writing of our goals, Dr. Klauser advises using positive instead of negative phrases. She also says that we should list the rewards these changes will bring. For example, one reward of achieving the goal of losing weight would be, "I would appear more presentable in my clothes and so feel better about myself." This technique also applies to the goals of a richer prayer life, a more generous spirit and greater patience.

ESCAPE TOOL #25 – MOLE HILL VICTORY PARTIES

Attaining freedom from our various forms of imprisonment and slavery is among the highest of human achievements. Just as high mountain peaks are successfully scaled by first climbing the foothills located at their base, the same is true for our life goals. When writing out your goals, include short-term objectives that you will need to achieve on your way to accomplishing the greater, long-range goals.

The very act taking up the challenging expedition of liberation is praiseworthy, and each small success along the way deserves to be acknowledged. The wise climber will celebrate each milestone passed, even the mole hills conquered in climbing toward the distant cloud-covered peaks. Eager for the fame of succeeding at great challenges, we tend to bypass lowly mole hills. Yet when we begin our ascent toward reform at some higher elevation, we usually falter midpoint from fatigue and surrender the quest. Just as happiness is to be found all along the road rather than just at the end of the journey, so too we best attain our goals by celebrating each victory along the way.

Chapter Nine
The Great Escape Keys of Gratitude and Discipline

In this chapter we take a break from our tour of life's prisons to take a closer look at two of the great keys to escape. The first key is gratitude.

GIVING THANKS ENDLESSLY

As we have seen, the action of giving thanks always and for everything is one of the three key elements of a spirituality of liberation. As the heart constantly pumps blood and life, so ceaseless gratitude pumps new life and joy into the soul. But even more, those who practice perpetual gratitude go to the heart of addressing the mysterious matter of doing God's will. Religious people often give "God's will" as an explanation for terrible misfortunes like a child born crippled, a deadly disease or some natural disaster. In their most popular prayer, Christians pray that God's will be done here on earth as it is in heaven. Yet, we still wonder: What is the will of God that each of us is to do here on earth?

The early Christians of the church at Thessalonica received a letter from Paul telling them, "Rejoice always, pray ceaselessly and in all circumstances give thanks, for *this is the will of God for you.*"[1] In that one sentence is found perhaps the primary holy rule of our liberational lifestyle. It is a simple guideline for holiness and a personal yardstick to measure our adherence to the will of God. If you want to be certain you're doing God's will, be always joyful, pray twenty-four hours a day and saturate every situation with gratitude.

FULL-TIME OCCUPATION

Being constantly grateful isn't easy. TGIF, "Thank God It's Friday," is that once-a-week worker's celebration of thankfulness. In North America a special day is annually set aside in the fall for thanksgiving. The devout are faithful in keeping the prayer ritual of giving thanks before they eat their meals. Spontaneous thanks is likely to burst forth when some misfortune is avoided by inches or when good fortune makes one of her surprise visits. Yet as beneficial as all these expressions are, thanksgiving is a more fundamental reality. The secret to perpetual gratitude is simple: Be awake. To Jack Kornfeld's saying, "Those who are awake live in a state of constant amazement," we could add, "and in a state of constant gratitude." Being awake to reality is to find ourselves living in the magical abounding garden of gifts for the soul and all the senses, the Enchanted Cosmos. Such awareness evokes a perpetual litany of thank yous. In fact, the constant repetition of those two words, "thank you" — as if chanting them in the midst of our unfolding daily life — creates the condition of enchantment. Gratitude is the secret magical formula for happiness and the great key to the door of the Kingdom of Heaven.

The mystical-enchanted world is one of endless gifts that are hidden under every stone. They are concealed within every blessing and even in every misfortune. This mystical world does not exist in fantasyland — it's at the heart of reality. We normally don't recognize it because of the layer of sleep in our eyes. Slightly editing the Prayer of Jesus so it says, "*gift* us this day with our daily bread" can help to expose the take-it-for-granted attitude that blinds us to our daily giftedness. Saying "*gift* us this day" might help us see the numerous blessings of our life as being more than the result of our sweat and labor or random benefits of fickle fortune. God is a generous lover, and the prayer of Jesus is addressed to that divine parent who, like any lover, delights in giving gifts.

What most delights gift-givers is when they see how their gifts are enjoyed and treasured: It is more precious than any words of gratitude. The daily delight and the appreciation of all the gifts we have received in life is, in turn, perhaps the highest form of gratitude. And constantly finding delight and fascination in the gifts that have already enriched us for two, twenty or forty years is one of the prime strategies for sainthood. Whatever is always before us seems to fade into the woodwork. The permanent and ever-present becomes invisible. On the other hand, giving thanks for the most common and least noticed of life's gifts gives praise to God as well as pleasure to us. And the sensual enjoyment of our possessions, abilities and blessings of creation grows us into our truest selves.

GENERATOR GIFTS

Gifts are magically electric engines that generate happiness. Adults tend to suffer from MP — Magic Privation — and are not easily able to experience gift-excitement. Adults also typically suffer from S & S — being Sophisticated and Stuffed with possessions. Classically, the best gift receivers are children, who are barefacedly enthusiastic in their joyful excitement over a new toy or gift. Jesus liberates sophisticated adults when he invites them to "become again like children,"[2] which he said was essential for those who wished to enter the Enchanted Kingdom of God. Heaven-dwellers are grown-up children who are able to enjoy a world where it is Christmas 365 days a year. Ex-adults freed of the apathy of sophistication can be tickled even to receive the simplest trinket. Such ex-adults are free and truly mature, more alive and happier even than their richly gifted brothers and sisters because they are living in God's homeland of gratefulness. Brother David Steindl-Rast summarizes the secret of this Enchanted Realm: "For happiness is not what makes us grateful. It is gratefulness that makes us happy."[3]

THE FREEDOM KEY

Gratitude is liberating. When upset over delays or disheartened by failures, find relief in the midst of these and all other negative circumstances by seeing something for which to be grateful. Thankfulness has the power to transform gray into gold. Gratitude dissolves anxiety and worry, as Paul of Tarsus said, "Have no anxiety at all, but in everything, by prayer and petition with thanksgiving, make your requests known to God."[4] In this admonition Paul also gives us a wonderful lesson for how to pray every prayer of petition. Petitions should be initiated with a preface of gratitude: "O Gracious God, I thank you for the gift of my health as I pray for the healing of my friend…" or "We thank you, Generous God, for the gifts of our homes that shelter us and for our abundance of food, as we now pray that you care for those who are homeless and hungry." Not only our prayers of petition but all our prayers should be saturated with thanksgiving. Indeed, when we pray with gratitude — rather than resembling ungrateful beggars at heaven's gate who ignore yesterday's bountiful gifts even as we seek more — we are liberated from smallness of soul and are blessed with an even greater bounty of God's grace.

The Man with a Gratitude Lifestyle

Recall St. Paul's counsel to give thanks "in all circumstances," which means we are to be thankful for what is annoying as well as agreeable, for that which is unpleasant as well as satisfying. This is no small challenge for those seeking to do the will of God.

A favorite story of mine tells about a man who practiced being grateful in all circumstances. One day, while driving to work, he had a flat tire and had to pull over onto the shoulder of the highway. Getting out of his car, he looked up and said, "Thank you, O God, for all your gifts. Thank you that out of this world's six billion people I belong to the small minority that owns a car. Thank you that it has rubber tires that can go flat, instead of those original iron-rimmed wooden wheels of the first automobiles. Thank you for the wide shoulder of this highway, on which I can safely change my tire. Thank you that it's good weather and that it's not raining or snowing and that I am physically able to change my tire. Thank you, O God, for these gifts on this day and for all your gifts."

The prophet Mohammed said, "Whoever does not express gratitude to people will never be able to be grateful to God." This gives us insight into how it was possible for the man in the above story to give such lavish thanks to God even in the midst of an uncomfortable situation. We can surmise that this man went about constantly thanking others — those with whom he lived and worked, those who packed his groceries or served him when he dined out. Gratitude is a habit, and it's also contagious. Perpetual gratitude toward people around us initiates habits of thankful prayer. It also starts a chain reaction of giving thanks, till our friends and loved ones and our whole world become imbued in grateful living.

GRATEFUL FOR OTHERS

It is important not only to be grateful *to* others but also to be grateful *for* others. We need to cultivate a gratitude for others' giftedness in the same way that we appreciate a beautiful sunset or a smile from a loved one. Others always seem to have been given gifts in life that we desire, and so it's easy to be envious. Riding sidesaddle with envy is a dangerous practice: I would be happy if I had what he or she possesses. By contrast, giving thanks constantly and in all circumstances liberates us from envy. Timothy Miller says gratitude is "the intention to count your blessings every day, every minute, while avoiding, whenever possible, the belief that you need, or deserve, different circumstances."[5] Being grateful does not require changing the situation we find ourselves in but only a creative change in how we view what has been put on our plate at life's surprise party. We may come to find that even when discomfort and troubles are dished out to us, it is possible to transform their taste by seasoning them with the stimulating spice of thankfulness.

THE MAGIC WAND

Indeed, gratitude is a magic wand. Wave it about you and it recreates the world around you. For millenniums we've prayed, "Send forth your Spirit and recreate the face of the earth."[6] When the Spirit of Thanksgiving sweeps across our personally troubled world, our life undergoes a face-lift. The old Shakers' hymn "'Tis a gift to be simple, 'tis a gift to be free," suggests the connection among simplicity, freedom and gratitude. Pray then for the gift of gratitude so that you can be twice-blessed: being simple, uncomplicated and natural — and, at the same time, free. Thankful people live simple lives since being overwhelmed with the gifts they already have makes it easier to be content. Those who are content are then freed of the addiction of needing more and more — whether more possessions or more of the gifts that others possess. Indeed, contentment requires a strange yet everyday form of giving thanks: negative gratitude.

NEGATIVE GRATITUDE

"No, thank you," is the polite response when we've had enough of anything. "No, thank you," is also an escape clause. We can use it when viewing an ad for new clothes: "No, thank you, my closet is already full." We can say, "No, thank you," to the itch to have a larger house, adding, "I have all the rooms I need." When tempted, say, "No, thank you, I don't need a new lover; I'm still finding great delight in exploring my first love." When facing the avalanche of advertising, we can say, "No, thanks," to more and more and more, "I have more than I need or can use." To live a simple life, make a rich, grateful, "No, thank you," one of your most frequently repeated expressions.

Katra and Russell Targ write, "...the absence of gratitude can create immeasurable suffering amidst plenty — not to mention insufferable people."[7] Peek into the hearts of those who are always crabby about the weather, life or their neighbors, and you will likely find they are suffering from a privation of gratitude. As privileged citizens in the Land of Plenty, the Land of the Free and the Brave, it is deplorable that so many of us live in a poverty of enjoyment of our plenty. Thankful hearts have signs hanging on them that read, "No Vacancy." They have no room to sublet their hearts to sadness, envy, anger, resentment, greed or self-pity. There is no vacancy because their hearts are already full to overflowing. Moreover, around-the-clock thanksgiving creates the craving to rejoice always. When "Thank you" springs effortlessly to our lips even in disagreeable times, being joyful becomes second-nature, for living gratefully, more than simply disposing us to receive gifts, brings joy.

HEARTS SET FREE

Natural and authentic gratitude sprints spontaneously to our lips in times of good fortune and blessings: the birth of a healthy child, escaping an accident by inches, the successful completion of an important project or finding a precious lost item. Words of gratitude at such times are stuffed with meaning and consequently set our hearts free. By contrast, our prayers of grace before meals are full of words of thanksgiving, yet how often are these words like a string of empty box cars? What percentage of the time are we truly grateful for the food we are about to eat? Eager to begin a meal or already engaged in table conversation, these mealtime gratitude prayers can easily become formalities, simply a sign of the good manners of religious people. Our challenge in living out a liberation spirituality is to invest these classic forms of ritual thanksgiving with as much meaning as our heartfelt spontaneous prayers of gratitude.

TOXIC RITUALS

Much of the power of ritual resides in repetition. A sacred repeated action is experienced at a subconscious level, which exerts a strong influence on the conscious mind. We need to be careful, however, because, by its repetition, ritual leads to mechanization. To be real, robot prayers must be liberated and made human. This work is an essential ongoing process of humanization for those of us who are involved in ritual prayers and actions. While starving people are typically and readily intoxicated with gratitude over being given a single crust of bread, meal prayers can be robotic for those living in the Land of Plenty. For many of us a full dinner plate usually evokes not thanksgiving but concern about the number of calories the food contains. An early name for the Lord's Supper is the Greek *Eucharist*, which means "thanksgiving." Yet we too easily come to this ancient act of table worship with little sense of thankfulness, with our pockets full of petitions instead of hearts overflowing with gratitude.

LOCKED DOWN HEARTS

The Catholic Liturgy of the Eucharist is proceeded by a preface prayer that begins with the invitation, "Lift up your hearts." That's a fitting way to approach the Meal of Thanksgiving since usually our hearts are *locked down*. Lockdown is a prison term for a time when inmates are locked in their cells for security because of some disturbance in the prison. Our hearts can similarly be "locked down," confined, imprisoned because of the disturbance of daily trials, struggles and disappointments. We might use the ritual prayer, "Lift up your hearts," in our personal prayer as an inner challenge to respond to life with generosity and gratitude. When a conversation becomes mired down in complaints and gripes or when we're preparing to greet some approaching pain or discomfort, we might pray to ourselves, "Lift up our hearts," as a personal ascension challenge.

The Great Liberator lifted up his heart in gratitude at his Last Supper before his day of great agony and pain. The night before his death, while at table with his small community, he took bread into his hands and gave thanks. More than a ritual expression of gratitude for the food, he gave thanks for *everything*, including the approaching shame and pain of his imminent death. Looking into the bread, Jesus may have seen his body dangling naked in pain from a shameful cross, and yet he lifted up the bread and gave thanks to God. As he looked down into the cup of red supper wine, he may have seen his blood, mixed with sweat, trickling from his crucified body, now covered with flies. Yet he was able to give thanks as he elevated the cup of the New Covenant. In his meal prayer of the Last Supper, we are given a pattern for our preparation prayers in the face of our approaching pains.

Do This in Memory of Me

This was a prayer of great generosity in which Jesus gave himself up to death, in which he gave his life and transformed the dark energy of his pain and suffering as a gift for his friends, for all peoples and for the world. Giving thanks at the first Eucharistic meal and giving up his life on the cross coalesce to form a single act of redemption-liberation. Gratitude consecrated the ugly energy of death into glorious life-giving energy. In Jesus' sacred act, we can see that giving thanks destroys any lurking human desire for pity or the temptation to see oneself as a victim needing sympathy or a captive of circumstances.

In the pattern of the Liberator we are invited to give away our sufferings, aches and pains instead of clinging to them or being imprisoned by them. With gratitude for the gift of being able to join our sufferings with his, we keep the memory of his gifting in a revolutionary, liberating way. We best keep the memory of his final meal by following his challenge that we make ourselves freely given gifts of love to others. The ritual meal in which we keep the memory of his Last Supper is a radical call to do with our sufferings what he did with his. If the Eucharist is attended only as a pious spectator supper, how can we say we are truly faithful in following him?

Gratitude is a great deliverer. Jesus was not "locked down" that night before his death. Thanksgiving sets free hearts pursued or captured by fear and dread. According to George Soares Prabhu, a Liberation Theologian from India, what shaped Jesus' lifestyle of generous loving was his core belief that God is a loving and compassionate Divine

Parent. It was Jesus' lived certitude that God was his *Abba, his* father, and that he was a beloved son, Prabhu says, that liberated him from "a law-based to a love-based norm of life."[8] In light of such a loving Divine Parent, how could convention, custom or even death lock Jesus down? Not only did the Liberator live a holy lifestyle, his was also a holy deathstyle. In life and in death he remained steadfast in his fidelity — even in the seeming absence of his beloved Abba as he died on his cross. Such unshakable love is truly a grace — a gift — of the Spirit, which reveals God as a beloved, extravagantly generous gift-giver. "Come, follow me," Christ says to each of us, "and make your lifestyle one that is love-based instead of law-based." Those who do so will experience God as an exceedingly generous lover and will begin to see creation as a cornucopia cosmos, a spiraling horn of plenty pouring forth infinite bounty.

THE MAGNIFYING GLASS OF GRATITUDE

Gracias, which means "grace" in both Spanish and Latin, is the mother word of gratitude. In the old translation of Luke's Gospel the Archangel Gabriel greets the future mother of God by saying, "Hail, Mary, full of grace."[9] This greeting also delightfully suggests the Spanish meaning of the term *gracias*, "full of thanks." Those who are constantly giving *gracias,* giving thanks, live in abounding grace since, as we have seen, they are doing the will of God. Mary's song of joyful praise, the Magnificat, begins, "My soul magnifies the greatness of God, and my spirit rejoices in God, my liberator."[10] Even though pregnant outside of marriage, young Mary thankfully proclaimed how God had gifted her with the honor of being the mother of the Savior-Liberator and for being the one to usher in a new age. Her song of thanksgiving poetically proclaims how gratitude is like a magnifying glass. Yet our mysteriously ever-present, invisible God is too easily eclipsed in the brilliantly visible and tangible daily world. Thanksgiving, however, mystically intensifies our awareness of the Divine Mystery, which is hidden from our senses. A person who is unceasingly grateful, even without mentioning the name of God, becomes a mystical magnifying glass that amplifies the invisible Giver of Gifts. Expressions of gratitude are never anonymous. "Thank you" is always said to someone, and so prayers like Mary's Magnificat are important because they bring the focus of our magnifying glass back onto the Source of all gifts.

THE HAZARDOUS MOUSETRAP OF GRATITUDE

Being thankful for all things and in all circumstances is, indeed, an indispensable key to liberation. This is particularly true in our practice of expressing our gratitude to others. It's an act of returning a kindness for a kindness that keeps us free from the prison of self-preoccupation. Yet like any powerful tool, this tool of liberation must be used with proper caution and safeguards. Paradoxically, when we strive to be faithful in always being grateful, we are at risk of getting caught in a trap. Being conscientious to always thank others can easily ensnare us in a booby trap. For then it's only natural to expect others to respond to our gifts with expressions of gratitude. Their failure to do so easily results in our disappointment and disillusionment. However, our chances for being caught in this trap in today's culture are greatly increased because there is much more to be disappointed about. It's becoming rarer and rarer to be thanked for a kindness extended.

In the more leisurely and courteous days of the twentieth century, expressions of gratitude were an integral part of good manners. Parents zealously taught their children to say "Thank you" when they received a gift or treat. The hearts of readers over the age of fifty probably contain memories of times when they were given a gift and their mothers said to them, "Now, what do you say to your Aunt Beverly?" Only retarded children didn't know the answer to that question. Among the first letters we were taught to write in our wiggly childlike handwriting were Thank You notes. Recently, however, the etiquette of gratitude is to be found in the Intensive Care Unit, lingering on life-support systems. Since, as Mohammed said, prayer habits are formed out of life habits, this is not a minor societal issue for those seeking to be Godlike. In exploring why expressions of appreciation for gifts are becoming an endangered species, it would be interesting to conduct a Gallup poll. This survey could question Americans by age groups to find out how many still send those old-fashioned Thank You notes — and perhaps why they have become antique expressions.

One of the main reasons given for the fading of gratitude would undoubtedly echo back to Timelock Prison: Our ebbing gratitude is significantly affected by our prolonged drought of time. Leisure having dried up, telephones and E-mail are used for messages since they require less time and personal investment than writing a note. Another culprit responsible for the demise of thanksgiving could be our consumptive consumerism. Being perpetual purchasers makes us better at getting than at giving, including giving thanks. And because many of us have too much, we are no longer hungry people who appreciate and are truly grateful for the nourishment our bodies, souls and spirits receive. When we're stuffed we're not hungry, and we of the Land of the Plenty are stuffed. Our closets are stuffed with clothes, our children's toy boxes and bedrooms are stuffed, our houses have become storehouses stuffed with things, and our lives are stuffed with activities and entertainment. When bloated people are gifted, it does not arouse delight, which produces gratitude. Any gift added to the ever flowing abundance only induces a ho-hum yawn. The twentieth century began with attention focused on one's duties to family, community and nation, and it concluded with an obsession about our rights. If fading gratitude is the result of a belief that we have a "right" to be treated with kindness and respect, to be gifted with others' time and love, then we are dispensed from the obligation of expressing gratitude. Who is roused to thanksgiving for our freedom of speech, for the freedom to worship however we please, for the ability to vote for our leaders? After all, these are our "rights"! It's easy to understand how readily we can get caught not only in the mousetrap of gratitude but also in the snares of bloated ingratitude.

NOTHING NOVEL?

Perhaps there isn't anything new about the absence of gratitude. The percentage of those who express gratitude may still be only one out of ten, the same as almost two thousand years ago. When Jesus healed ten lepers who begged to be cleansed of their disease, only one, a non-Jew, a Samaritan, returned to thank him. Jesus' surprised response was edged with sadness: "Were not all ten made clean? Where are the other nine?"[11]

Sharing the disappointment of Jesus when people fail to thank us can itself be a gift. It can be an opportunity for solidarity with the One whose gifts so often go unappreciated. It can be a backhanded blessing in the order of the Beatitudes. So, each time you send a gift and fail to receive a response — even to confirm that your gift arrived safely — rejoice and give thanks. One of the classic sayings of Christianity is, "It is more blessed to give than to receive." Applied to thanksgiving, this means it is more delightful to give than to receive gratitude for what we give. To be blessed means not just to be holy but to be happy. Not being acknowledged for our generosity is truly an opportunity for happiness because it helps ensure that we properly gave the gift. Real gifts are stringless, and the more we grow in our capacity to be real givers and mature lovers — being able to give without expecting a return — the more godlike and, therefore, the more happy we become. While every "Thank you" is a gift, every absence of a "Thank you" can also be a gift.

THE GIFT OF A THANK YOU

Reverencing every expression of gratitude as a gift will free you from regarding it as an IOU — a debt payment for your kindness. When you're disappointed by the lack of such a grateful response to your gift, in order to escape the Blue Dungeon of Disappointment examine yourself on how grateful you have been for the gifts of your life. Ask yourself how often you have taken the glorious gifts of creation for granted and have failed to express gratitude for them. When we're aware of our own poverty of thanksgiving, we can escape being imprisoned by others' ingratitude.

SUMMARY

It bears repeating that cultivating a heart crowded with constant thanksgiving is the magical way to live daily in the Enchanted Kingdom of God. Remembering the Prophet Mohammed's wisdom that it's difficult to be grateful to God if we are not grateful to people, practice being grateful to everyone around you. Being grateful to God for all things and in all circumstances is the inspired wisdom of Scripture. Become rich in that wisdom and never tire of daily saying "Thank you" to all creatures: to flowers for their beauty, to trees for their shade and the life-giving oxygen in their leaves, to birds for their songs and free flight and to pets for the companionship and joy they bring. Neverending gratitude is liberation: from sadness, self-pity, greed and melancholy moodiness.

The Key of Discipline

It is appropriate to include the practice of discipline in this chapter because remaining free from what imprisons us and being ceaselessly grateful requires discipline, the art of disciples. Not only is a good disciple self-disciplined, the practice of discipline is also a key to liberation. Being faithful to the various exercises of a spirituality of liberation requires the same kind of disciplined patterns that make it possible to play the piano or drive an automobile. We might rephrase the teaching of Buddha that "with our thoughts we make our world"[12] to say, "with the discipline of our thoughts we make new worlds possible for ourselves."

The discipline of any daily exercise causes the neurons in your brain to grow microscopic filaments that branch from one section of the brain to another. This neuron growth process is called *arborization,* which means taking on a "a treelike shape." It's a term also used for those formations contained in fossils and minerals. Studies show that when you stop practicing a skill or behavior these neuron branches of the brain begin to wither away. Each day you do not engage in the disciplined exercise, the more difficult it is to begin again because the neuron path has begun to disintegrate. Walking, praying, being grateful, meditating — all these good habits begin as thought-paths in the brain.

THREE WEEKS TO GROW A HABIT

It takes about three weeks to build an established habit-path. Think of your mind as a green lawn. Envision yourself "walking on the grass" daily as you perform an exercise. This three-week process of *arborization* — neuron branch-making — establishes a habit-path in the lawn of your mind. You also have an ally in creating a habit: As you learn a new skill or acquire new knowledge, the neurons in the chemical factory within your brain secrete growth hormones that fertilize this process of arborization. These chemicals also stimulate the growth of neural pathways in neighboring sections of the brain.

DRILL YOUR WAY OUT OF PRISON

A *drill* is a tool for boring holes. It is one of the classic tools for escaping from prison. To *drill* also refers to the process of repeating an activity again and again. Each repetition makes the activity easier to perform. The more you pray, for example, the easier praying becomes. The more you are generous, the more effortless generosity will be. Dedicated, disciplined drills of spiritual exercises establish microscopic pathways in the brain that reinforce a positive behavior. These pathways also lead away from prison and toward freedom. Indeed, these two connotations of the word *drill* are connected. We are best able to escape from our prisons by developing positive physical and soul skills as well as thought habits, particularly habits of gratitude. Assisted by various chemical agents of your brain, three to four weeks of drilling will not only make any spiritual discipline seem second-nature, it will expand pathways in your heart. Become your own demanding coach, your own tough *drill* sergeant — or, if that seems too harsh, your loving but persistent teacher. Keep the branches of brain pathways open by continued practice and, in addition to the newfound freedom you will gain, you will be amazed at what you can accomplish.

THE ATTIC CLASSROOM

Learning is usually restricted only to the young and to a special schooling period in life; it is rarely thought of as a lifestyle. Yet each of us was designed by God with a special department in our brain reserved for learning, which we might call our Attic Classroom. Have you been playing hooky from your Attic Classroom? Is learning new skills and ideas or solving new problems part of your daily routine? Is study part of your life-orientation? The reason many of us are easily frustrated and stressed out by the problems of life is that we have been truant from school. Those who drop out of being lifelong students also jettison the part of the human brain designed for taking in new knowledge, meeting new challenges and creatively contending with problems. They are more likely to respond to difficulties with frustration and anger since their mind's resourceful problem-solving section has grown dormant. When you withdraw from disciplining yourself to learn new skills and experiment with new things, your Inner Classroom shuts down to a flat, unimaginative, sterile mode of automatic pilot. Psychiatrist Martin Groder says that this neglect has other consequences:

"Motivation is often the major victim of this process. Once you let your skills decay, it's harder to feel excited."

Exhilarated About Life

Being zestful, excited about life, doesn't have to be reserved for the young. Assisted by an oversupply of bubbling hormones, the young are usually motivated by a passion to know or learn — even if it's something that will get them into trouble. Because of their zeal for life, they are students actively engaged in learning. Those who passionately pursue the enrichment of ongoing education are usually highly motivated people. Such motivation is essential for liberation and for holiness, for our personal evolution in becoming more Godlike.

Motivation is the mother of discipline, and discipline helps our motivation bear fruit. To maintain an excitement about life, discipline must be romanced rather than endured. One way to make our drills less rote and more romantic is to add variety to our disciplined acts. Variety, along with being the spice of life, is the secret of great loving and learning. When we bring a great love into our drilling, repeated practice and self-discipline, we empower our personal inner coach, confessor and spiritual director, who, in turn, can help grow our springtime zest into abundant fruitfulness.

No one escapes — and no one evolves — without disciplined practice. And no one's discipline becomes truly effective without love and passion.

Chapter Nine Inventory of Escape Tools and Unshackling Reflections

Escape Tool #26 – X-Ray Gift Inspection

Carefully inspect any gift you are about to give to see if you may have unconsciously attached any strings. Just as hand luggage is inspected at airports for weapons and bombs, playfully x-ray scan your gifts for strings. Gifts can be wrapped in ribbon, but never in strings with hooks. A true gift must be stringless, devoid of expected responses of gratitude or possible paybacks. Do not give "Mafia" or "payback" gifts. If your scanner detects even the smallest string, snip it off before your act of giving in order to make your gift truly a gift — and also to free yourself from disappointment if it is not gratefully acknowledged.

Escape Tool #27 – No Strings Islamic Generosity

> The poor, the orphan, the captive: feed them for the
> love of God alone, desiring no reward, nor even thanks.[13]
>
> *— The Koran*

Islam encourages acts of love toward God in the form of a stringless, genuine generosity to the needy. Giving your money to erect churches may be a praiseworthy expression of your love of God. But giving without expecting a return is the highest form of love. Jesus says it is liberating to make our gifts such well-kept secrets that one hand doesn't even know what the other is doing. With such sleight-of-hand giving the donor is unknown, and so no thank you notes are possible. The only gold benefactor name-plaques would bear the name Mr. & Mrs. Anonymous. Such free and stringless giving is a passionate sign of our love for God. Moreover, such sharing of our wealth with the poor is all the purer when our good deeds are performed simply as acts of justice.

Escape Tool #28 – Make Extravagant Generosity Your Greatest Vice

A lavish way to show your gratitude for all things is to be extravagantly generous. Being generous with your money, time and presence is far better than words of gratitude to God. When you have been gifted with an inspiring teacher, mentor or coach, the best way to express thanks is unsparingly to be the same for others. Being extravagantly generous is an enchanting way to become holy and Godlike, for God is awesomely extravagant — as is revealed by even a casual glance at creation.

ESCAPE TOOL #29 – "THANK YOU" A HUNDRED TIMES A DAY

In their book *Spiritual Rx,* Frederic and Mary Ann Brussat suggest an excellent exercise: saying short thank-you prayers called *berakhot* blessings throughout the day.[14] An example of such Jewish blessings is the meal prayer, "Blessed are You, Lord our God, King of the Universe, who has given to us this bread" or the morning prayer, "Blessed are You, Lord our God, King of the Universe, for the gift of a new day of life." In this Jewish tradition there are countless short benedictions for almost every situation in daily life, and the devout Jew would say at least one hundred of these one-line prayers of gratitude daily. Consider composing your own contemporary form of these mini-gratitude prayers. Here are a few samples to get you started:

Blessed are you, Giver of Gifts,
   that I found a parking place so close to the door.

Blessed are you, Generous God,
   for my good night's sleep.

Blessed are you, Gracious God,
   that my doctor's appointment is on time.

If you think you would have difficulty finding a hundred things for which to be grateful each day, take another look at your day. If you practice this daily exercise of a hundred thank yous, I assure you that your humdrum day will be transformed into a treasure hunt.

ESCAPE TOOL #30 – MAKE A FORTUNE OUT OF MISFORTUNE

The next time you are helplessly trapped inside some unpleasant situation, do not curse and don't call 911. Instead, escape from the nasty condition by being grateful. Search through your predicament to find something — anything — for which you can be grateful. If after you have looked high and low, you end up empty-handed, be grateful that something worse didn't happen to you. Trust me, there is always something for which to be grateful. Be creative in searching for it.

Remember that frequently in life blessings come like fortune cookies. The good fortune is hidden inside a misfortune. Break open the shell of your misfortunes, trusting in this infallible law of the universe: Nothing is totally evil, and every dark rain cloud has a silver lining.

Escape Tool #31 — The Golden Prayer of Prayers

The golden prayer of prayers is only two words long: It's the potent phrase, "Thank you." True followers of a liberation spirituality are addicted to saying "Thank you" as many times a day as possible. Like a chain-smoker, become an addicted chain-thanker.

Escape Tool #32 — Fasting and Abstinence

The most neglected of our blessings are those commonplace ones we take for granted. Under normal circumstances the only way we are awakened to them is when they are suddenly taken from us by sickness or loss. A good antidote is to practice abstaining from your blessings in order to appreciate them more fully. If you are right-handed, fast from using your right side for a day or two. Struggle to button a blouse or shirt with your left hand or try writing left-handed. Fast from the presence of one you love by setting aside three or four minutes to imagine your life without that person. As another spiritual exercise, intentionally park your car at home and ride the bus to some destination. These and other forms of gift-fasting can open doorways to rejoicing in the great bounty of common things in the feast of life.

Tao Training

Ancient China's spiritual tradition of the Tao teaches, "Extend your help without seeking reward. Give to others and do not regret your generosity. Those who do this are truly good."[15]

The Vocation of a Troubadour

In Mark's Gospel is found the charming story of a man who eagerly asked to become a companion-disciple of Jesus, but was turned away. This Gerasene man had just been liberated by the Prophet of Galilee from being possessed by many demons. So he was "pressing" to accompany Jesus as a disciple. His urgency is understandable, for what better way to express gratitude than by becoming his healer's follower. After all, blind Bartimaeus of Jericho had done the same. However, Jesus tells this man his vocation isn't to be one of the companion-disciples. Rather, Jesus tells him, "Go home to your family and make it clear how much the Lord in his mercy has done for you." That he did, and more than just with his kinfolk. Mark says he "went off and began to proclaim through the ten cities what Jesus had done for him."[16]

If you've been liberated — gifted by the mercy of God — consider that you may have a vocation, like the Gerasene man, to become a Troubadour of Thanksgiving.

Escape Tool #33 — Let Your Fingers Do the Walking

The old Yellow Pages telephone book slogan, "Let your fingers do the walking," suggests a playful way to remind yourself of *arborization,* the mental process by which habits are grown. In this discipline, drilling and repetition are essential. Select an exercise from among the tools in this Escape Manual, and in the first days of practicing it reinforce the habit by pretending that the index and middle fingers of your hand are feet. Use them to walk across the top of your head, saying aloud,

"Walk on the grass, walk on the grass, and soon you'll tread yourself a path."

Hope for AWOL Discipline Deserters

Are you among the majority of us who at one time or another have deserted a discipline? Boot camp is a place of discipline and hard work, and those who are able, frequently go AWOL. Have you, for example, gone AWOL from your regimen of physical exercise? If so, there is good news from professor Avery Faigenbaum of the University of Massachusetts in Boston: Our muscles have memories! The muscles of people who have exercised regularly and then stopped, even for a period of many years, responded more quickly once they began again than did those who had never exercised.

Disciplined practice encodes both mind and body. Since we are body-mind-souls, we can tap into encoded memories of prayer, meditation and other spiritual disciplines. Professor Faigenbaum's findings are good news if for whatever reason you have stopped practicing some spiritual exercise. If you return to it, you'll likely find the practice easier than you thought.

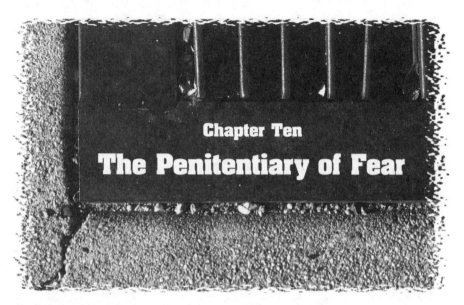

Chapter Ten

The Penitentiary of Fear

Daily, fear imprisons millions upon millions. I once read that there are some 366 entries in the Bible that in one way or another say, "Fear not."[1] That's one for each day of the year, including leap years. A challenging way to begin each day would be to quote the Bible, saying aloud, "Do not be afraid." It would prod us not only to trust more fully in God's care but also to confront our fears. This might prompt our conscience to ask, "Afraid of what?" But then it would force us to face into our response. Theologian Robert Barron says, "Fear is the 'original' sin of which the church fathers speak; fear is the poison that was injected into human consciousness and human society from the beginning; fear is the debilitating and life-denying element which upsets the 'chemical balance' of both psyche and society."[2]

How easily fears shackle our freedom with chains stronger than iron. Those who boast, "I'm not afraid of anything," should ask themselves if they fear snakes, flying, cancer, heights, public speaking, being robbed, deadly viruses like AIDS or a host of other terrors. Interestingly, according to the data of several polls, the greatest of all fears is having to give a speech in public. A humorist once noted that second place goes to having to listen to someone giving a speech.

Fears come in two styles: reasonable and unreasonable. It's reasonable, for example, to experience fear when hearing a tornado siren in Kansas. On the other hand, large numbers of people will not travel by air because of a relatively unfounded fear. A study of the validity of that fear was done by Dr. John Paulos, a professor of mathematics at Temple University in Philadelphia. He calculated the ratio of airline disasters to the number of passengers flying, and his test revealed surprising results. The average person's chances of dying in the crash of a domestic flight are one in seven million. The reality is that a person would have to fly every day on a commercial airline for 19,000 years before exhausting the odds of dying in a crash! The chances while on an international flight aboard any U.S. owned airline are somewhat greater, but still only one in 1.5 million flights! This translates into having to fly every day internationally for 4,000 years before reasonably expecting to die in an airplane accident. These facts proclaim: "Be not afraid of flying!" Yet the statistics will not erase the fear of flying because fears are often unreasonable and defy logic.

A "BE NOT AFRAID" FEAR LIST

Fears also come in at least two forms: clinical phobias and commonplace anxieties. The following is a partial list of phobias with their companion apprehensive anxieties.

Agylophobia (a-gill-o-fobia): *the fear of crossing busy streets*.

Changeophobia: the household-variety of *agylophobia*. It keeps you frozen on the same, old side of the street in life. Those beset with this folk phobia dread changes in their surroundings or religion. They shudder at the prospect of new ideas or crossing over to new ways of thinking and acting.

Climacophobia (klim-a-ko-fobia): *the fear of falling downstairs*.

Ascensionphobia: the cousin of *climacophobia*, this is the fright of climbing higher by using all your gifts and talents and assuming more responsibility in life. This bizarre yet common fear of our own potential causes the neglect of our abilities. This condition keeps us in the security of the basement of life where embarrassing mistakes and shameful failures are less likely to happen.

Aichmophobia (aik-mo-fobia): *the fear of needles and pointed objects*.

Controversyphobia: the fear that restrains us from engaging in controversial conversations or discussions of topics in which people are sharply divided. This nonclinical fear prevents us from *pointing out* the sins of injustice or hypocrisy in our religion and government.

Algophobia (al-go-fobia)*: the fear of pain.*

It-will-hurtphobia: the folk fear that causes us to avoid facing unpleasant situations or the painful struggle involved in breaking an addiction. This fear blocks achieving greatness of soul, since escaping from our ego-addictions is impossible without the often pain-producing realities of discipline and denial.

Anuptaphobia (an-up-ta-fobia)*: the fear of staying single.*

All-alonephobia: the domestic fear that compels people to become one with the crowd and echo the majority opinion. It forces those afflicted to fade facelessly into the herd instead of taking a lonely stand on issues of justice, exploitation and oppression. This fear easily camouflages itself in various ways to enable us to appear respectable.

Catagelophobia (ka-te-jel-o-fobia)*: the fear of being ridiculed.*

Uniquephobia: one of most widespread fears and a cousin to all-alonephobia. It includes being afraid of taking risks and appearing different from other people, which is a crippling affliction for Christian discipleship. This ailment prevents us from following the Redeemer-Rescuer, who dared to act so differently that some people thought he was mad! This fear appears first in the early teenage years and continues to develop and to debilitate. Those unable to escape from its grip never become creative, adventuresome or inventive.

Eremophobia (er-am-o-fobia)*: the fear of loneliness.*

Solitudephobia: the common version of its clinical cousin. Those in its grips dread being alone in prayerful solitude and are apprehensive of the emptiness of doing nothing. This fear securely blocks the door to experiencing the universally acknowledged fruit of the liberating prayer of solitude.

Ergaslophobia (ur-ga-slow-fobia)*: the fear of work.*

Laborphobia: the generic anxiety that prevents liberation and growth in holiness because they require disciplined work. It is also expressed in a rejection of personal responsibility and a refusal to volunteer for extra work. It causes a self-inflicted blindness to problems, so that others must take up a disproportionate burden in shouldering the unpleasant tasks in life.

Automysophobia (ot-o-mys-o-fobia)*: the fear of getting dirty.*

Proximityphobia: the common form of the above clinical fear. It's the dread of personal contact with social outcasts, the poor, aliens, convicts, those with different sexual orientations and those judged as living immorally — the very ones with whom Jesus associated and even identified himself.

Gymnophobia (jim-no-fobia)*: the fear of nudity.*

Stripteasephobia: the domesticated form of being afraid of being naked. It often causes hypocrisy and the wearing of respectable masks and costumes to disguise oneself. This common phobia prevents any depth of intimate friendships and love relationships since it abhors vulnerability as well as honest disclosures and revelations of weaknesses. Those so afflicted are prone to employ an ingenious variety of fig leaves.

Erotophobia (er-o-to-fobia)*: the fear of sexual love.*

Incorporationphobia: a fear, paradoxically, not limited to the unmarried; in fact, it most poignantly afflicts married persons. From one perspective this is a reasonable fear since God declared that by sexual union, "The two shall become one."[3] The divinely designed end of sexual love is incorporation, becoming one body, which requires an increasing capacity for personal death, the demise of the self. So great is the common form of *erotophobia* that it has almost all of us always practicing "safe sex." This fear compels us to use the prophylactic of protecting our egos, thus cleverly shielding our precious psyche so it isn't fused with our beloved.

We pause temporarily in this catalog of common fears in order to reflect on how fear may be healthy and serve a positive service in our lives.

FEARS AS LIFE-MOBILIZERS

"Hunger, sexual desire, fear and avoidance of pain are deeply ingrained, hard-wired if you will," says Christian Wertenbaker, "instinctive-emotional drives that protect the individual from death and the species from extinction."[4] Our human emotion of fear is a blessing when it mobilizes us to act for our survival. After the body's hunger signals the need for nourishment, thoughts about food begin to occupy the mind and affect the nervous system. The same healthy, natural process is involved with our sexual hungers and our fears in the face of physical dangers.

Walter Cannon's now famous "fight or flight" response to danger is an accepted reality, yet consequences are frequently forgotten. Cannon's rule is that when we are faced with some physical or psychological danger, our body issues a spontaneous 911 signal for the energy needed to either escape from or attack what threatens us. The body scrambles to mobilize itself to respond to the perceived danger by increasing blood pressure and the heart rate, rerouting blood from the digestive system to the muscles and dilating the pupils of the eyes. The ESCC, or Emergency Survival Control Center, is located deep within the brain and directs this response to danger without instructions from the conscious mind. The complex reaction response of the ESCC is good, life supporting and necessary for survival.

A REAL OR ERRONEOUS ENEMY

Recent research has revealed that our ESCC defensive mode reacts not only to real survival dangers but also to a wide variety of phobias, anxieties and emotional fears. Wertenbaker provides important information when he states, "The emotional brain has its own memory, distinct from the conscious memory."[5] When the body, without any instructions from the mind, energizes itself either to make war or to retreat from a feared enemy, the logical mind struggles to make sense of what is happening to the body. The conscious mind attempts to rationalize the sudden change in the body's behavior by proposing some logical explanation. This clarification may not be correct, however, since our emotional memory is directing the behavior.

As we've already noted, what people fear the most isn't flying or even cancer: The greatest fear is having to stand up before a crowd and give a speech. This is a prime example of fear being generated by an emotional memory, since the perceived danger has no reasonable grounds, at least as a physical threat. After all, the speech is not going to be given to an audience that's actually an armed mob intent upon injuring the speaker. Nor is it likely that any threats have been issued to the presenter. Perhaps the source of this greatest of all fears is found in a submerged emotional memory from early days in school. The thought of having to stand up alone before others to give a speech may arouse childhood memories of the palm-sweating fear of being ridiculed when called upon to give the correct answer in class. Those fears, in turn, may be triggered by an even more primal fig-leaf fear of being naked or exposed.

LEARNED AND ABSORBED FEARS

Ophidiophobia (o-fid-i-o-fobia): a fright caused by snakes that is fundamentally a learned and wholesome fear. Small children might pick up deadly snakes and play with them unless they've been taught to be afraid of them. Yet snake fear can also be unhealthy. Some serpents are, indeed, poisonous, and caution must be exercised when encountering them. However, our fear can lead to the hatred of snakes and to making it virtuous to kill them, even if they are harmless and even beneficial. It is wise to make a distinction between acting out of fear and approaching with apprehension and caution whatever is potentially life-threatening. Like some snakes, electricity can be dangerous and so should be treated with appropriate attentiveness. When the White House was first wired for electricity in 1891, President Benjamin Harrison and the first lady were afraid of getting electrical shocks from turning on the light switches. A servant would turn the electric lights on at dusk to illuminate the White House and would find them still on when he returned to work the next morning.[6] Be gentle with the old, fearful Harrisons, however, for you and I suffer from similar unrealistic fears.

Small children, who have not yet acquired adult discernment, can easily absorb the fears and anxieties of their parents. Mothers and fathers' highly infectious fears become the unconscious foundation of children's lifelong anxieties. When parents are fearfully anxious of not having sufficient money for their needs, their infected children can become penny-pinching and miserly as adults. Our logical minds attempt to make sense of this fear absorbed in early childhood, intermingling it with the praiseworthy virtue of thrift and a prudent concern for money.

THE FANTASY FEARS LURKING IN THE DARK, UNDER THE BED OR OUT IN THE NEIGHBORHOOD

We continue our catalog of fictional fears with another childhood fear, *bogeymanphobia* (boo-gey-man-fobia). It is not named after

Colonel Bogey, the fictitious English gentleman who is the patron saint of golfers. The origin of bogey is from the old word "bug," meaning a ghost. In time it began to be used for any imaginary scary creature, particularly those who frighten children into being good. As a teaching tool, fear is rarely ever a healthy way of instruction. Yet bogeymen and bogeywomen, in all colors and sizes, are also frightening to adults. At election time, politicians cleverly conjure up a variety of these frightening creatures from whom they'll protect innocent citizens — if they are elected. Their scare parade includes bogeys such as liberals, advocates of gun control, undocumented aliens, those on welfare, big government, corporate giants, paroled prisoners, criminals on the loose and even those who mix religion and politics.

Gossipphobia (gos-sip-fobia) is a domestic dread expressed in the query, "What will the neighbors say?" This freedom-stealing anxiety inhibits original behavior and creativity. The fear of our neighbors' gossip is another childhood-learned phobia. Socially, it acts as a mechanism to control unusual behavior and, in turn, breeds hypocrisy and pretense. The dread of the negative opinions of others blocks the original thinking necessary to engender an authentic personality. Eccentrics, who behave contrary to convention, are a rare breed in an age obsessed with the outward appearance of being mentally healthy. Yet being truly yourself is a spiritual duty. Like Jesus, each of us is a one-and-only incarnation of God. We are each originals, divinely designed not to be copies or clones of others.

JESUS AND GOSSIPPHOBIA

Our Liberator-Lord demonstrates in his own life the necessity to escape from the fear of what others think or say — even if it means we will be considered demented, as was he.[7] Jesus is the patron saint of eccentric saints and the holy hero of all of those who dare to be truly themselves and those bold enough to live out as fully as possible the embodiment of God in their flesh. Jesus was a healthy eccentric — which sounds like a contradiction in terms, since the word implies someone or something slightly off center. The center is defined by what is conventional, the socially and religiously proper way of behavior. God's ways are not our ways, however, and the enfleshment of God we see in the post-baptized Jesus was not a crowd-like clone, but a dynamically different sort of person. By who he was, Jesus calls us away from the comfortable centers of our lives to come out to the edge, where, led by the Holy Spirit, he was bold enough to live his life.

Healthy eccentrics are those who are faithful to living out the unique, never-before-seen-in-history enfleshment of God in them. Gandhi, Joan of Arc and Francis of Assisi are a few of history's healthy eccentrics. On the other hand, unfortunate are the social eccentrics whose behavior, speech and dress are peculiar because they are afflicted with a mental illness, making them prisoners of phobias. They live on the edges of society because they are psychologically unable to live anywhere else. They truly deserve our prayerful support and our personal and social assistance.

Fear-of-failurephobia is a paralyzing dread of making a mistake. Once again, the roots of this phobia are often found in childhood. Escaping from this fear as an adult involves recognition of how early in life it was implanted as the thought, "If I do everything perfectly, I'll be loved." Parents, family and teachers unknowingly sow this erroneous seed-thought by their glowing praise of high grades, excelling in sports or even maintaining a tidy bedroom. And whenever parental figures express disappointment at any failure to be less than the best, they reinforce these counterfeit grounds for being lovable. This dread of not being the very best is further nurtured by society in adoration of winning in athletics and admiration of success in business. Those incarcerated by a fright of failing or being wrong find criticism and correction to be extremely painful. Not infrequently, those held captive by this affliction engage with hidden delight in pointing out the failings of others. By being evangelizers of others' errors, they erroneously believe they will appear to be superior by comparison. Striving to be perfect is, indeed, a mental illness, for who in his right mind would consider himself to be infallible? An offshoot illness of this phobia is *postponemania*, an abnormal tendency toward procrastination, the foot-dragging delay spawned by perfectionism.

ESSENTIAL CRITICISM

Escapees from *fear-of-failurephobia* are not only freed from the dread of criticism, they are eager for it. They consider it to be essential evaluation-feedback necessary in the desire for excellence, which is different from perfectionism. In this light, criticism is simply useful information for learning and growth. Those free of this fear also readily discern the difference between legitimate and illegitimate criticism. Bastard criticism is envy thinly disguised as correction. It is expressed in a masqueraded delight at finding blemishes in another's work, which frequently the cynical critics themselves are incapable of creating or executing.

Be your own greatest critic. Anyone who passionately loves what he or she does, be it making dinner or making love, should constantly strive to make it even better the next time. Personal evaluation challenges us to excellence. Critics of religions and governments are repeatedly condemned as detractors, rebels or hatchet men and women. True critics, however, are first and foremost lovers of what they appraise. The prophets of Israel and the Prophet Jesus were passionately in love with their religion and yearned to see it lived as God originally intended. Jesus has many titles: Christ, Savior, Lord, Master, Teacher and the Good Shepherd, along with Prophet. We might add another to this list: Jesus the Good Critic, the patron of all who criticize and expose the hypocrisy of their religion and its leaders. Yet because he was a good critic of organized religion, of the institutional Temple establishment, he was crucified. So beware: Indeed, the truth will set you free, but the truth may also get you killed.

THE COUSIN OF CLIMACOPHOBIA

As we have seen, those suffering from *climacophobia* (kli-ma-ko-fobia) are stricken with the fear of falling downstairs. Another domestic version of this affliction is *scandalphobia,* the fear of being exposed in some scandal, resulting in a shameful falling down the stairs of status. This fear haunts those who have skeletons in their family closets (which is just about everyone), and those living a double life or engaging in any activity which society might view as immoral or illegal. The actual number of those who live shadowed by this fear is unknown, but it certainly must be large. At high risk are public figures, especially political and religious leaders who are expected to live by unrealistically high moral standards. This cultural expectation breeds hypocrisy, which generates the fear that exposure and public scandal will rip off one's mask and disguise.

In past centuries, perhaps more than today, one of the most powerful deterrents against private immoral behavior was the haunting thought that "Everyone will know!" The Last Judgment was preached as a cosmic courtroom, where all our sins, including those performed in secret darkness, would be made public by God the Judge in the presence of everyone we knew, as well as everyone who ever lived. The dread of being shamed before parents, family, clan and community made this exposure of every single sin more horrible than hellfire.

EMMANUEL THE EMANCIPATOR

Jesus the Savior-Emancipator says, "Do not be afraid" to those suffering from these and other fears. To those afraid of being a victim of scandal he says, "You will truly be my disciples and you will know the truth, and the truth will set your free."[8] Humility is unpretentious truth. Humble people are aware of the truth of their gifts and abilities; they do not deny the existence of their gifts, and neither do they boast of them. They are similarly aware of their flaws; they acknowledge them but do not despair of them. Humility, like truth, sets us free, which is certainly good news for those whose present or past private lives would fail to get the Good Housekeeping Seal of Approval. Along with being liberated from this diabolic fear of disgrace comes the stunning news that it can even become a grace. Dishonor holds a secret key to humility, which is one of love's most essential attributes. Living the truth in harmonious union with Christ includes living harmoniously with yourself, every part of yourself! No one is perfect. Even Jesus, it seems, made mistakes. After all, he chose Judas as his close companion and apostle. He also mistakenly predicted the imminent end of the world within the lifetime of his disciples.[9] Yet Jesus' human flaws do not diminish his divinity. Moreover, Jesus, as the enfleshment of God, delighted in spending his time in the presence of sinners, mistake-makers and those who were failures at observing the social and religious codes. Embracing the truth about ourselves leads to integrating our weaknesses with our strengths, blending our gifts with our drawbacks. Furthermore, embracing with love our own flaws makes it easier to embrace others' shortcomings. Loving self-clemency empowers us not so much to be tolerant with our enemies as to accept others as they are. That embrace of acceptance, by necessity, must be a wide one since it includes those whom we find disagreeable and even the authoritarian oppressors and dictators in the political and religious world.

"Be Afraid," Says Jesus

Yet we are also wise to heed Jesus' caution to be afraid: "Be not afraid of the powerful who can silence you and even destroy you; rather, be afraid of the one who has the power to destroy your soul."[10] "For what profit is it to gain the whole world and lose your soul?"[11] Jesus, who was tempted to his core, knows firsthand that loss of the soul is more deadly than poisonous vipers, cancer or AIDS. Yet, if the soul is immortal, how could anyone be able to destroy it? Your soul, your inner-life, the breath of God breathed uniquely into you, can be slowly suffocated to death by continuous compromises. Those who have lost, or are losing, their souls, are the walking dead: impotent underlings with fearfully sealed lips, ambitious ladder-climbers wearing blindfolds to the evil of systemic injustices and those incognito cowards who, when exposed, whimper, "I was only following orders," or "The canon (or civil) law says...." As much as any sexual sins, cowardly silence and spiritual sloth destroy the soul. Neglecting to exercise and nourish the soul cause a once-vibrant soul to become "zombieized."

The Torch of Liberty

When Old Zechariah prophesied in his canticle about the coming Messiah, he said the Savior-Liberator would "rescue us from our enemies and *set us free from fear....*"[12] He promised that a great light would shine for all those living in the darkness of fear. The Great Liberator was to be like our American Statue of Liberty holding high a flaming torch to banish the darkness in which lurk many of our fears. Let the Savior's torch illuminate whatever darkness covers you as you strive to live according to the miracle-laden implications of his words, "Do not be afraid" — words Jesus spoke numerous times to his disciples and which the Risen One continues to repeat today.

Believe in the Good News, believe that the power of love is the greatest power. God is love, and Jesus is the incarnation, the full embodiment, of that love. The author of John's letter wrote, "The one who dwells in love is dwelling in God and God in him/her.... In love there is no room for fear; indeed perfect love banishes fear."[13] For anyone reared on a steady diet of sermons about God's wrath toward sin and vivid accounts of the tortures of hell, these are, indeed, words of wondrous liberation. As the letter of John continues, "For fear has to do with punishment, and anyone who is afraid of punishment has not attained the perfection of love." So let us strive for excellence, for perfection in our loving. How is such excellence in loving achieved? By opening to the powerful influence of "practice, practice, practice."

THE BODY-SOUL GUARD

Bodyguards are a status symbol, a sign that you are an important person. Yet even if you are not the president, a Mafia boss or some movie star, there are agencies where you can rent a pair of bodyguards for the evening as a way to impress the other guests at a restaurant. There's no need to rent one, however, for each of us has a personal bodyguard who is always with us. So says the writer of Hebrews: "God said, 'I will never leave you or desert you.' So we can take courage and say, 'The Lord is my helper, I will not fear; what can anyone do to me?'"[14] Indeed, what can frighten you if you truly believe these words of Scripture about God being constantly at your side as your bodyguard, as your soul's secret service agent? Perhaps only one unquestionably frightening thing remains to fear, so terrifying as to shake even the bravest of Jesus' disciples.

BEWARE OF PLAYING GOD

The writer of Hebrews addressed the most dangerous of fears: "It is a terrifying thing to fall into the hands of the living God."[15] Just prior to this sentence, Hebrews' author quoted God saying, "Justice is mine: I will repay." Today, those who assist others who are dying of a painful disease and no longer want to live are denounced as "playing God." Yet are not those who promote or even approve of capital punishment equally guilty of playing God? Those presumptuous enough to believe they are administering God's justice by taking the life of one convicted of a capital crime should shudder in fear at falling into the hands of God, who has reserved judgment to God's own hands.

BEWARE OF PLAYING WITH GOD

Viewed from another angle, these words from Hebrews can be a warning about how terrifying it can be when we are embraced by the hands of God. Jesus, the village craftsman, apparently was living an ordinary life when he was enfolded in God's hands at his baptism — and look at what happened to him! Mystical writers in all of the world's great religious traditions advise spiritual seekers to approach playing with God only with great caution. In various ways they say, "Don't invite God into your daily world unless you're willing to have your world turned inside out and upside down." While such a warning should, indeed, be heeded with prayerful caution, it also needs to be viewed from another vantage point. Thomas Wolfe gave us such a perspective in his classic book, *Look Homeward Angel*: "Naked and alone we came into exile. In her dark womb we did not know our mother's face; from the prison of her flesh we have come into the unspeakable and incommunicable prison of this earth. Which of us has not remained forever prison pent?"[16] Not to invite God into your world as your constant companion is to remain forever prison pent — and that is surely a fate to be feared more than having your world turned upside down. So, perhaps better advice would be: Risk being stripped naked of your personality, that elaborate defensive mechanism, and risk losing your very self in order to find your most authentic self. Risk playing with God in the game of life to find a freedom no one can take from you. Risk letting God play you like a rare Stradivarius violin so that the soul-song of the cosmos will flow from you. The only other option is to remain forever in slavery.

THE FIRST ENCYCLICALS

An encyclical is a letter from the bishop of Rome intended to be circulated among the bishops and faithful of the world. The apostolic encyclicals of the early church, called epistles or letters, are all interlaced with themes of freedom and liberty. A prime example is the apostle Paul's encyclical to the catacomb Christians of Rome, in which he says, "The spirit you have received is not a spirit of slavery, leading back into a life of fear, but a spirit of adoption, enabling us to cry, 'Abba! Father!'"[17] He further admonished them to live "in the glorious freedom of the children of God."[18] These encyclicals continue to call us to allow the same Holy Spirit who filled Jesus to be active in us and daily to inspire us forward toward liberation. Paul wrote more about this abiding presence of the Spirit of Freedom in his second letter to the Corinthians: "Where the Spirit of the Lord is, there is liberty."[19] Those of us who long to read inspiring instructions about liberty from our church leaders need only to return to reading the original apostolic encyclicals. They provide more than enough encouragement — if you receive them with eyes of faith. Read and believe them; let them be the sources for forming and strengthening your lifestyle-spirituality.

WORRIES — LOW-GRADE FEAR INFECTIONS

"Do not worry or be anxious," Jesus tells us. Worry is a habitual fearful concern that seriously impedes the enjoyment of life's great adventure. Worry may take the form of occasional low-grade fears about various things and situations in our lives. It may manifest as an undue concern about the future, whether an hour from now or twenty years down the road. It is the kind of uneasiness that chews on us, as is expressed in the old saying, "a dog worrying a bone." It comes from an Old English word meaning "to strangle." Indeed, the ancients knew how to name things! Once, prisoners were confined not just by iron chains on their hands and feet but also with a strangling iron collar around their throats. Now, as then, however, we are more likely to be strangled by our worries.

The Great Liberator encourages those imprisoned by worry, "Do not be anxious, worrying about tomorrow and whether you will have enough money to sustain you in retirement. Do not fret about what you will wear and eat, and do not brood about the amount of money in your stocks and savings. Look at how God cares for the birds and flowers with great love. Learn a lesson from all of creation, and do not worry but instead trust in the providence of God."[20]

While worry and anxiety are often interchangeable words in daily speech, anxiety carries the connotation of highly agitated worry. Anxiety is an ancient affliction. Our prehistoric ancestors did more than worry about their next meal, they were anxious about their food supply. Anxiety's mother word *angere,* meaning "to choke," gives a vivid picture of the reality. Anxiety has the power to clutch us by the throat and squeeze the spirit-life out of us. In psychological terms, anxiety is an intense fear usually lacking a specific threat, and so it can imply an abiding state of imprisonment. Because it doesn't need any object that focuses our fear — one that in time will be resolved — anxiety makes us live in a constant state of fear.

A Thief in Both Day and Night

Worry comes as a thief in the night, robbing us of peace of mind and sleep. The stronger the worry, the more frequently it appears in our sleep as a nightmare contender. But, of course, worries aren't limited to nighttime warfare. They can wrestle with us on the mat of our mind 24 hours a day. Worry and her cousins, anxiety, dread, stress, panic and agitated apprehension, are all fears related to the future.

An adventure is an undertaking that holds the potential risk of facing the unknown and uncontrollable, which is exhilarating but also gives rise to fears. When these fears are great enough, they immobilize us, which explains why so many of us choose a safe, stay-at-home lifestyle. Contemporary urbanized, highly organized and sanitized life is not very adventuresome. Yet as a lingering memory from primitive times, humans still retain a hunger for adventure. Otherwise, we wouldn't have sports like mountain climbing or go on safaris, and theme parks with roller coasters would be out of business. But, indeed, daily life, even in the suburbs, can be adventuresome.

When our belief system contains the dogma that God passionately and deeply loves us and cares for us, then we can embrace a lifestyle of adventure. Such was the core belief of Jesus of Galilee, and it empowered him with the confidence to engage life as a high adventure. At times the crowds attempted to kill him, throw him over a cliff and stone him, yet he remained calm and serene. One of his personal dogmas was Psalm 23:

> You, O God, are my shepherd; I fear no harm,
> for you are with me;
> your shepherd's staff and crook give me comfort....
> Goodness and unfailing love will follow me
> all the days of my life."[21]

The deeper our realization of this ever-abiding care, the more we make tangible the reality of a loving God and the more boldly we can confront life's alien anxieties. When we allow such a belief to impregnate our life, we are more peaceful and calm even in threatening situations. Jesus was not fearless, and neither should his disciples be. Rather, like him, they should be love-filled. It is this capacity for love that dissolves fear and allows us to face our worries and anxieties, the unpredictable and uncontrollable, with calm trust and courage.

A Spirituality of Liberation is an adventuresome lifestyle in which, regardless of the hazards, daily life can be experienced as a soul-expanding expedition, a spiritual safari. It doesn't require leaving home to climb snow-capped mountains or trudge through dangerous jungles to experience adventure. The only necessity is being fret-free.

Fretting is a form of worry that involves brooding. To fret is more than just to stew over something; it's like living in a bubbling stew pot. When you realize some worry has captured you, escape the pot. Repeat aloud the words of our Liberator-Savior, "Do not worry. Do not be anxious." He goes on to say, "Worrying is so useless! Can an anxious thought add a day to your life?"[22] Instead of worrying, he calls us to focus our hearts on the enchanted reign of God and to believe that we are loved and protected by God. By living immersed in his core belief of God's love for him, Jesus lived a freeing, magnetizing life that drew to himself all those who desired to likewise live in such liberty.

PRODUCTIVE WORRYING

To worry can be good. Productive worrying involves calculating the possible difficulties and disasters of some projected situation. This is a kind of fire-escape planning, creating a checklist of possible problems that can be faced in advance. Apprehension is natural, and it is wise to plan prudently for tomorrow. Jesus advised taking care to build our house on solid rock rather than sinking sand.[23] He also counseled sitting down before engaging a challenging situation to calculate whether we can beat the odds.[24] Of course, we need to be cautious even with *productive* apprehension. There is always the hidden threat, as the term *apprehension* literally suggests, of being arrested or taken into custody. Indeed, even productive worrying can imprison. Yet apprehension also has the positive meaning of *understanding*, as when we grasp the implications of a situation. Wise disciples are those who use their intuitions to anticipate and avoid possible problems. The Master-Deliverer encouraged his disciples to live a balanced life: on one hand being carefree and innocent as doves and on the other being as apprehensive and clever as serpents.[25] What begins as productive worry can subtly and involuntarily grow into a full-blown anxiety that feeds upon itself. So, whenever you feel your wary anticipation of an approaching situation growing into a fear, take preventive action. Retreat at once into your core belief in God's abiding love and providential care for you.

Xenophobia — the Next Chapter

The next chapter will address a particularly deadly fear, *Xenophobia*, the fear of strangers and those different from you. This is a deadly phobia because of its serious social and personal implications. Xenophobia is always imprisoning. This fear of strangers includes any foreign or unusual person in society as well as anything out of the ordinary within ourselves. As such, it can include a variety of psychological or sexual fears. It's paradoxical that the folk term for our human sexual organs is our "private parts." Sexual actions are called "intimate," implying that they are familiar and close, yet they, along with certain parts of our bodies, can be feared as strange.

Chapter Ten Inventory of Escape Tools and Unshackling Reflections

Escape Tool #34 — Live in the Now

Worries and anxieties all deal with something in the future. So, one way to avoid being captured by a worry is to focus the fullness of your attention on the present moment. Remember that the mind can only think one thought at a time. If you attend only to what is going on in the "now," being fully present with all your senses to its feel, smell, sight and sound, you can't stew and worry about something in the future. Experiment with this escape tool whenever you are about to deliver a presentation or report. Let go of being anxious in anticipation of what you are about to do, and instead be present to the present moment. Carefully examine the details of your surroundings as if committing them to memory, be fully attentive to those seated around you and, if possible, engage them in conversation. You will likely find that you are too occupied to worry.

A Short but Powerful Morning Prayer

Begin each day praying aloud, "Be not afraid."[1] Use this three-word prayer by itself or as a conclusion to your formal morning prayers. Whenever the dark shadow of some fear falls across your day, you can repeat those three calming prayer words of Jesus. They can remind you of the source of your confidence: your faith in the reality that you abide constantly in God's embrace and so have nothing to fear. The way to inhabit the same mind frame as the Galilean Master is to practice living unafraid.

Escape Tool #35 – Be Disobedient

This is not an easy tool to handle, for we have been trained from childhood to be obedient. Yet you can escape from fear by practicing being disobedient. Whenever your fearful inner voices whisper that you should be afraid of (___fill in the blank___), be naughty and do the opposite of what those old, echoed fear messages are telling you. Fears can only hold us prisoner as long as we agree to comply with their voices. Schizophrenics are not the only ones who hear voices. As you are bombarded with the prerecorded voices of your fears, prayerfully listen for the quiet voice of the Spirit of Freedom encouraging you to be brave and to escape from your fears. That same Spirit-Voice of God prompted Jesus to be disobedient to the narrow, small-minded voices of the religious leaders and self-righteous. He listened to and obeyed only the Spirit's voice when being tempted by the primal voice that cried out to him, "Forget about others; save your own skin!" Each time you follow his example and disobey your inner-voices of fear, know with confidence that they will grow fainter and fainter until they are swallowed up in silence.

THE PRISON-FORTRESS OF FEAR

Robert Barron says, "When we fear, we cling to who we are and what we have; when we are afraid, we see ourselves as the threatened center of a hostile universe, and thus we violently defend ourselves and lash out at potential adversaries. And fear — according to so many of the biblical authors and so many of the mystics and theologians of our tradition — is the function of living our lives at the surface level, a result of forgetting our deepest identity."[26]

Father Barron's words should be recalled whenever you find yourself suddenly in "attack mode," about to strike out at someone or to escape from some difficult situation. The defensive position you've taken is a reaction to fear. You may not feel afraid, but at some level you are. The first step to disarm yourself is found in *Escape Tool #36*: the practice of moving beneath the surface layer of life by taking the elevator.

ESCAPE TOOL #36 – USE THE ELEVATOR

While they're named elevators, they descend as well as ascend. When a fear takes away your freedom, making you a hostage, remember that you are living only on the surface level of life. Take a deep breath and ride down an imaginary elevator to a place deep within yourself. With each breath descend downward another floor, until you reach your deepest level, wherein resides your Image. All you will see there, however, is darkness because your Image is of the invisible God. To experience your Image, you must see it with the braille eyes of faith, feeling the presence of the Divine One residing in the center of who you are.

That Divine Presence is the All-Powerful, All-Luminous, All-

Energizing One, who enlivens the universe with all its 200 billion galaxies. As you rest in that inner darkness, breathe in the permeating, passionate love and quiet power of the Divine Mystery. When you feel saturated with the Sacred, take another deep breath and let yourself be elevated back up to the surface level of life, there to face with confidence what once terrified you.

FREEDOM MAGNETIZES

Henri Nouwen said, "When you are interiorly free, you call others to freedom, whether you know it or not. Freedom attracts wherever it appears.... Whenever we meet a truly free person, there are no expectations, only an invitation to reach into ourselves and discover there our own freedom. Where true inner freedom is, there is God. And where God is, there we want to be."[27]

ESCAPE TOOL #37 – TALKING TO YOURSELF

Like the previous escape tool, this one may be awkward to handle when you first begin to use it. Mentally disturbed people carry on conversations with themselves. Mentally healthy people usually do not talk to themselves, but they could find it helpful! Smile and step over the fear of appearing odd or senile, and frequently chat with yourself. The more senses we employ in practicing any exercise, the deeper will be the influence. Thus, to the discipline of changing negative thoughts to positive ones, we can now add the act of giving ourselves verbal instructions. Be your own personal coach and guru-guide as you give yourself audible directions concerning your desired new behavior and new thought patterns. Be aware, however, that for most of us it doesn't work to be polite when faced with difficult problems. So, be your own boot camp drill sergeant and shout out tough commands to yourself.

Enjoy playing with these multiple personalities of personal coach, guru-guide and drill sergeant. You may even find it helpful to add the persona of a private secretary. Dictate aloud to your personal secretary reminders about the tasks and things you need to remember. You might even consider giving your secretary a name. You will be surprised at how much more easily you remember things with the use of this exercise. You can also add to your enjoyment and enlightenment by including a personal court jester in your cast of characters. This private clown-comedian can poke fun at you for your silly mistakes or ride you when you come off as righteous or pompous. Not only will living with such colorful inner personalities assist your liberation, it will provide great companionship and great fun.

PROCRASTINATION FEAR RELIEF

Often we postpone making out our will, shelve for another day the cleaning of our closet, delay addressing an important interpersonal issue with our spouse, or put off any number of other projects because we fear we don't have sufficient time to accomplish these tasks. While fear in this case is a folk term for *apprehension* rather than *dread*, it's still beneficial to learn how to "fear not." In our overworked, time-short society, we are even more likely to postpone indefinitely tasks that need to be done.

Relief for this malady of procrastination fear comes by practicing organization. It's wise to begin with the old-fashioned exercise of "making a list" of priorities. Good organization is a cure for inertia. Less important tasks tend to be louder and pushier, yet finishing them doesn't give nearly the satisfaction as completing truly important tasks. When we successfully complete our higher priorities, we can then build momentum on the resulting satisfaction to take on the rest of our agenda. Moreover, to manage our large, time-consuming tasks, it helps to divide them into smaller portions and assign manageable sections for specific days. Lethargy has several sources, among them is the proper allotment of our limited amount of time. As with all disciplines, be gentle yet firm, reasonable yet uncompromising, and build on small successes. Your fear will dissipate as your tasks get done, and you will know the added blessing of strengthening the fiber of your soul as you increase your ability to respond to life's challenges.

THE CONTAGIOUS FREE PERSON

In an article titled *Thomas Merton's Asian Journey*, Harold Talbott depicts Merton as a liberated man:

He tipped Sikh taxi drivers like a Proustian millionaire. He was on a roll, on a toot, on a holiday from school. He was a grand seigneur, a great lord of the spiritual life. He radiated a sense of "This is an adventure, here I am folks," and he woke people up and illuminated them and enchanted them and gave them tremendous happiness and a good laugh. People knew his spiritual quality. People in planes knew it. There was no question about it. Merton was not an object of scrutiny, he was an event.

"FEAR NOT," SAYS THE HOLY SPIRIT

The Spirit has spoken the message of freedom from fear in every age and spiritual tradition:

God is our refuge and strength, a very present help in trouble. We therefore do not fear, though the earth should vanish and the mountains disappear into the sea.[28]

— Judaism

Deep within each abides another life, not like the life of the senses. It is unchanging. This life endures when all created things have passed away.[29]

— Hinduism

If the traveler can find a virtuous and wise companion,
  let him go with him joyfully and overcome the dangers of the way.
If you cannot find a friend or master to go with you,

travel alone rather than in the company of a fool.
Do not carry with you your mistakes.
Do not carry your cares. Travel alone.[30]

                    — Buddha

Not one sparrow falls to the ground without your Father's knowledge. Even all the hairs of your head are counted. So do not be afraid; you are worth more than many sparrows.[31]

                    — Jesus

Trust in Allah, but always tie up your camel.

                    — Persian saying

YOU SAY YOU'RE NOT AFRAID OF ANYTHING?

If so, consider reading Melinda Muse's book, *I'm Afraid, You're Afraid: 448 Things to Fear and Why*.[32] Among her long list of things to fear, you may be surprised to find Mondays and Saturdays. She quotes an American Association of Suicidololgy report that the majority of suicides occur on Monday. Also, most heart attacks and car accidents occur on that first day of the week. Saturdays are to be feared since they have the greatest number of fatal motor vehicle crashes, the most dangerous hours being between 4 P.M. and 4 A.M.

If you prefer an aisle seat when flying, request it with some apprehension since every year items falling from overstuffed luggage bins strike 4,500 airline passengers. You may have reason to be afraid, for you could be hit by such potentially lethal objects as heavy briefcases, backpacks and laptops.

Finally, pet lovers should beware of showing affection to their dogs. Each year more than one million Americans get parasites — roundworms, hookworms and panoramas — from kissing their pet dogs! These difficult to diagnose canine infections cause headaches, liver ailments or sinus infections for their owners. Melinda Muse encourages teaching your dog to shake hands.

Chapter Eleven

The Prison of Prejudice

Fear is the mother of hatred.[1] That causal relationship describes the subject of this chapter's prison: prejudice. It's roots lie in *xenophobia*, which is a social fear, the anxiety aroused by strangers and by the strange, by anything different from ourselves. In prejudice, what once functioned as a healthy prehistoric survival mechanism becomes a false fear that imprisons. The stranger, because of skin color, language, custom, dress or behavior, is blindly or unconsciously judged as a threat and, therefore, becomes an enemy. This prehistoric judgment of prejudice is based on insufficient evidence to substantiate the fear. This is exactly the kind of discrimination that the Liberator from Nazareth was addressing when he said, "Do not judge and you will not be judged; do not condemn and you will not be condemned."[2]

As a mirror exercise to help us gain insight into how irrational our prejudices can be, let's reflect on the predicament of those born left-handed. Since the majority are right-handed, the use of the right hand is customarily considered natural and good. By contrast, using the left hand has not infrequently been judged to be unnatural and, therefore, wrong. Left-handers have often been discriminated against by their parents or early teachers, who forced them to eat or write with their right hand, which was also assumed to be their "correct" hand.

School desks, tools, machinery and other objects have been designed for those who are right-handed, and this prejudice is reinforced by our use of language and humor. Those born left-handed have to endure such expressions as "a left-handed compliment," which means one has received an insult under the guise of praise. "She's out in left field" means she's eccentric, odd or mistaken. Some say this idiom originated because early baseball parks had left fields larger than right fields, causing more balls to be lost, thus resulting in greater confusion. Yet many left-handers dispute such an "excuse" explanation.

THE SIN OF SINISTER

Left-handed prejudice is ancient. The Latin root of the English word "sinister," one meaning of which is left-handed; it has the connotation of threatening, evil, wicked, dark, mysterious and ominous. The "bar sinister" in the code of heraldry is a band or stripe running to the left across a coat of arms, symbolizing that the owner was a bastard. In some pre-industrial countries the only practical use reserved for the left hand is to wipe one's behind. Moreover, the social prejudice is given a divine underpinning when Jesus places the sheep, who are righteous, at his right hand and the goats at his left; then he proceeds to cast those on his left into eternal fire.[3]

Consider the consequences if in Leviticus the Lord God had commanded, "You shall not use your left hand for writing, working or grasping your sword; such a thing is an abomination." And what if in the epistle to the Corinthians St. Paul had said, "Neither fornicators, nor adulterers, nor sodomites, nor the left-handed...nor the greedy will possess the kingdom of God." Imagine if most religions forbade left-handed people from marrying right-handed people and left-handed people were barred from most country clubs, from living in certain suburbs, from seating on public transportation and eating in certain establishments.

This last paragraph is obviously a caricature, but many of my left-handed friends would suggest that it is only a slight exaggeration. Now, take this mirror exercise and substitute for left-handers any of the following: black-skinned, women, gay, Jewish, fat people, Chinese, the NRA, fundamentalist Christians, Moslems, aliens, Catholics, or the object of your favorite prejudice. Before you say that you don't have any prejudice, consider that our prehistoric xenophobia, our fear of strangers, lingers deep in our DNA and very often unconsciously restricts our freedom to interact with those who are different from us.

Discrimination is prison behavior based on prejudice, and the degree of our discrimination determines the length of our prison term. As we might expect, our conviction and subsequent imprisonment happens as a result of a courtroom procedure. Our path to prison goes through a *kangaroo court*. This term isn't Australian; it was actually coined during the American Gold Rush. It referred to quickly jumping to a judgment to hang claim jumpers. Prejudice is always jumping to a conclusion. No evidence is needed for a prejudiced judgment since bigotry, intolerance and discrimination are learned fear-hate behaviors. Freedom from prejudice, however, is also a learned acceptance.

COME, FOLLOW ME

Escape from Prejudice Prison begins with an acknowledgment of the existence of a prejudice. Don't be ashamed of the reality of your prejudice, for apparently even Jesus the Liberator suffered from prejudice and overcame it. While traveling outside Galilee in the area of Tyre, he was approached by a Canaanite woman. Being a product of his culture, he would have been taught to treat her with aversion since she was a non-Jew. When she begged him to heal her daughter, he refused and responded with what sounded like an insult, saying, "It isn't right to give the food of chosen children to dogs." And she replied, "Please, even the dogs eat the scraps that fall from their master's tables." I imagine Jesus smiling as he said, "O woman, great is your faith. Your wish is granted." Her daughter was healed at that moment.[4]

This passage from Jesus' life is liberating since it reveals that we can rise above our indoctrination about people of other religions or nationalities. Matthew's account of this scene leaves us empty-handed as to the reason for this seemingly sudden change of mind, but since Jesus was led by the Holy Spirit we can surmise that he was inspired. The Spirit of God is inclusive, a Spirit of unity and love. So, the next time you are taken hostage by some prejudice, you might try breathing in the Inclusive Spirit and asking to escape from your kangaroo court.

THE HOLY DISCRIMINATING SPIRIT

Escape from social or religious discrimination by being discriminating. The very word is a two-edged sword that has a double meaning. On one hand, it speaks of intolerance, chauvinism and bigotry. Yet it can also mean discernment, perception and insight. This latter sense of discrimination is a work of the Spirit of God. It involves the ability to distinguish what exists beneath apparent reality. As a gift of the Spirit, discernment is the graced ability to see into what seems threatening or different and to see God. The Spirit's gift of discrimination sees beyond the surface of skin color, age, sex or social status. The Spirit's gift of perception is blind to the labels of our culture and church, and it sees God enfleshed in pagan, Protestant, Jew, woman, divorced and gay. It discerns God embodied in all persons and delights in the differences.

The Spirit of Creation is extravagantly diverse. Those led by the Spirit thus find great joy in the endless variety within humanity and creation. According to Edward Wilson, within a space of only 2.5 acres (about two and half football fields) in Brazil's Atlantic forest, 425 different kinds of trees have been found. In Peru's Manu National Park scientists have counted over 1,300 butterfly species.[5] The social necessity to embrace diversity in all its forms is a required evolutionary step forward over the grave of xenophobia. Each time you rejoice in what makes others different from you and what makes you different from others, you are growing in soul and becoming more Godlike.

Ultimately, there is only one race — the human race! This radical revelation that is increasingly reinforced by twenty-first century anthropologists has profound consequences. They suggest that the division of humanity into various races was an unsubstantiated, arbitrary mechanism created by Anglo-Saxon scholars of the nineteenth century. Thus, to speak of interracial marriages or the intellectual differences between races or the need for racial divisions is an antiquated falsehood. The division of humanity into various races gave those early classifiers authorization for their own social superiority. The poison of their invention continues to infect societies throughout the world. To neutralize this poison, we need at every opportunity to live in the glorious variety of the creation of God.

APOSTOLIC ANTI-XENOPHOBIA

The beginning of chapter 13 of the Letter of the Hebrews contains an important part of the lived message of the Liberator of Galilee. It states, "Remember to always welcome with hospitality those who are strangers, for by doing so some have entertained angels unawares."[6] Aware of our deeply ingrained fear of those who are "other," Jesus encouraged his followers to welcome strangers as more than mere angels, saying that when they welcome strangers, they welcome him.[7] The ancient world was very conscious of spirit-beings visiting earth disguised as strangers, and those who treated them with respect and hospitality were always rewarded. This welcoming — this religious, social inclusion of those who look, speak or dress differently — is a sure antidote for our ancient fear of aliens. This cure of our fear involves acting completely contrary to the fearful voices that denounce strangers by treating them as family, clan or fellow villagers.

Contemporary parents are faced with many moral dilemmas, but one in particular stands out in this discussion. How do we simultaneously teach our children to be Christians by welcoming a stranger on the street and still be wary of those strangers as potential predators? From television news programs of child abductions to milk cartons bearing the faces of kidnapped kids, today's children are fed a continuous diet of xenophobia. Childhood fears, some real and others unfounded, remain submerged throughout our adult lives. Yet they strongly affect our behavior when triggered by some emotional situation. Realizing the impact of our childhood fears, how do we protect our children and at the same time keep them from becoming fear-bound? How do we form them as healthy Christians?

CONVERSION AND OVERCOMING OUR FEARS

Is the Kingdom of God — living fully and radically in the holy Kindom — only possible for adults? Consider the possibilities of a twenty-first century ritual: reserving the conversion experience of Baptism until the age of 21 or having everyone who was baptized as a child undergo a process of adult conversion at that age. Either of these ritual options would give each person the freedom to reject or accept adult conversion to discipleship. It would clearly identify the two groups present in every Christian church, regardless of the members' chronological age: Child Christians or Adult Christians. Such a classification would greatly reduce the accusation of hypocrisy in Christian churches since people would not expect Child Christians to live out an adult religious and moral life.

Adult conversion would include not only embracing a theology about Christ and a set of moral principles, but would also involve these Christians in a Gospel way of life. It would educate them on how to control fears that prevent many of the works to which Jesus called his disciples: welcoming the stranger and alien, visiting those in prison and feeding those who are dirty and homeless. Matthew's Gospel account of the Last Judgment tells how those who will be welcomed into heaven are those who overcame their ancient fears by caring for Christ hidden in the stranger, the prisoner in jail and the ragged, dirty and hungry.[7] Real and inclusive conversion always involves controlling and overcoming our primal fears.

As with racial discrimination, this revolution has only begun, since prejudice exists on both sides of the color and sexual lines. Continued work must be accomplished to eradicate the poisons of prejudice.

SEXUAL LIBERATION

Radical social actions in the second half of the last century saw landmark advances in overcoming the prejudice toward those with colored skins. At the same time, another liberation from prejudice began to take shape in the area of sexuality.

Another name for discrimination is bias. It's a kinder and softer sounding name for what is always a harsh reality. Yet despite its cosmetic qualities, it's actually another face of bigotry. Literally, a bias is a slanting or diagonal view. When tailors cut diagonally across the grain of a fabric, they call it "cutting the cloth on the bias." Interestingly, deviate is another name for moving diagonally, for cutting against the grain of established norms, social customs or moral standards. It is the term we use for those whose sexual expression is different from the majority. Yet when we practice discrimination against gays or lesbians, we are the ones who deviate, for we are violating the most foundational of commandments, "Love your neighbor."[8]

"Judge not and you will not be judged,"[9] said our Liberator-Savior in giving us the most comprehensive insurance for eternal life. When we judge others as perverts because of their sexual behavior or orientation, we are setting ourselves up to be judged as perverts since we are violating one of the most basic moral standards of Christ. The letter to the Galatians declared, "There does not exist among us gentile or Jew, slave or free, male or female, for we are all one in Christ."[10] Unity in the Risen Jesus, the Christ, implies not only equality but also inclusive acceptance. Those words of the early church are not just wishful thinking or even an ideal to be strived for, they are a statement of a present reality and a Declaration of Equality. Those who believe in the Good News are obligated then to make that declaration part of their lifestyle, their lived spirituality.

SEXUAL PREJUDICE IN HOLY PLACES

Sexual discrimination flourishes in holy places. Women being denied ordination and leadership in communal Eucharistic worship simply because they are a different gender is a prejudice contrary to the norm of Scripture so beautifully expressed in the above passage from Galatians. Indeed, any organization or institution can make arbitrary rules to determine who may or may not function as its representatives. Moreover, the church is not alone in its historical discrimination against women, which to some degree continues in all strata of society. The removal of the discrimination that limits what professions, positions or other opportunities are available to women — along with biases based on sexual orientation or the color of one's skin — is an important part of the work of a liberation spirituality. The process of releasing those imprisoned by prejudice begins with our thoughts, and then proceeds to our speech, which is enfleshed in our deeds.

FREEING THE VICTIMS OF PREJUDICE

Prejudice can be internal as well as external. Any socially ingrained bigotry, especially when blessed by religion, imprisons in shame and damaged self-worth those whom it targets. Young girls can easily be indoctrinated by parents, family, teachers and society at large to limit their expectations of what they can accomplish in life. This internal self-prejudice is strengthened when their religion reinforces their limited capacities as women by restricting them from worship leadership roles and suggesting that they blindly subject themselves to their husbands. Any self-limiting of the gifts and abilities given at birth by God is not only tragic, it is stealing from God. Our whole society is also robbed whenever we inhibit ourselves by failing to use our gifts because of the effects of fear or prejudice.

A person who enters life as a woman in a patriarchal society, or with dark-colored skin in a white culture, or with a genetic sexual orientation toward persons of the same sex, begins life in prison, a captive of prejudice. As they grow up, it doesn't take long for women and blacks to realize they are looked upon as second-class citizens. And as for gay people, as soon as they begin to become aware of their sexual orientation, even if no one else knows of it, they experience condemnation. Denounced by religion and society as being evil or deviant, they are taken hostage by shame and disgrace. Social ridicule, jokes and racial, sexual and gender slurs only buttress the imprisonment of these groups. They must not wait for society to free them but must find an escape route within themselves so as to live in the glorious freedom of the children of God. Most of the time, unfortunately, they must learn to be like salmon and swim upstream.

SALMON SPIRITUALITY

Prejudice is a powerfully surging river. When the mighty River of Religion flows into it, it creates a compelling current that can easily carry us away. When you are the subject of prejudice, resist the current. Find for yourself some quiet pool where you can reflect on the truth that you, like Jesus of Galilee, are an embodiment of God. The incarnation is not restricted to Jesus, nor did it end when he ascended into heaven. In light of Jesus' liberating, redeeming resurrection, God does not just reside in your heart; the Divine Unlimited Mystery is embodied in every cell and organ of your body. At sunset each day of creation, God looked at what had been created and proclaimed, "Ah, that's good." At the divine moment of your creation in your mother's womb, God echoed the very same words about you. Each one of us, regardless of our race, gender or sexual orientation, is a uniquely beautiful, embodied word of God. The Divine Mystery longs to have the divine word that is you spoken clearly and truly in the world. Each word of God has a purpose. The world needs each and every word made flesh to be fully him/herself if the divine mystery in its awesome wholeness is to be revealed.

Repeat to yourself the words Jesus heard at his baptism in the River Jordan, where he was empowered to be a Salmon Savior: "You are my beloved, and upon you my favor rests."[11] God aches for each one of us to hear that message so we might find the courage to be divinely different. The Salmon Savior swam upstream against the tides of his village culture and codes of behavior, his family's expectations, his religious laws, the powerful temple priesthood and even the mighty torrent of the Roman Empire. To you and to all enslaved by bigotry and shame he cries out, "Come, follow me." Like him, you may have to swim upstream against ingrained social customs and moral codes, against misguided Scriptural quotations and sociological studies, against accusations and denunciations by the clergy or the machinery of the state. Whenever you feel the strong current of Prejudice River beginning to sweep you back into shame and guilt, find that quiet pool again and repeat to yourself the words of God, "You are my beloved, upon you my favor rests."

The following creed is a faith-prayer for those who suffer discrimination. It can consolidate your faith in moments of doubt, in times when the current of the River of Prejudice seems to be too strong.

A Credo of Liberation

I believe that God is love,
    and that love is infinite since God is infinite.
I believe God shows no partiality in loving:
    Divine love is passionate and all-inclusive.
God does not love others more than me.

I believe that Christ is the Vine,
    and that on this Vine I am a living branch.
Through me flows the sacred energy,
    the life and grace of the Vine.
I believe that God loves others
    through me and with me and in me.

I believe God is embodied in my flesh,
    as God was incarnated in Jesus of Galilee.
The Divine Unlimited One fills
    every cell and organ of my body,
    making nothing about me unholy or unworthy.

I believe the Holy Creator made me as I am,
    for a special and holy purpose,

and that I give glory to God
by being fully and wholly myself.

I believe the same Holy Spirit
who filled and inspired Jesus
also fills me, leads and inspires me.
I believe I am God's beloved
upon whom constantly rests
God's full favor and blessing.

FOLLOW THE INNER VOICE

Even if all the world condemns who you are, if you do not feel condemned you are free of condemnation. Conscience is the personal supreme court that overturns any decision by a lower court, whether it be the state, the Council of Churches, the Vatican or even the Bible.

LIVE TOMORROW TODAY

Be patient with prejudice. Inherited, entrenched, ingrained are many of the prejudices present in society. It's not just a passage of years but often of generations that's required to abolish them. Patience is easier when you know what time it is! Steward Brand, the creator of the *Whole Earth Catalog*, speaks of time lags and lead times. He says it is useful to understand that any civilization operates at a different number of speeds. Business and fashion change quickly, while nature changes slowly. Religion and government change at a rate somewhere in between. Although vast cultural changes occurred in the final thirty years of the last century, usually culture moves much more slowly, and prejudices are entrenched in cultures.

Brand adds that because we usually pay more attention to fast-changing elements, we can forget that real power resides in slow, deep changes. While commerce and clothing and automobile fashions respond or "learn" quickly, culture integrates lessons steadily and remembers. He says, "The combination of quick learning and deep remembering makes a civilization strong against shocks and profoundly adaptable."[12]

While Brand's evaluation of the speeds of change may be realistic for culture and religion, it is too slow for God. The Divine Liberator does not say to someone in chains, "Be patient, your great-grandchildren may someday be free." In removing injustice and discrimination, religion and culture embody nature's process of slow, gradual change. Yet the urgency of the Great Liberator's desire to set the prisoners free was captured by his apostle Paul when writing to the Romans: "Now is the hour...."[13] Realistic liberators inspired by the Great Deliverer must learn to practice the twin virtues of holy urgency and holy patience. While culture moves at a turtle's pace and religion at a snail's pace, Net-Time, a revolution toward globalization, will radically alter the rate of social change. Would that St. John the Baptist, that urgent prophet of tomorrow, even though he lost his head by being ahead of his time — of the timetable of his culture and religion — might become the patron saint of religion.

THE INTERNAL PREJUDICE PRISONS OF ENVY AND JEALOUSY

Internal prejudice is judging oneself out of fear. Bound by the anxiety that we don't measure up, we judge that somehow we are lacking for physical or intellectual reasons. Two other painful forms of imprisonment branch out from this personal prejudice: envy and jealousy. When I judge myself as being less gifted than others or judge myself as being in competition for the seemingly limited resources of honor, pride or love, I am as isolated as anyone in solitary confinement.

ENVY'S INCARCERATION

Envy and jealousy are often considered to be interchangeable terms, but they are really distinct emotions. We begin with envy, which is a desire for and a begrudging resentment of others' good fortune and gifts. Envy-coated resentment is often the source of veiled verbal abuse, crude kidding and malice-laced humor. Since envy is a strong desire to have for oneself what others own, thievery is a stepsister of envy. Coveting is a secret desire to steal from others that which we desire for ourselves.

Envy involves a particularly heart-wrenching imprisonment since it is a longing to possess what is usually beyond our reach. As a result, envy typically poisons life and is self-destructive. Incarcerated by the need to compare ourselves with others, we are incapable of being grateful for the unique gifts we've been given. This is especially crippling and constraining because being grateful for all things and at all times is one of the cardinal elements of a liberated lifestyle.

Throw Away Your Tape Measure

Check your pockets. If you are like most people, in your pocket you carry around an invisible tape measure. When we go to a business or social gathering, we instantly get out our tape measure. We use it to measure ourselves against those present in a variety of categories. These tape-measure judgments are made instantaneously as we calibrate ourselves compared to others' degree of physical beauty, levels of education, wealth and social skills. Then we take our calibrations and judge ourselves as being inferior or superior.

Throw away your incarcerating tape measure and know the intoxicating freedom of entering any gathering and being able simply to enjoy other peoples' companionship because you no longer need to measure up. Furthermore, you'll receive the bonus prize of being eager to learn new things from each person present. For those who never outgrow learning, life is jammed with teachers. As you mingle with people, you can delight in the infinite variety of ways God is incarnated in time and space. See with the eyes of love.

Awaken also to the easiest escape route from envy. It lies in cultivating the consciousness of your incorporation in the Body of Christ. For when you're connected to the Body, the good of another is no threat to you since as a member of the Body it is your good as well. The entire body rejoices and shares in the victory of a marathon runner whose feet carried him or her across the finish line first. The arms don't lust to become feet; the lungs and heart rejoice in their hidden yet vital part in the victory; nor do the veins and arteries demand to be acknowledged for their essential participation. The whole body rejoices. In the same way another's success does not lessen your status but truly increases it since you share directly in the success.

Do not measure and you will not be measured. Indeed, using the tape measure of comparison as a criterion of your worth is only another form of judging. Even when others are competitive and are unaware of their connection to the Body of Christ, you can escape the chains of judgment. Even when others are addicted to their secret tape-measure, you can still be free. Conduct constant tape measure searches, and if you find one in your hand, throw it away. With practice and discipline, you can put other things in your pockets in its place, like gratitude and joy.

WHOLEHEARTED CONGRATULATIONS

Rejoice always by congratulating constantly. Indeed, congratulating is a holy communion of joy. In fact, its Latin root meaning is to express joy, to rejoice with another. While at times it's no easy challenge to celebrate another's success, offering congratulations is freeing. When we sincerely share in the delight and good of others, we not only free ourselves from the Evil Eye of Envy, we free ourselves to love and be loved more deeply. To wholeheartedly rejoice in another's good can deliver us from the chains of competition. While polite congratulations may be socially correct, it is not liberating. It takes a wholehearted delight in another's accomplishments or good fortune to free us and enlarge our hearts. The more we can consciously share in God's Global Body, the more expansive will be our souls, our spirits and our whole lives. There is great deliverance in the expansion of our capacity to love in this way.

JEALOUSY, THE GREEN-EYED JAILER

Whereas envy deals with possessions, property or talents, jealousy is connected to love. Love can be freeing, and love can imprison. A suspicious, confining love gives rise to jealousy, which arises from the fear of being supplanted by another. It's born of a dread of being robbed of affection and expresses itself in a fierce and possessive passion. While our word jealous comes from the Latin and Greek for zealous, sadly it is a freedom-stealing zeal.

Yet the good news for all of our fears is found in the first letter of St. John: "Perfect love casts out fear."[14] The author prefaces this by saying, "God is love, and whoever remains in love remains in God and God in him or her." What is perfect love? Perfect love is a love that our sufferings and trials have made exquisite. It is a love that has become unshakable because of its awareness of participating in a communion with God, who is love. The infinite, infallible escape tool from the prison of jealousy — the place of terror and dread at the loss of something precious — is such a love. Use this tool often and with confidence.

Chapter Eleven Inventory of Escape Tools and Unshackling Reflections

ESCAPE TOOL #38 —
PREJUDICE SNIPPER

As we have seen, the mind seems obsessed with making judgments, even when lacking solid evidence for coming to a conclusion. Prejudging others based on religious, social, sexual and ethnic reasons is an inclination all of us possess. Yet those who carefully monitor their thoughts and attitudes quickly realize the presence of the discriminating judgments toward others that arise spontaneously. To free yourself from these negative judgmental thoughts use your Prejudice Snipper, the principle behind which we introduced in Chapter 4.

Be an observer rather than a judge. Rather than thinking, "John is bossy," liberate your mind from it's prehistoric need to make snap judgments by making an observation: "I've observed that John enjoys being in command and giving orders. I wonder why?"

LEFT-HANDED CHARITY

And Jesus said, "When you lend a hand, don't let your left hand know what your right hand is doing."[15]

THE HOLY OIL OF SURVIVAL

Rabbi Hugo Gryn told of an experience when he and his father were in the Lieberose Nazi concentration camp in 1944. When his father, who did not survive the war, lit the Hanukkah lights secretly using margarine for oil, his son protested. When Hugo complained about wasting food on a religious ritual, his father replied, "We have often lived for as long as three weeks without food, yet we cannot possibly live for three minutes without hope."

Prejudices are only slowly drained of their poison. Hate dies a long death. Bigotry is a cat with more than nine lives. Patience and, even more importantly, hope are required of victims of discrimination and those who labor to remove it. Patience does not mean acceptance of an evil; it is, rather, productive waiting for justice and full acceptance and communion. It is a waiting that is full of redeeming, liberating words and deeds. And as Rabbi Gryn's father said, it is essential, for "we cannot possibly live for three minutes without hope."

To Escape from Internal
Prejudice – Don't Surrender

In a speech to inner-city African Americans, the Rev. Jesse Jackson spoke about the prejudicial labels society has pinned on them:

> ...every one of these funny labels they put on you: call you outcast, low-down, you can't make it, you're nothing, subclass, underclass. I was born in a slum, but the slum wasn't born in me. And it wasn't born in you, and you can make it.... Hold your head high, stick your chest out. You can make it. It gets dark sometimes, but the morning comes. Don't you surrender. Suffering breeds character. Character breeds faith. In the end faith will not disappoint. You must not surrender. You may or may not get there, but just know that you're qualified, and you hold on and hold out. We must never surrender. America will get better and better. Keep hope alive. Keep hope alive. Keep hope alive.

A Pauline Quote to Escape Prejudice

Accept one another just as Christ accepted you,
by so doing you will give glory to God.[16]

— St. Paul, writing to the Romans

Bias Blindness

Prejudice is the logical consequence of a failure to see reality. It's the inability to see beyond one's beliefs and prejudgments. Another name for this affliction is *Kalaharitis,* from the Kalahari tribe of the Botswana plateau area of South Africa. This tribe believes that the world ends about 250 yards beyond an invisible line at the edge of their local area. And if you were to take a Kalahari to this place and attempt to point out the landscape that extends beyond, he or she would see nothing, only a vast void. Or if you walked over to the other side of this invisible line, the Kalahari would no longer be able to see you! Such is the strength of the acquired self-limiting mental framework with which these people view themselves and their world. Similarly, imprisoning beliefs can hold enormous power over our thoughts and actions.

Chapter Twelve
Workhouse Prison

In 1921 Karel Capek gave us the word "robot," which he invented for his play, *R.U.R.*, about mechanical men manufactured by the Rossum Universal Robot Corporation. Capek's resource for the term robot was the Czech word *robata,* meaning "work" or "slave." The word has since come to include people who are devoid of human feelings and who act automatically. In the course of his play these mechanical men revolt and threaten to conquer their creators. While the world was ultimately saved when the mechanical work slaves miraculously became human, unfortunately the same has not been the case with humans who have become robots.

In 1984 the U.S. Census Bureau's first survey on robots in American industry listed their number at 5,535. As the last century ended, that number was estimated to be in the tens of thousands. The Census Bureau defines a robot as "a reprogrammable multifuctional manipulator designed to move materials, parts, tools or specialized devices through variable programmed motions for the performance of a variety of tasks." In light of this definition, not only assembly-line workers, fast-food service people and checkout stand clerks, but all of us at one time or another have been involved in robotic labor.[1]

Indeed, robotic labor is designed for work slaves, mechanical or human. Entering data on a computer or washing the dishes or any number of other tasks can be robotic when done mechanically. Moreover, since a large part of today's work is done by humans operating machines, we easily become nonhuman extensions of our machines. This kind of human labor is not only demeaning, it imprisons. And this fate not only affects those who do menial work; large corporate offices have white collar robots involved in a variety of "reprogrammable multifunctional performance of a variety of tasks."

Office cubicles are cells. Thirty years before the twenty-first century, Robert Propst creatively invented modular cubicles as a new breakthrough in office design. Like Dr. Frankenstein, he began with a good idea that turned bad. Desiring more for the inch, management converted his creative concept of free workspace cubicles into crammed, fluorescent-lighted cells for prison-like assembly-line work. Like all prisoners, cubicle-mates lack privacy. As in prisons many inmates of cubicles are constantly being watched, counted and having their E-mail read — all under the close eye of the office warden. The crystal-ball readers of business predict that within the next twenty years large corporations will require employees to wear I.D. badges (as prisoners do), which will be electronically coded. This will allow superiors, says Daniel Eisenberg, to know where the employees are at all times, whether they are visiting vending machines or going to the bathroom.

Vacation-Famished Americans

Among the top fourteen Western nations, Americans have the fewest legally mandated vacations! Sweden leads the top fourteen, legally requiring 32 vacation days a year; Spain, Denmark, Austria and France require 30 days; Ireland 28; and the Netherlands, Japan and Portugal legally designate 25 days. At the bottom of the list comes America with an average of only 16 days. According to Joseph Robinson, an adventure-travel magazine editor, America is the most vacation-starved country in the Western World. While American small-business employees get an average of eight days off annually, Europeans and Australians receive from four to six weeks of paid vacation. Between 1995 and 1999, the number of American employees calling in sick because of stress has more than tripled. Robinson also states that half of all Americans report some kind of stress with their work, and 63%

say they would rather have more vacation time than more money.

There ought to be a law! If you would like to be elected President of the United States, consider promoting a Month of Sabbaths Law. This would require all employers to give their employees an entire month, 30 days of paid vacation every year. Yet even if such an extraordinary and admirable law was passed by Congress, would not compulsive, utilitarian Americans find it impossible to rest and relax for thirty days? Should not America, which is known as the Land of the Free and Brave, be renamed the Land of the Enslaved?

GOD LIBERATES THE ROBOTS

God freed the slaves. The Exodus was the liberation of Jewish slave labor in Egypt. The Great God Yahweh, aware of how work enslaves, instructed the Israelites to set aside one day out of seven exclusively as a day of absolutely no work. This became one of the Great Commandments. Yet at the beginning of this twenty-first century few if any observe complete absence of work on their Sabbath or Sunday. And most of us are still waiting to be liberated from our slave labor.

Indeed, Americans today work more and longer hours. In fact, as the above statistics on vacations would indicate, of all the people in the industrialized world Americans work the most. An average American works at least 1,966 hours a year according to the International Labor Organization in Geneva, Switzerland. So, in addition to having fewer days off from work, Americans labor the equivalent of almost seven hours a day for seven days a week. If work is the curse of Eden, then it seems Americans are doubly cursed.

Because of their garden crime of disobedience, God sentenced woman to painful childbearing and man to toil by the sweat of his brow for their bread all the days of his life.[2] No retirement for Adam. And, indeed, most of the world's billions of men — and women — still live under that sweaty sentence. While pensions and social security allow Americans and those of Earth's richer countries to retire from work, such options do not exist for the vast majority of the people on this planet. Their children are their only source of social security and health care in their elderly years. Meanwhile, among many of us in richer nations who are work-addicted, retirement is a kind of death sentence, as our primary source of life-meaning and purpose is taken away. Yet even as we're addicted, we long to be set free of our chains of slavery.

Throughout the last century's South Sea Island fantasies, which echo our primal hunger to return to Eden's paradise, the common theme is complete absence of work. In these idyllic flights of fancy, ex-work slaves enjoy endless leisure surrounded by bountiful food, drink and sex. We working slaves are limited to two-week vacations in some Tahiti-like paradise, after which we always have to pack up our fantasy and go "back to work." This return-to-Eden dream was bred out of the industrial revolution, which turned humans into mechanical workers on assembly lines, in sweatshops and coal mines. That dream is still awakened each day as millions of alarm clocks announce the opening of day — or night — prisons for legions of slave workers.

Another spin on the South Sea Island Paradise dream is the Win-the-Lottery fantasy: that winning the "big one" will enable us to retire to a life of leisure. Casino addicts lust after a variation on that theme, where money equals freedom from work. Of course, the odds against achieving these dreams are overwhelmingly stacked against us. Still, the odds may be better than the possibility of release from slavery suggested in Karel Capek's 1921 play *R.U.R.*, in which the world doomed to a robot takeover is saved miraculously when the machines become human. That also seems true for us work robots — only a miraculous desire for liberation can set us free to be human once again.

I HAVE COME TO SET THE PRISONERS FREE

Jesus the Redeemer offers to all who desire freedom a way to restore the world, all of it: people, creation, art, music, play and work. The way of the Holy Returner leads back to Eden, to enter humans' original intimacy with their Creator. Rather than any exodus from this so-called "evil" world, he offers a U-turn. Paradoxically, he calls us to return by staying right where we are and breaking our work chains of bondage. He invites us to turn around and live again here and now in loving harmony with God and with all creation — and with our work. He encourages us to embrace his life-work as a way of life.

At its roots, work is not a curse. Like all great myths, the story of the first humans in Eden contains truth and insightful wisdom about the good life. And there we see that the curse of work doesn't occur until the second creation story. In the first account of Genesis' sacred saga, Adam, the first human, is found working, "cultivating and caring" for the garden.[3] It seems that God must have said to Adam, "My son, it is not good for you to do nothing, so I will give you work to do." Work was part of paradise. The Liberator Christ sets all of us work-robots free not only by returning us to our original relationship to work but also by inviting us to see our daily labors as redemptive.

CHRIST THE WORKER

No billionaire or king ever led a slave worker's revolution. And certainly Christ did not come to set us free from the curse of work while dressed in princely robes or from a privileged position. Jesus was no idealistic romantic. Jesus knew sweat. He knew, firsthand, hired-hand exertion and even backbreaking labor. While honoring Sabbath rest, he toiled six days a week from sunrise till sunset. The Gospel writers take care to point out that the Savior-Liberator belonged to the working class and not to the priestly caste. Like his father, St. Joseph the Worker, he was a carpenter, craftsman, laborer and jack of all trades. His hands were not soft and clean like the hands of scholars and princes; they were the hands of a poor peasant laborer. While Joseph of Nazareth is the patron saint of workers, Jesus of Nazareth became a hard-working savior of workers. In contrast to Christ the King, imagine how the working class would identify with a special feast as well as churches dedicated to Christ the Worker. Such a model would spur a work spirituality with profoundly practical implications for lay people, who because of religious conditioning have rarely considered Jesus of Galilee an integral part of their workaday world.

A LIVING SPIRITUALITY OF WORK

Since work consumes the major part of the life of the laity, how can we cultivate a richer, fuller spirituality of work? The fact that our divinely enfleshed Liberator Lord was a stone mason, carpenter and laborer should open our eyes to the spiritual potential in our daily work. For Roman Catholics and all catholic Christians, the Second Vatican Council's document *The Church in the Modern World* offers this emancipating good news: "When men and women provide for themselves and their families in such a way as to be of service to the community as well, they can rightly look upon their work as a prolongation of the work of the Creator."[4] Such a profound doctrine requires daily meditation so that it can become a living reality, for it cannot help but enhance our work and raise it to a divine level.

The balance of work and prayer, once the twin pillars of monastic life, leads to an integral spiritual life. Ronald Rolheiser quotes the monk and spiritual master Thomas Merton: "The biggest spiritual problem of our time is efficiency, work and pragmatism; by the time we keep the plant running there is little time and energy for anything else." This excessive focus on work is no stranger even to monastic life, as Merton's quote implies. Rolheiser adds, "It is not that we have anything against God, depth, and spirit, we would like these, it is just that we are habitually too preoccupied to have any of these.... We are more busy than bad, more distracted than nonspiritual."[5] The first step in escaping is always to acknowledge being a prisoner. The words of Merton and Rolheiser surely must hit home in our lives, whether we live in a monastery or on main street, U.S.A. Step two for escapees, if you recall, is to have a lifestyle that grows out of our beliefs.

The greatest task of life according to the saintly French Jesuit Teilhard de Chardin is to realize our beliefs.[6] As we saw in the Chapter Two Inventory of Escape Tools, to *realize* does not mean achieving some high intellectual insight but, rather, making our beliefs real, concrete and tangible. Indeed, a spirituality is a lifestyle that flows from our belief system. If we believe God is everywhere, then our work is to make that faith ever-present — to make the invisible God tangibly present — in our workplace and our daily tasks. If we *realize* our belief that God dwells within us, then we must live out that reality in our attitudes and behavior. Our lifestyle should be one of intimate communion as God works with, in and through us in the mystery of perpetual creation. Once the daily labor of our hands and minds is *realized*, then as an average American we will be praying between 40 and 60 hours a week!

Any kind of work, then, from collecting garbage to programing computers, is a sacrament of the divine work of ceaseless creation. Once the enfleshment of God in each of us is comprehended in its fullness, the lived implications become breathtaking. Our workplaces are miraculously consecrated, transformed into sites of holy coalition where we and God are working together. A glorious ascension occurs when the secular work we do becomes, to paraphrase the Lord's Prayer, our work done here on earth as it is done in heaven. The words of the Second Vatican Council about being a co-creator are truly work liberating: Indeed, how could sweating side-by-side with God ever be seen as drudgery?

According to the Jewish mystical tradition, we are shaped and formed by the work we do for a living. We become our work and our work becomes us. The ancient rabbis insisted that a rabbi must do some honest craft in order to earn his daily bread. The Master followed that tradition by earning his bread as a carpenter, and the apostle Paul of Tarsus practiced the honest craft of a leather tentmaker. Mahatma Gandhi was likewise insistent that his followers earn their own bread and not live on charity. Like Jesus in his woodworking and masonry and Paul sewing tents, Gandhi's weaving of cotton helped him find the Holy One in his labors.

HOMO FABER – THE WORKING HUMAN

Work is a significant part of the evolutionary process. The origin of our species began with the first humans being able to stand up and walk: *Homo erectus*. Possessing an enlarged brain, Homo erectus' successor was *Homo faber*, the human worker. Now, the simple human, who was a fruit-, seed- and grain-gatherer advanced to the state of a worker who made stone tools, enabling humans to become hunters of food. Writing for the *Smithsonian*, author and professor Roger Lewin proposed that the creation of sharp-edged stone tools to cut up meat was one of the major technological breakthroughs in human evolution. The shift from being vegetarians to meat-eaters required tool-weapons for hunting in groups, creating a radical shift in *Homo sapiens'* lifestyle.

This shift was necessitated by radical changes in the environment that forced those early humans out of the trees and onto the vast grasslands, which abounded with game. The more early humans worked with tools, the larger their brains grew. Inspired by their work, their hunting tools soon evolved into artistic tools. The epiphany of a spiritual age was ushered in with the awesome painting-carvings of the sacred caves in France and Spain some 30,000 years ago. This evolution continues today with electronic tools that are changing lifestyles and enabling artistic epiphanies of bewildering beauty. All tools can be door-openers to new lifestyles and sacred instruments to uncover the divine.

WORK CONSECRATORS

The Liberator-Carpenter invites us to further evolve: to find God embodied in our work and to consecrate our work into the work of God. God needs us. God's ongoing redemption of the world requires our cooperation. When Jesus' disciples returned from the town of Sychar with food, they offered some to the Master. "I'm not hungry," he said. "My food is to do the will of the one who sent me and to finish his work."[7] His lunch had been liberating a loose-living Samaritan woman at the well — treating her as an equal and sharing with her his Messiah mission of liberty. Each day we have similar opportunities whenever we encounter occasions to treat with dignity anyone considered an outcast, an alien or unclean.

Workers of the world, arise! Let that cry of the Union of World Workers ring in your ears. Each of us is ordained to Laborhood in the Age of God. We are called to work for the completion of creation and the reign introduced by God, set in motion by Jesus, continued by the apostolic community and now passed on to us. Creation was not finished at sunset on the first Saturday. So, approach your labor as a co-worker with the Creator in the daily continuing creation of the world. Appreciate how each new invention, each new breakthrough in technology and each act of creativity may be part of the ever-expanding act of creation. Invest yourself in each task at hand, saying, "This is my body; this is my lifeblood, which I give with love."

The billions of workers around the planet have to work for their bread. "Putting bread on the table" or "Bringing home the bacon" express why so many of us endure the bondage of work, the lost hours commuting and the unpleasant conditions at our place of employment. Laboring for our bread was part of the curse cast by God upon Adam, who would only earn his bread by the sweat of his brow. Then Jesus came and disturbed his listeners by saying, "Do not work for food that perishes but, rather, for food that remains fresh into infinity." This caused them to ask him a question that we continue to ask: "What can we do to accomplish the works of God?" Jesus responded with an answer within an answer within another answer: "This is the work God desires, that you believe in the one that was sent."[8] Belief in Jesus includes belief in his message — belief that the Time of God has begun — which, in turn, includes living out that belief as our daily lifestyle.

SLAVES OF SUCCESS

Indeed, work is human, and work is holy. Work is also a primary source of identification. It's the focus of one of the first questions asked upon meeting a stranger: "What do you do?" Others' occupations frame how we view them. And this often becomes a "frame-job," where persons' professions blind us to who they really are. Certain professional titles of respect and prestige conveniently keep their bearers safely insulated from others — and often from self-scrutiny.

Moreover, our occupation can occupy not only our time and energy, but, like a foreign dictator, it can occupy our very selves. There are many such tyrannical dictators, whose forces are ready to occupy the realms of our souls and imprison our spirits, preventing our work from being human and holy.

One of these opportunistic dictators is the desire for success. As with all fascist-style dictatorships, the image of the tyrant and his ideology are drummed into us from early childhood. Even before preschool, parents, peers and the media instilled in us the necessity to be successful, to be a winner, top of the class, number one, superior to others. Our hunger for success is turned into a voracious appetite when fueled by the creed of competition, which prevents us from working in cooperation *with* others and *for* others' real benefit. This creed creates anxiety, worry, stress and the compulsion to achieve. After all, losers are losers. No rewards are given for being at the bottom of the class or the last to cross the finish line — except the "prize" of shame. America's obsession with success in school and athletics, in business and throughout life, creates a nationwide concentration camp crowded with competitors. It's an enslavement that deprives us of the joy of engaging life, of working hard, of being truly productive and creative.

Escape from this prison doesn't require leaving our culture, but it does require a liberating attitude. Author William Faulkner suggested one escape route when he said, "Don't bother just to be better than your contemporaries or predecessors. Try to be better than yourself."

Channeling the craving for success into healthy competition with oneself or into a spirit of cooperation that engenders "success for all of us" can go a long way toward our liberation.

PRISONERS OF FAILURE

Fear of Failure is a sister prison to Desire for Success' concentration camp. This fear lurks in every new enterprise. It is based on society's judgment of guilt by association: Those who have failures *are* failures. We become our mistakes. When possessed by this fear, innocent-looking situations, like school, sports, jobs, professions, marriages and daily life all become deadly mine fields. We enter into these fields with extreme caution, for at any moment we might stumble on a failure. Daily failures of all shapes and sizes explode, wounding and maiming millions of innocent or guilty children and adults. And our culture offers no sympathy or healing for these walking wounded.

Yet by his death on the cross, our Liberator-Savior heals our wounds and frees us from our fear of failure and shame. We can be saved from disgrace by his death as a failure. The crowds that had just acclaimed him as a king have deserted him. His disciples have fled to save their skins. His entire mission appears to have died as a disaster with him. Indeed, God's ways are not our ways. There is no way we would choose failure as a climax of our life work. The crucifixion is anti-American. A cross is the last image we'd find in a sports stadium or business meeting. Failure is heresy to our American obsession with achievement. Yet it seems God prefers failure. God's favorite work tool appears to be defeat. The Divine Worker delights in twisting and turning it around and around to create life, victory and new unseen possibilities.

So, if you want to escape the prison of this pervasive fear, remember how God used the failure of Jesus to introduce the world into a new order of life. When failure comes into your life, also be aware of how in science and art, many mistakes, when reexamined, have become great breakthroughs. Remember how failure in the early political lives of people like Lincoln, Churchill and Gandhi became a springboard to success. Do not hide ashamed from your failures but, rather, be a co-converter with God in transforming them into something useful. Indeed, the fear of failure or being seen as a failure incapacitates the Holy Inventor Spirit, who is constantly experimenting with the

New. "Let's experiment," may be the Spirit's favorite invitation. Accept it. In these pregnant early years of this new millennium the Spirit's call to experiment offers immense possibility in addressing the problems facing society, business, the arts and religion.

GOD NEEDS US

Our work has an eternal dimension; it calls us toward the infinite. So, regardless of whether you're cleaning the house or building a house, managing stocks or stocking grocery store shelves, work on your infinity. By making every act of your day an expression of your liberation lifestyle, you are working for bread that does not perish. The Divine Mystery embodied in Jesus — in his life, death and escape from the tomb — give us a clear picture of the occupation of God. The continuous work of God certainly involves making good out of evil, bringing life out of death, synthesizing suffering into meaning. Thousands are the daily opportunities to mirror such miracles — to cast a spell over a fellow worker's mistake and find in it something valuable, to work a miracle and bring to life someone deadened by defeat.

In this light, no work is lowly or demeaning. Whatever is done with love and care is a divine work. At the Liberator's Last Supper he transformed bread into his body and slavery into a sacrament when he washed his disciples' feet. As he performed his task of a slave, he instructed them, "Free yourself by becoming slaves to each other."[9] Whenever we do humble service or any work with love and attention, we are busy at God-work. Recall the fourteenth century German mystic Meister Eckhart's formula that holiness consists in doing the next thing you have to do with your whole heart and finding delight in doing it.[10]

The other day at the grocery store my purchases were being bagged by a good-looking young man in his early twenties. Subtle clues suggested that my youthful sacker might be slightly mentally challenged. I was pleased that the store had given him employment. When I thanked him for the thoughtful way he had doubled-bagged a particularly heavy item, he beamed a large smile at me and replied, "Thank you, sir. That's my job — and I always try to do it the best I can." I was momentarily in awe at this grocery store sacker who was living out the way of holiness proposed by Meister Eckhart. The unskilled task of sacking groceries was in no way demeaning for him, nor did he do it robotically. His pride in a job well done indicated that his work gave him meaning and inner satisfaction. Imagine what our world would be like if each one of us worked as mindfully and wholeheartedly at our jobs?

PUT YOUR SOUL INTO IT

Whenever you are absorbed body and soul with great love in whatever you are doing, you are making love with that activity, and "the two shall become one." Theologian Diarmuid O'Murchu writes about how the hidden mystery of the quantum universe is present in our lives. He uses the example of his desk, something normally considered to be composed of dead, inert materials. Yet if you take a fragment of it, he says, and place it under a very powerful microscope, you will see a sea of diminutive moving particles. It's alive! The life in the wood is crystallized and condensed but composed of the very same particles that make up your fingers holding this book — in fact, the particles present in everything in the universe. He says, "My desk may be described as a pulsating conundrum of crystallized energy. Even the sweat, toil, devotion, and creativity of those who made my desk belong to its essential nature and may have a minute but nonetheless real effect on my feelings and thinking." [11]

Our senses are typically zombied. They are almost completely desensitized by our constant contact with machine-made objects. As such, we usually struggle to believe that an original piece of work somehow contains part of the maker. We doubt this soul connection even as we are aware of millions being paid for a great artist's original painting or as we treasure as relics our handmade family heirlooms. Even the loving work taken to craft a letter or thank-you note makes the pieces of paper they're written on repositories of cosmic energy and tabernacles containing the love energy of the sender. If the mail carrier delivers the letter with love and care, then the carrier's touch is upon it as well. In the same way, all our labors, even the work we do electronically, may through the mystery of electric energy also be a courier of the soul-love of the sender. That awareness can help us treat all our tasks with great love and care.

Donald Nicholl tells the story of Saichi, a Buddhist Japanese cobbler. He was a poor but talented craftsman who made a special type of wooden shoe known as a *geta*. Because he could not afford paper, he would save the wooden shavings from his shoes. In tiny print he would then inscribe on them his spiritual reflections! All those who purchased Saichi's wooden shoes found them delightful, for they were filled with the same joy that the cobbler had derived in making them.[12]

The joy of Saichi that tickled the feet of those who wore his wooden shoes leads us into the subject of the next chapter. Investing yourself, heart, mind and soul in everything you do requires total attention. That art of total absorption in your work is a truly great achievement, and it only comes by traveling the challenging path of joy and delight.

Chapter Twelve Inventory of Escape Tools and Unshackling Reflections

SAINTS MAKE BAD ROLE MODELS

Athletes, movie stars and presidents are expected to be role models for the youth. Some are good role models, while others are not. Saints, however, make bad role models since they are not playing any kind of role. Saints are authentic ideals. Holy people are not one person in public and another in private; they are truly who they are, both "on" and "off" stage. Saints set a good example by not trying to be an example of anything but themselves. Saints are free.

EYE TEST FOR IMPRISONMENT

Mrs. Byrne's Dictionary has an entry for the word *Eyeservice*. Definition: "Work done only when the boss is watching."[13] Do you find yourself doing eyeservice? Along with your boss at work, you might perform eyeservice for your bishop, the pastor or elders, your parents, teachers or peers, or even that ever-present internal critic. If you find yourself in eyeservice prison, seriously consider escaping now.

Escape Tool #39 — Dress Appropriately for Work

Various occupations have their own uniforms or special clothing. Large corporations often have dress codes that define appropriate attire when in the office. Some new companies permit "anything-goes" dress on the premise that it will increase creativity and the employees' enjoyment of their workplace. Regardless of what's appropriate attire for your place of employment, check the mirror before leaving to go to work to ensure that you're properly dressed. Paul said, "Put on Christ...for I no longer live; rather, Christ lives in me."[14] When we believe that — and when the Word has become incarnate in us, as God so passionately desires — then Christ is enfleshed in the work we do. Christ waits on customers. Christ replies to E-mail orders. Christ picks up the trash.

Time to Go To Work

"We have to do the works of the One who sent me while it is day. Night is coming when no one can work,"[15] said Jesus to his co-workers. Those with eyes to see will recognize that the work they have to do is the same as Jesus did: They will heal by acceptance, teach by example and liberate by their love — and they will find joy in this work.

The Moses Principle

Overworked spiritual seekers frequently go on retreat to some quiet monastic setting in order to have an encounter with God. This is a commendable spiritual exercise, following in the footsteps of that famous frequent retreatant, the ever-busy Jesus. However, as the founding editor of *Praying Magazine*, Art Winter, points out, it is wise to note where Moses found God — or, more correctly, where God found Moses. Moses was not wrapped in prayer in the temple but was at work caring for the flock of his father-in-law Jethro in the wilderness when he encountered the God Who Is Everywhere. This can be a liberating pattern for each of us: to encounter God in our workplace as well as in our prayer and church.

Yet think of the implications of God coming to visit me at work! What a frightening and potentially embarrassing proposal. What would my co-workers say? How could I explain it? How would I be expected to act?

Imagine the scene in an office if a worker seated at her desk suddenly removed her shoes as did Moses before the burning bush. What a refreshing and liberating image: to see God at work where Moses was at work — or at our workplace. Yet we twenty-first century pilgrims struggle with skepticism at the possibility that our workplace could be the site of such a visitation — and, even more, a place of the abiding presence of God.

As St. John of the Cross said, "We receive from God what we expect." So, in the spirit of St. John, seriously consider expecting God to speak to you at work, not in a burning bush but in a luminous computer, a burnt-out co-worker or a fiery telephone call. Expect God to be working alongside you in your every task. If you cultivate faith in that Abiding Omnipotent Presence, you can share Adam and Eve's original joy at being a companion worker with the Creator in the garden.

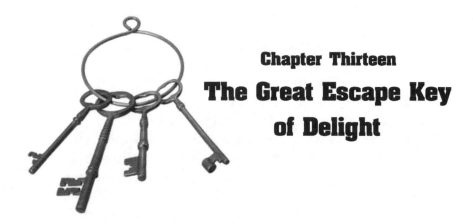

Chapter Thirteen
The Great Escape Key of Delight

Delight is not a prison.
Indeed, it and joy are the way to stay out of prison.
Rejoicing is the third branch of this path to holiness.

This chapter offers another reprieve from our prison tour, taking us on a liberating excursion into the wonderful realm of delight. Yet for delight to be an effective escape route it needs to be more than a momentary experience. It requires cultivating a lifestyle of enjoyment, of simply living in joy. Puritans, both the original seventeenth century dour-dressed variety and today's Puritans of heart, frown on such a fun lifestyle. For them, God is serious; life is supposed to be hard work, struggle and stress. Puritanical saints don't laugh. Perhaps they may smile — on Easter. The favorite liturgical season for such Christians is Lent: purple penance, fast and denial. Hair-shirt Christians believe pleasure is to be reserved for paradise; enjoyment comes only after this life.

Surely, Puritans believe, the admonition in Paul's letter to the Thessalonians to "be always joyful"[1] must have been a mistake scribbled by some scribe monk who copied the manuscript in the Middle Ages. Yet it is no mistake or heresy — but an invitation, valid, orthodox and divinely inspired. Inspired, indeed, but very nearly impossible. It's akin to Paul saying, "Climb to the top of Mount Everest every day." To be always joyful, happy and cheerful truly seems unachievable for us who are living in this vale of tears. How many people do you know who, regardless of the situation, are always cheerful and happy?

The Three Mystical Musketeers — rejoice always, pray always and give thanks always[1] — work as a team. They support one another and fight side-by-side against the Anti-Kingdom, a term used by the Spanish-born Jesuit theologian, Jon Sobrino, for the forces that crucified the Great Liberator.[2] How do these Musketeers stay together? Gifts delight. A lifestyle grounded in perpetual gratitude for our daily avalanche of gifts leads to being continually delighted and, thus, to constant expressions of rejoicing. Praying always is being ever present to the presence of God, who is Unsurpassed Delight and Unlimited Bliss. How can some of that not rub off? A lifestyle of always rejoicing, finding enjoyment in even the most trivial of things, leads, in turn, to being constantly grateful. This addictive thanksgiving overflows into incessant prayer. And so these Three Mystical Musketeers are linked together arm-in-arm to fight for the Kingdom of God.

THE MARK OF JOY

The sure trademark of a contemporary saint is not a halo, it's mirth. As a form of happiness, mirth is "rejoicing, especially expressed in merrymaking."[3] Rejoicing is a work project whose end product is being merry. It's not merry in the sense of being jolly. Rather, it's more the Old English sense of *merie* as found in the carol, "God Rest ye merry, gentlemen." Notice the comma in that song and then read the olden-days meaning of merry: blessed, pleasant or peaceful. Merry England was, indeed, blessed, peaceful England. A merry woman or man is a peaceful blesser. A blesser is a person who happily goes about making everything blessed simply by his or her presence. This act of enchantment is done naturally and almost unconsciously by those living in the Kingdom of God. This process of becoming a blesser begins with the healing of their eyes. Blessers bless by seeing what exists beneath the crust of the common, which then causes them to handle everything with wonder and delight. In turn, their out-of-the-ordinary behavior can awaken the sleep-closed eyes of others to the magnificent, mystical, ever present reality of the sacred.

Those becoming Godlike can't hide their private lives. They tend to look like a man who has just won a ten-million dollar lottery or a woman who has discovered an original Picasso painting buried in an old trunk of junk she has just purchased at a garage sale. One of the infallible signs of someone who has found the Reign of God here and now is that they're always smiling.

The Joyful Liberator

As he was preparing to die, Jesus compared himself to a grapevine and his friends to the branches. Knowledgeable about what's necessary for vines to produce great harvests, he tells his friends that God is the vine grower and is about to prune him so he can bear more fruit. He explains to them that as God's life flowed vine-like through him, it will also flow through them if they remain in him. He says that remaining loyal in their love, regardless of what happens, glorifies God, since God is love. Then he sums it up, saying, "I have told you these things so that my joy might be in you and your joy may be complete."[4]

Our drab, cheerless Puritan discipleship fails to fully explore or celebrate the joy of Jesus. Centuries have dismissed that joy as simply a spiritual foretaste of heavenly delight instead of it becoming a basis for a lifestyle of rejoicing. Saviors must be serious to match our image of God. Yet small children, who are not attracted to grim, staid, joyless adults, flocked around Jesus — so much so that the apostles wanted to shoo them away. Jesus' very presence exuded that Holy Trinity of prayer, joy and gratitude. Jon Sobrino adds that Jesus not only announced the Kingdom of God but, by being the embodied Word of God, he *was* the Kingdom![5] And the apostle Paul describes the nature of that Kingdom when he says, "the Kingdom of God is not about food and drink but about righteousness, peace and joy in the Holy Spirit."[6] Jesus was so imbued with joy that he spoke of it even on the eve of his crucifixion.

The answer to the riddle of how joy abounds at the edge of great suffering may be found in the letter of James: "Consider it all joy, my friends, when you encounter various trials, for the testing of faith-loyalty produces endurance. Let your endurance be perfect so that you may be perfect and complete."[7] Jesus could be joyful since the loyalty of his love for God and his friends would be put to the test and come to completion on the cross. Endurance, hanging on and fidelity in love even unto death leads to the fullness of joy and to victory. By his endurance through his passion, seemingly abandoned by God and his friends, the Liberator freed us from living cheap love to a love lived without limits or conditions.

We've all got our share of problems, yet we're called to "consider it all joy." Consider your problems as experiments in endurance. One such experiment on a spring Friday in Jerusalem two thousands years ago proved that even under extremely painful and abusive circumstances love can survive. The subject of that gruesome experiment perpetrated by the Anti-Kingdom invites us along: "Come, follow me, and prove that your love is invincible." Follow his example, but not with a grit-your-teeth-grin-and-bear-it smile. Rather, be extravagantly joyful. Apostolic believers of Jesus were told, "...rejoice, although now for a little while you may have to suffer through various trials...although you do not see him now yet believe in him, you rejoice with indescribable and glorious joy."[8]

JOY IS EVOLUTIONARY

Homo faber's (the working human's) successor was *Homo ludens* (the playful, laughing human). In the evolutionary ascent, the human laborer became the playful human. The Latin *ludicrus* suggests Homo ludens' new ability to laugh at incongruity. Of course, play has always been an activity of nonhuman creatures. It's easy to imagine cubs and pups playing together and finding pleasure in it. Yet Spirit-inspired humans elevated animal play by gifting it with a dimension of sacramental laughter and joy. Animals cannot laugh. And the ability to laugh at life's inconsistencies was a great evolutionary leap forward, infusing humanity with a capacity for joy as well as an invaluable tool for balance.

Homo ludens learned to see tools as something more than work instruments. The drudgery of tasks done with primitive tools evolved into a new kind of work that provided delight, joy and even fun. The ability to work not as survival labor but as joyful play is born from the marriage of hand and mind that enables us to create art. What sheer delight must have absorbed those millenniums-old ancestors of Walt Disney and Michelangelo who first transformed the walls of caves into cathedrals by their paintings. That mystical, magical power to create images remains alive today — for those who are awake to their potential for joy.

The handicraft of holiness is accomplished, Meister Eckhart said, by doing everything with all your heart, soul and attention — and with great delight. Is the last part of his equation the greatest challenge of liberation? Or perhaps taking delight in everything you do is not a challenge but rather simply the fruit of wholehearted activity. Recall something you love doing so much, something that so fully absorbed you, that you forgot what time it was — wasn't it also great fun? Being totally engrossed means being enraptured, and rapture has the same meaning as ecstasy, bliss, enchantment and heavenly delight.

Usually, rapture is considered the occupation of high-octane mystics, not blue-white-or-no collar workers. And only the simpleminded, and the saintly minded, are thought to have fun at work. Yet taking delight in what you're doing flows organically from making love to it. So, we don't need a doctor's degree in mystiology to experience delight. Taking joy in our job does not require wearing a halo to work but only investing ourselves totally and completely in whatever is before us at the moment.

Adam and Eve knew rapture. They found it tending the garden. They found their bliss in the Eden of God's company. You can too. Living in rapture is as simple as following Meister Eckhart's Rule, which is the same as being faithful to the Thessalonian Trinity Rule: Rejoice always, pray without ceasing and give thanks for whatever happens to you.[1] Calling it simple may sound like poetic exaggeration — for who can actually live that way — yet our Christian life challenges us to practice that simple threesome daily.

Even though work has been redeemed, it still often seems to be a grind, as if the curse of Genesis still had the power to turn all our best efforts into toil. And, indeed, finding fun and enjoyment in our tasks seems to require becoming simpleminded. Only in fairy tales like Walt Disney's *Snow White* do people go off to work as happy as those whistling Seven Dwarfs, singing, "Hi ho, hi ho, it's off to work we go!" Perhaps, but the Redeemer consecrated the curse into a blessing by restoring Eden's intimacy with God. As his disciple, enter into your work or occupation seeing it as redeemed, liberated from the curse of drudgery. Those who enjoy their work, who find delight in it, are also creative.

I read once about a supervisor of a research laboratory at a large American corporation. He would daily go from one laboratory station to another asking his research scientists only one question: "Are you having fun?" When asked why he did this, he replied, "I believe that if my team of research scientists is having fun, even if they haven't created a new product for years, eventually and consistently they'll make great breakthroughs."

Chapter Thirteen Inventory of Escape Tools and Unshackling Reflections

IN TOUCH INSIDE

The wisdom of Confucianism teaches that "What the undeveloped person seeks is always something outside; what the advanced person seeks is always within."[9] The happiness that leads to constant gratitude and delight comes from perpetually exploring and touching what's inside us. Even though that inner reality is as invisible as an atom, those who are never out of touch with this inner source of joy shimmer on the outside.

THE PERFUME OF PLEASURE

The Sikhs of India ask, "Why do you go into the jungles? What do you hope to find there? Even as the scent of a beautiful flower abides within the flower, so God within your heart ever abides."[10] Flowers are naturally pungent, and we smell them as soon as we enter a garden. Their perfumed beauty instantly transforms a hospital room simply by their presence. Wakes and watermelon feeds leave off a scent that lingers long after. Similarly, those striving to be Godlike by becoming more human give off a fascinating, alluring perfume. Those with Spirit-anointed noses sense their presence, and those with clogged noses ponder how such people can always be so pleasant and joyful.

THE FACE INFLUENCES THE HEART

The more your smile, the easier it becomes to find delight in your routine daily activities. The muscles of the face seem to tug at your heart strings, so that smiling while doing the dishes or taking out the trash works the miracle of making that task enjoyable.

If you doubt this simple exercise has magical powers, try it when driving to the store, mowing the lawn or even tackling some difficult problem.

THE MIRROR MIRACLE

"Bless me, Father, for I have sinned," John whispered through the aged wooden confessional grill, "but I also want to be holy."

From behind the curtain of the screen the voice replied to this unusual opening line of a confession, "Hmm, interesting." And at the end of the brief litany of sins, he said, "Yes, yes, my son. Now, for your penance say one Our Father and one Hail Mary and go in peace."

"Father, I do not want to go in peace," John said. "I am restless until I can begin to become holy. Will you help me? I have been told you are holy, so you must know the secret. Please, share it with me."

In the darkness, he could hear the priest sucking his tongue as if it were rummaging around in the moist cave of his mouth for the right words. "You were misinformed," the old priest said through the grill, "I'm not holy. Only God is holy. Now, go in peace, and try to sin no more."

"Father," John pleaded, "are you telling me that the secret to holiness is to be virtuous and sin no more?"

"No, my son," the priest answered, "that is not the secret, but it does help."

Leaning closer to the grill, John begged, "What else must I do to be holy? Please, give me some clue!"

A cough and throat clearing preceded the message from the other side. "Others are waiting, my son, waiting to confess their sins. The confessional is a place to take secret things away, not to give them out. Now, go in peace."

His fingers gripping the confessional grill, John answered, "I will be glad to go, Father, but only after you've told me the secret."

"Communion with God is the gift given to the virtuous," the priest said with a great sigh, "but it is an incomplete communion and so comes short of true holiness. To be holy is to...to be Godlike, for God alone is holy."

Pressing his face as close as possible to the wooden, sin-stained grill through which so many dark secrets had passed, John said, "Yes, yes, Father, but how, then, do I become like God?"

"Ah, my son, you must return to the beginning. Yes, yes, it is there in the garden that you'll find the secret, for in the beginning were not humans made in the image of God? Alas, now that image is turned upside down. Go home and look in the mirror. Now, go in peace." Then the old priest slammed shut the sliding grill door of the confessional.

"He just wanted to get rid of me," John said to himself as he left the church, "with that stuff about going home and looking in a mirror." He drove home, his heart filled with disappointment. Three days later, awakening from a restless night's sleep, he recalled the old priest's words, "...now that image is turned upside down."

He immediately went into the bathroom and tried to turn his head so he could see his image upside down, but all he saw was a contorted face. Then going to a full-length mirror, he stood on his head and looked at his image. He screamed aloud — not from the blood rushing to his brain, but in delight. "Thank God, the old priest did share with me the secret of holiness!"

Now, John lived in a small town where everyone knew everyone else, so soon all the townsfolk were talking about the "new" John. While he continued to practice his faith, going to church each week, he also daily practiced something else. John was now constantly checking his image in every mirror, store window and shiny surface he passed.

The parade of years marked by fidelity to his daily discipline bore fruit in two strange ways. John became known for his vanity, as he was always looking at his reflection. But he was also known as the happiest and most contented man in town.

To be sure, no one ever called him holy, since he was not known to be particularly pious or saintly. Instead, he was known for his smile!

Everyone agreed that it left a lasting impression. Some even called it "John's autograph."[11]

THE INFLATION AND DEFLATION PRINCIPLE

Experiment with ballooning your activities as a way to experience delight. Take some common endeavor that is of little significance, such as drinking a glass of water, and blow it up. Balloon up that simple act of drinking the crystal clear water by doing it slowly and gratefully, aware that you are among the minority among the billions in this world who have safe, clean drinking water.

Conversely, whenever some big fat difficulty lands in your lap, stick a pin in it and deflate it to almost nothing. When your problem looks like a limp balloon, you'll smile with delight that you ever found it oppressive. Ordinarily, 90% of our daily difficulties are blown up out of proportion, so use your Delight Pin to shrink them to their proper size.

ESCAPE TOOL #40 – CHRISTMAS CAROL DELIGHT

The Christmas carol "Joy to the World" is typically placed on the lips of the angels who announce the birth of Jesus by singing, "Joy to the world! The Lord has come: let earth receive her King; Let every heart prepare him room...." The Liberator Lord and the Reign of God have come, bringing the gift of delight to the world.

Every heart is to make room by sweeping out gloom and doom, boredom and apathy, so as to be filled with delight. This heart-house eviction and resettlement can be made easier when we are addicted to celebrating. Birthdays and significant anniversaries along with national and religious holidays are our primary celebrative days and so are occasions for delight. Yet since birthdays come only once a year and holidays are few and far between among the year's 365 days, you may need to create your own celebrations!

Commemorate and throw small parties for your personal historical dates. These could be the birthday of your dog (or the day you acquired your dog), the purchase-anniversary of your car or house, or the anniversary of the first time you met your spouse. Ah, indeed, you could have a crowded calendar of small festivals of delight.

Jesus, the Usher of the New Time Zone of God, spoke frequently of the Age of God in stories about big parties thrown for small things. A woman who loses one coin among many, finds it and throws a party for her neighbors.[12] The shepherd who has a large flock goes out and finds a single lost sheep and hurries home to celebrate with joy.[13] Use the finding of lost car keys or a misplaced credit card as an occasion for a party, even if it is a solo jig of delight. Laugh aloud when good fortune smiles on you, and you will finally find the missing life for which you have been searching.

ESCAPE TOOL #41 — RECONCILIATION REJOICING

While a long lost son's return is no small event, the father does something surprising on the sinfully wasteful prodigal son's return.[14] He rejoices by celebrating. The son's sins, his abandonment of the family farm and family responsibilities are not met by some parental penance. In fact, they are not even acknowledged. To the surprise of all, including the elder brother, the father's delight is expressed by declaring a holiday and throwing a grand celebration for the village. This is no minor celebration; rather, it's complete with the prize fattened calf, with music and dancing. Those living in the Reign of God are invited to live every day in such a festive, joyful, delightful way.

Express delight whenever you and another are reconciled by celebrating as did the father of the wayward son in Jesus' parable. This is no time for a drab shaking of hands or even an embrace. Instead, with extravagant joy, throw a party. Celebrate and live in delight. If you help others celebrate special occasions and their personal holy days, you will find delight filling your heart.

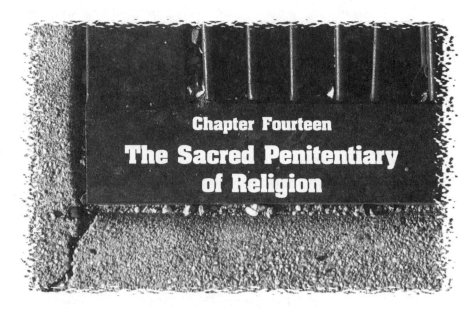

Chapter Fourteen

The Sacred Penitentiary of Religion

Yes, there really is a Sacred Penitentiary — literally! Once known as the Sacred Apostolic Penitentiary, and now shortened to the Apostolic Penitentiary, it's the office in the Vatican that judges cases of absolution, dispensations and issues of conscience.

Yet, indeed, all of religion can be a Sacred Penitentiary, regardless of whether it bears the name Roman Catholic, Baptist, Islamic or Hindu. The Latin *poenitientia,* the mother word of penitentiary, means "repentance." It implies the hope that incarceration will lead inmates to repent of their past mistakes and reform their lives. As we have seen, Jesus required reformation for entrance into the Reign of God, and so it is not surprising to find a parallel between penitentiaries and Christian churches. Too often, however, churches can resemble prisons where the inmates contemplate their guilt due to their past sin-crimes. These prisons with stained glass windows can perpetually incarcerate their members in a sense of fearful unworthiness.

A PRISONLESS RELIGION

Churches can also be places where the People of God gather to experience community, to rejoice in their glorious freedom as Children of God and to be inspired to live lives of justice and truth. A religion that deepens our abiding sense of freedom and promotes a joyful awareness of our great dignity as God's beloved daughters and sons who are unconditionally embraced with divine passionate love — such religion is not a prison. Whenever religion is a reservoir of holy tradition, an organizer of life in harmony with the cycles of life and death, it is not a prison. Whenever a religion provides us with a language for prayer, reinforces our perpetual communion with God and emphasizes that the sacred is found in ordinary lives, it is not a prison. Whenever a religion helps us ritually celebrate the significant events of our lives and at the same time stretches us out in a global inclusivity toward those of all religions as well as those of no religion, then it is no prison. Whenever a religion guarantees us a freedom of conscience with which to judge the morality of our personal actions, while at the same time calling us toward a life committed to justice, peace, nonviolence and compassion for the poor, then it is not a prison. A religion that does these things is a way to the sacred rather than a sacred penitentiary.

THE PRISON OF RELIGION

Just as fear, anger and hate can imprison us, so too can religion. In light of all the benefits and blessings that we've just recounted, we may wonder how that's possible. Yet, unfortunately, we don't have to look far to see the imprisoning effects of religion in our culture and in our lives. What's more, Jesus' life and ministry reveal an ongoing confrontation with the confining, constricting face of religion. Our Deliverer-Savior liberated and continues to set free those held in bondage by their religion, regardless of its name. Because the prophet of Galilee was an escaped prisoner of the chains of religion, and as such was a danger to the powers of the religious establishment, he was executed. Religion, even one that bears the name of the Liberator, can be an imprisoning institution. Churches can imprison their members by holding to rules and regulations rather than to love, compassion and service — by holding to the letter rather than the spirit of the law. Churches can chain their members in a sense of unworthiness and inferiority as well as a sense of superiority over inferior religious expressions, thus caging the faithful in blatant or subtle discrimination against those of other faiths.

Even worship can be a prison activity. While worship can be a ritual action recalling and embodying memories of the great liberating deeds of Moses and Jesus, it can also be a service that enslaves. Weekly worship can be an hour of indoctrination at which the congregation's sense of failure and sin is reinforced by the clergy and by prayers such as, "O Lord, I am not worthy." Emphasizing prayers that beg God for mercy only affirm the secret feelings of failure and shame of those with low self-esteem. Such feelings of inadequacy are reinforced when we compare our lives with religion's high ideals and moral laws. Hymns and rituals can further weave a web that says our sinfulness requires continuous pardon from God — through the ministry of the church.

Religious images buttress this belief system based on personal sinfulness and inferiority before an omnipotent God who sees and judges every hidden deed. Images of an unmarried, asexual Jesus Christ and an immaculate, ever-pure Virgin Mary, along with sinless, celibate saints can create deep-seated anxiety about ever being acceptable, let alone being loved by God.

THE PRISON OF THE OPEN DOOR

The Sacred Penitentiary's doors are open to welcome all, and the inmates of this holy prison are many and varied. Some are born in the prison of the religion in which their parents were inmates. Often they are then educated in prison schools, married in prison and usually die there. Others freely enter religion as adults for various reasons, such as marrying a partner who is an inmate. Or they may enter because they find life threatening or meaningless and so choose religion as a way to cope with the pain of existence and the fear of death. Indeed, Karl Marx's observation that religion is the opiate of the people can be true. Those who for physical or psychological reasons feel themselves unlovable and lack loving relationships are often drawn to churches because of Jesus' moral code that guarantees unconditional love. Others, overwhelmed with personal, emotional and interpersonal problems, enter churches seeking relief by abandoning themselves and their problems to God. This can border on a religious rejection of personal responsibility found in expressions like, "Just leave it in God's hands" or "All we can do now is pray" or "It's God's Will. Trust in God." Trusting in God, while a holy and positive stance of any lover of the Divine Mystery, can also sadly be a pious excuse to avoid growing up and confronting life's hard issues. Such a "soft" trust can absolve religious inmates from responsibility for their spiritual evolution.

These pewed inmates are kept subservient by their clergy-guards by repeated calls for conversion and the necessity of frequent confession. The prisoners' sense of sinful imperfection is renewed yearly by cycles of penance and revival services. It's no wonder that guilt addicts feel comfortably at home among the sacred penitentiary's population. Those incarcerated by guilt are frequently beset with the fear of never being able to perform enough penances or acquire enough indulgences to escape from the punishment due for their sins — which are most frequently identified by the prison guards as sexual in nature. The sacred penitentiary is the most unique of all prisons: It has no high stone walls, razor-like barbwire fences or guard towers. Unlike those in ordinary prisons, its inmates feel no shame at being imprisoned. On the contrary, they feel shame at not being in prison. In fact, the greatest shame is paradoxically showered on those who become ex-cons, escapees of this pious prison. The prison court condemns these escaped inmates to the ultimate capital punishment: hell.

HOMO RELIGIOSUS

In taking our tour of this sacred penitentiary, it might be helpful to explore the origins of religion. How old is religion? Did Adam and Eve go to church on Sunday or the Sabbath? Theologian Dr. Anne Foerst uses the term *Homo religiosus*, the praying human, for an important evolutionary stage of *Homo sapiens*.[1] She states that neurologists maintain there is a special part of the evolved human brain that functions specifically when someone is having a religious experience. This section of the human brain is especially active when a person is praying. Interestingly, studies have shown that when the neurons in this area are externally stimulated, even if the persons are not engaged in prayer or worship, they report having a religious experience! In the process of human evolution the once primal human brain has gradually enlarged and developed to allow humans to engage effortlessly in a variety of tasks, and this is increasingly true of prayer and spiritual activity. Indeed, spirituality has been part of the evolutionary ascension of humanity and has been part of the fabric of human experience long enough to have wired the brain, disposing it to spiritual thoughts and deeds. Yet while spiritual and religious experience can be traced back scores of millenniums, religion itself is a rather recent human development, perhaps no older than 5,000 years!

Homo erectus, the upright walking human, evolved about two million years ago, and Homo sapiens, who has evolved into today's human, appeared around 200,000 years ago. Advance the evolutionary calendar 130,000 years to somewhere around 70,000 years ago, according to Diarmuid O'Murchu, and spirituality makes its first appearance.[2] The earliest evidence of human spiritual activity is found in ancient burial customs that are dated 65,000 years before the arrival of religion! Homo religiosus, the first praying humans, began burying their dead with flowers and with other symbolic objects, implying a belief that life continued beyond the grave. This means then that prayer and ritual, the activities of spirituality, appeared thousands of generations before organized religion.

HOMO SPIRITUALIS

The 35,000-year-old Ice Age caves of France and Spain also reveal the activity of what more correctly might be termed *Homo spiritualis*, the spiritual human. These underground cathedrals, the original catacombs, were decorated thirty-five millenniums ago with breathtaking paintings that reveal a developed spiritual awareness combined with stunning artistic imagination. About this same time in various places throughout the world there appeared carved stone statues of the Mother Goddess, expressing a blending of a spiritual sensitivity to fertility with an intentional portrayal of divinity in a human body.

Our earliest spiritual ancestors were also aware of invisible life-forms, which O'Murchu calls, "energy-forces."[3] These unseen spirit beings, which were present throughout creation, were regarded with reverence and awe. These invisible powerful forces that commonly dwelt in certain trees, stones and pools were more often experienced as friendly than as evil spirits. Instances of this primal spirituality can be found today in various places around the world where special trees, standing stones and pools are reverenced as sacred and decorated with tokens of piety. Typically, the latter-day, advanced religions of Judaism, Christianity and Islam have denounced such practices as pagan and have attempted to banish them. Yet perhaps we need to consider a broader approach toward this evolutionary acknowledgment of the presence of the spiritual energy within creation. After all, Christianity teaches the belief that God is everywhere. Could not those who are highly sensitive to the subtle presences legitimately reverence the Divine Mystery abiding in trees, rocks and streams? The answer to that question contains a seemingly haunting threat to organized religion that leads us to ask: How today should we express our belief in the abiding presence of God in all creation and throughout the cosmos?

THE SPIRITUAL GROUND OF RELIGION

As we have seen, formal religion is perhaps no more than 5,000 years old![4] The mother of religion was the Agricultural Revolution that swept across the earth 8,000 to 10,000 years ago. The shift from a society of hunting and gathering of food to one that cultivated crops began around 8000 B.C.E. (before the Christian Era). This stage of cultural development would last until the Industrial Revolution of the seventeenth and eighteenth centuries C.E. (Christian Era, or A.D.). The oldest sustained religious expression is Hinduism, which can be traced back to around 3000 B.C.E. Hinduism incorporated into its practice previously existing pre-religious spirituality and animal worship, just as Christianity would do with the pre-religious spirituality of those peoples it converted. For example, most of the religious images and customs of such feasts as Christmas, Easter and the Feast of the Holy Dead were baptized and absorbed from Northern European pagan spiritualities. Even a brief thumbnail history of religion reveals not only that spirituality existed for thousands of years before religion but that primal spiritualities became part of the fabric of the religions that followed.

THE RISE AND FALL OF PRE-RELIGIOUS SPIRITUALITIES

The pre-religious spiritual person looked at creation and was able to see not a collection of inanimate objects but an integrated web of life. Our spiritual ancestors' dawning awareness that life did not cease at death was raised by the fundamental spiritual question, "What exists beyond the grave?" From the perspective of the evolving human spirit, the answer to that inquiry is not as important as the question itself. Only humans can ask questions, and questions lead to enlightenment. By asking questions we continue to ascend upward on the ladder of human spiritual evolution. Often, unfortunately, religions tend to denounce as evil any questioning of their teachings, dogmas and rituals.

By contrast, spirituality requires questioning as a critical component of the quest of the soul. In fact, questioning is the evolutionary tool for plumbing the infinite depths of sacred mystery.

The Holy One of the Paleolithic Age, around 5400 B.C.E., is depicted in the magnificent cave wall paintings of France and Spain as the Mystical Mistress of Animals. At that time large herds of bison, elk and other animals roamed freely, and many were reverenced as divine, particularly the bear and, later, the bison. Climactic changes caused the gradual disappearance of the vast herds of bison, which besides being sacred were a major food source for these early humans. Along with their food supply, these primitive peoples' spirituality also became an endangered species as primitive forms of religion evolved. Spiritualities had their shamans, holy medicine men and women and spirit-guides. These would also become endangered roles with the formation of the first religious caste, the holy cowboys.

THE HOLY COWBOYS

According to William Thompson, as the divine image of bison was beginning to disappear, their worshipers began to capture selected wild cattle and place them in corral-sanctuaries.[5] The sacred bison cow, once only a mystical image on a cave wall, could now be a real cow that was constantly nearby to grant blessings and protection. The corralled god/ goddess, however, needed chosen caretakers to properly feed and care for it. These sacred cow caretakers — the holy cowboys — were the predecessors of ordained priests. The sense of the sacredness of all life that was part of the spirituality of the hunters and gatherers would be mutated by the process of corralling divinity. The corralling of sacred cows cared for by holy cowboys began religion's divorce of sacred space from the rest of life and created the division of the sacred and the secular. Along with the holy space of the sacred corrals and the increasing domestication of cattle, people of the early religious era began to build walled cities with grain storage bins. The growing of the food supply required some magic or craft to manipulate and accommodate to the erratic gods of weather, planting and harvesting. Religion, with its priestly rituals, would ensure the friendly and beneficial relationship with these gods. Previously, the kinship of small clans combined with ancient taboos were sufficient for social order. Religion would now also become an effective agent to control the behavior of the many diverse inhabitants of the new walled cities. Cities needed strong and wise leaders, so kings also appeared, commanding a new social status. Kings needed more than armies to ensure order, they needed an elite priesthood to affirm their authority and to keep their records. The evolution from holy cowboys to clerical clerks would soon be complete.

These earliest cities had no temples, for every home had its own shrine to a family god. Humanity, once at home in nature, was now becoming divorced from creation by living safely behind city walls. Another division would be created with the appearance of the magical divine art of writing, which separated the literate priestly elite caste from illiterate commoners and even nobles. (The effects of written language and more developed civilization would progressively place the needs of the individual above those of the community.) The sacrifice of animal and human victims to the gods then appeared as a means of placating the fickle divine overseers of life. Now the walled cities would need an innovative new building, the temple. The gods and goddesses who once had dwelt in the heavens, now took up residence in their magnificent houses of worship, which would also be the sacred sites of sacrifice. In time, extensions would be added to these god houses for the domiciles of their priests and scribes.

While it took only a few minutes to read this brief account of the beginning of formal religions, the evolution actually required thousands of years and was extremely diverse in expression.

The suggestion that churches evolved may appear heretical in light of the belief that God ordained religion from the beginning of time. Yet who created Christianity? Did not the church come into being as a cooperative product of human and divine evolution? "Ongoing creation" would be another good name for evolution, which means that God has both set things into motion and continues to be at work. Teilhard de Chardin adds that it is impossible to see God, "as a focus at the summit of the universe without, in doing so, simultaneously impregnating with his presence even the most insignificant evolutionary movement."[6]

Thank you for your patience with this evolutionary-historical review of religion. It has been a necessary preparation before treating the relationship between the Great Liberator of Galilee and religion.

Obedience to God

While *E Pluribus Unum,* "one from many," was finally chosen as the motto for the official seal of the new American Republic, Benjamin Franklin had urged the adoption of this option: "Rebellion to tyrants is obedience to God." Franklin's motto easily could have belonged to Jesus the Liberator in light of his mystical mutiny against religion's tyrannical oppression.

Jesus the Rescuer appeared in the fullness of time and in obedience to God, announcing the arrival of a new era of God's rule. Embodied in his flesh was the Divine Earthquake, who would again shake up the world with something new. Even temples are not earthquake proof. In both word and deed, Jesus foretold the destruction the Temple of Jerusalem[7] — which would take place in 70 B.C.E. and would effectively end its cult of animal sacrifice. His cleansing of the Temple, which turned into a riot, was a slow-motion encore of the final scene of the story about Samson, one of the great Jewish folk heroes.[8] Samson, renowned for his great physical strength, had been captured by the Israelites' enemies, the Philistines. Tortured and even blinded as a prisoner, God invested him with a final burst of extraordinary physical strength, and he single-handedly pulled down the Philistine temple dedicated to their god Dagon, crushing all who were within it. Jesus, the New Samson, was likewise invested with the extraordinary power of the Holy Spirit to bring down God's holy temple in Jerusalem, since God had no further use for it.

Jesus the Holy Founder or Holy Flayer?

Jesus is universally acknowledged as the founder of the Christian religion. Yet his words and actions reveal him to be more a Samson Savior who came to pull down religion. The Gospels describe him not so much as a holy founder as a holy flayer of religion. The term speaks of one who "assails with stinging criticism, and strips away." He denounces as no longer necessary or valid the compulsory rituals, clerically imposed obligations and countless extensions of the religious laws of Judaism and of religion itself. Faithful to the prophetic tradition of Israel chastising the perpetuators of religious sham, the Prophet of Galilee exposes religion's hypocrisy and oppression of the poor. He signals God's impatience to begin a new age, which is a radically new return to ancient times, to a Spirit-inspired age empty of temples and the division of life into sacred and secular zones.

Moses was Israel's religious architect. He is acknowledged as the founder and great lawgiver of Judaism. Unlike Moses, Jesus does not give to his followers a single instruction for sanctuary rituals. Unlike Moses, he gives no blueprint instructions for constructing any kind of temple, sacred space or church building. Nor is he the creator of an elaborate system of laws as was Moses. Unlike the six hundred different laws that the priests extended out like tentacles from the Ten Commandments of Moses, Jesus gives only one expansive law: the necessity to love God and neighbor. He gives no instructions for the creation of a priestly caste; he mandates not a single regulation about liturgical or religious garments or any particular symbolic clothing for his disciples. Unlike Moses, he decrees not a single ritual action for the forgiveness of sins beyond offering it without bounds. Contrary to Moses, he institutes not a single religious festival or holy day and even refrains from obliging worship on the Sabbath; he calls his disciples only to repeat his last meal as a memorial of him. He gives them no instructions on how often they are to celebrate this meal or how they are to remember it, nor does he limit the menu. Rather than a founder, Jesus is both a returner and an advancer. He ushers in a radical return to the ancient days when every house was a temple, and he opens doors to every place becoming a shrine and every situation an opportunity for encountering the sacred. He makes every home a sanctuary and every household's threshold a doorway where God can be experienced in the stranger or friend. He makes every family table as sanctified as the Temple's altar and every room a Holy of Holies. He fulfills and realizes the original dream of Moses that God's people would be a priestly people.

Moreover, Jesus is depicted by the Gospels as a nonreligious man! Being religious in that context implied a public demonstration of prayer and piety, including the wearing of religious symbolic objects and clothing as well as a fidelity to various daily rituals and customs. The religiously pious Pharisees were shocked that Jesus' disciples disregarded important public rituals such as fasting and the ceremonial washing of hands before eating. Yet those disciples clearly were the followers of their master, who, it seems, didn't observe this kind of religious practice. In response to his harsh religious critics, Jesus chided them as hypocrites and whitewashed tombs who kept the surface requirements only, calling them, "Blind guides, who strain out the gnat and swallow the camel."[9] He further quoted to them the words of Isaiah, "This people honors me only with their lips; their hearts are far away."[10] The Redeemer-Liberator lived the reality of true religiousness, which resides in the heart. This religious spirit is measured not by keeping external practices — even going to church every Sunday, reading the Bible every day or saying pious prayers — but by a great capacity to love and to be deeply concerned for the afflicted and those in need. The writer of the letter of James expresses well Jesus' attitude towards religion: "Religion that is pure and undefiled before God is this: to care for orphans and widows (the poorest of the poor) in their affliction."[11]

THE GALILEAN BYPASS

Instead of the elaborate sin-removing rituals of the Temple, the Liberator gives an uncomplicated way for forgiving sin. Each time, he simply says to the sinner, "Go in peace, your sins are forgiven."[12] He never asks those he forgives to confess their sins but rather simply announces that they are freed of them. Some believe that Jesus had divine knowledge of their sins, and so there was no need to list them. But the most compelling reason for the Master's attitude can be seen in his parable of the Prodigal Son, where the father would not let his son recite the list of his sins but in great love swept him up in forgiveness.[13] For Jesus, it seems, all that was necessary was an awareness of the separation from God caused by sin, not a precise listing of sinful actions or thoughts. His prodigal — extravagantly generous — acts of forgiving angered the religious establishment. They were outraged at his audacious disregard for their laws about how sins could be forgiven, his radical bypassing of the required temple rituals for the removal of sins.

He shared with his disciples this revolutionary power to forgive sins, most notably when he instructed them to pray, "...forgive us our sins as we forgive those who have sinned against us."[14] That prayer of Jesus containing the non-ritual act of forgiveness has been known by heart since childhood by devout and even casual Christians. Ron Rolheiser speaks of the prayer's sin-absolving power when he quotes the great theologian St. Augustine. In one of his homilies to the newly baptized, St. Augustine asks why the Lord's Prayer is recited before receiving the Body and Blood of Christ. He answers by saying, "Because of our human fragility perhaps our minds imagined something which was not decent, our ears heard something…which was not fitting…they are washed away by the Lord's Prayer at the moment we say, 'Forgive us our trespasses' so that we can safely approach the sacrament [of Holy Communion]."[15] Jesus freed his followers from the religious rituals required to be pardoned by telling them simply to forgive each other, and to do so seven times seventy times if necessary.[16] Christians of the first several centuries experienced this glorious liberation from their sins without the need of confessional rituals. In the early church the Sacrament of Penance could be received after baptism only once in a person's lifetime. It would require another thousand years before the concept of yearly or frequent confessions would become the norm.

Early Christians did not have immaculate conceptions. Like Christians of today, they were not sinless and failed as easily as do we. At the same time, Baptism was understood to be a major life conversion, and they were expected to live lives devoid of serious sin. So, in the context of the early Christian communities, ritual forgiveness was administered only for grievous public sins such as murder, adultery and a formal denial of the faith. For centuries the vast majority lived in the glorious freedom given them by their Liberator Lord. But enslavers hate liberators and so, in time, seek to hunt down, remove and imprison rebels and outlaws like Jesus who go about freeing the enslaved.

JESUS THE OUTLAW

Jesus lived outside the law. The carpenter-now-prophet of Nazareth did not break those religious laws penned by the scribes and temple lawyers, he simply dismissed them as invalid. He embodied a love that went beyond the law and encouraged his followers to cultivate that same capacity for love. By telling his disciples to forgive each other's sins, he invited them to live outside the law that required they be pardoned only by a temple priest. He ignored the sanctimonious sub-laws forbidding eating with sinners and was notorious for sharing meals with such sinners as tax-collectors, prostitutes and social outcasts. He sidestepped the rigorous Sabbath laws whenever the human need for love and compassion was required, and he even dared to challenge the commonly accepted purpose of this day of holy rest. He publicly refuted what for centuries had been taught was absolutely required and most pleasing to God: the great Temple of Jerusalem, its animal sacrifices, its rituals of purification, its holy priesthood and festivals. He discarded the promise of the religious establishment that obedience to their numerous laws would bring the reward of heaven and instead proposed that prostitutes and sinners were entering heaven before the law-abiding, self-righteous religious people. Again and again he denounced the leprosy of religion, exposing its hidden pestilence of hypocrisy. The crucifixion didn't take place because from the beginning of time an act of sacrificial redemption was required by the will of God. It was rather the will of the religious Temple Establishment that Jesus be executed on the cross because of his radical disregard for their priestly office, traditions and laws. If the gentle Galilean Prophet walked among us today speaking the same caustic words of judgment toward the religion bearing his name, would he not once again be silenced by excommunication or some other form of crucifixion?

THE SACRED SLAVERY

Religion enslaves by making its members docile and obedient. I once read that the nineteenth century slave traders in the South Pacific sought to capture a certain type of island native. In their quest for ideal slaves they intentionally sought out baptized natives recently converted to Christianity! The slave traders had found from experience that these people were more docile and easier to capture and manipulate as slaves than pagan or unconverted natives.

Religion has a long history of manipulation. The word comes from the Latin *manipulus*, "of the hand," and it means artfully controlling or insidiously exploiting others for one's personal gain. Religion stands on two legs: Scripture and Tradition. It's interesting that the latter is from the Latin *traditio,* meaning "to hand on or over," and refers to the transmission of customs, doctrines and practices that are handed from one generation to the next. Religion, which passes on wonderful traditions like the Lord's Supper and Christmas across the ages, is also skilled at having "hands on" control of its members. As the old slave traders of the South Pacific knew, docility and submission are prime qualities of religious people, making them easy to manipulate.

The Holy Outlaw Jesus was not docile when the righteous observers of the religious law challenged him on why he and his disciples openly disregarded and violated the law. He boldly responded that he was bound only by the freeing law of love. Jesus was a holy escapee who, without guilt, lived publicly outside the restrictions of religious regulations that limited life and love. He invites all domesticated, docile, nonresistant church members to "Come, follow me, and stand tall as a holy outlaw."

A story is told about a pre-Civil War slave auction in New Orleans that was being watched by some visitors from the North. As the African slaves wearily shuffled across the square toward the auction block, one middle-aged slave stood out in striking contrast. He walked with his head erect and with all the proud bearing and dignity of a conqueror. One of the Northerners asked, "Who is that man? Is he the straw boss of that gang of slaves?" The former slave owner who was auctioning some of his slaves answered, "No, even after all these years that fellow just can't get it out of his head that he is the son of a king. It seems he was captured as a slave when he was a small child, but it had been drummed into him that he was a chief and not an ordinary person. We've never been able to break his spirit."

At the trial before his death, Jesus stood tall, proud as a king, before the most powerful religious figure of his religion, the High Priest. He did the same before the Imperial Roman Governor, Pontius Pilate, and King Herod. His born-free standing tall was consistent with the rest of his life when he was challenged by the leaders of the Pharisees and learned lawyer-scribes. He was not a groveling bootlicker of the religious or political leadership. The authoritarian power of those in high places did not diminish his dignity. In this independence he is a liberating model for all of us who are so easily enslaved. Like the African slave in the story, even when under the rule of religious, political and corporate structures we can stand nobly tall, and our spirits, when united with the Sacred Spirit, are unbreakable.

Yet don't act on impulse. Before accepting Jesus' invitation to join his band of outlaws, seriously consider the consequences. First of all, there are the repercussions that Jesus faced in being an outlaw, namely angry opposition, persecution, legal action and finally crucifixion. But there are also social and developmental implications to going outside the law. Many laws are intended to maintain order and protect the innocent. Civil and religious laws are boundary lines, legal fences that can imprison but can also liberate. In certain situations and at certain stages of personal development — like the toddler or teenage years — setting limits gives a healthy sense of security and is often necessary. Yet fences that limit human growth, eliminate personal responsibility and restrict basic human freedoms must either be torn down, jumped over or slipped through. While restrictive religious fences usually have posts that are set in concrete, these fences must be scaled, even if they are topped with razor-like barbwire.

A FENCELESS SPIRITUALITY

The Holy Outlaw of Galilee calls us to live outside the limiting confines of the commandments and to follow him in living lives of unlimited love as members of a fenceless community. Those who religiously tithe often use that 10% Old Testament yardstick to feel they have fulfilled their obligation to God and church. But the High Jumper Jesus easily bounded over that holy fence, saying, "Love God not with 10% but with all your heart. Don't just give 10% of your love to your neighbor; rather, love your neighbor as you love yourself — with all your heart." In today's web-world, our neighbor is not restricted to the family across the street, but includes the Hindu living across the world in India and the Muslim in Mecca. As one who lived in the space outside the law, Jesus was a highwayman — not a robber, but one who lived on the high road of conscience instead of the easy low road of legal compliance. Inspired by the Holy Spirit of Liberty, his actions were not contrary to the law but *beyond* the law.

Only the brave follow. The fearful sit and chew their fingernails. Those disciples courageous enough to follow the Highwayman are liberated from the pious craving for the assurances of religious authority. They let go of the secure sense of having God's blessing — via the church — upon their behavior and moral decisions. God's Spirit inspired in Jesus a wondrous freedom of conscience, which is also available to each of his disciples. The Vatican Council spoke to all Christians when it said in the Document on *The Church in the Modern World*, "Only in freedom can people direct themselves towards goodness...an authentic freedom is an exceptional sign of the divine image within humanity." [17] The Council also affirmed the personal freedom of conscience to determine what is or is not God's will for us. *The Declaration on*

Religious Freedom said, "This Vatican Council declares that the human person has the right to religious freedom...that in religious matters no one is to be forced to act in a manner contrary to his or her beliefs."[18]

To assume personal moral responsibility by exercising your freedom of conscience requires maturity. The mature formation of a wholesome and holysome conscience can be liberating, and it can also be scary. It calls for prayer, reflection, spiritual counsel and a respectful consideration of the moral teachings of one's religious tradition. The majority of us desire to do what is morally right in God's eyes, so faithfully following a pronouncement of conscience is difficult when that inner directive is contrary to religious or national laws. To live beyond the narrow boundaries of religious rules and commandments requires heroic love. To scale faith-fences and follow Christ beyond merely being a Baptist, Methodist or Catholic — to move beyond even being a Christian, in order to belong to a fenceless community — requires courageous loving. To live above the law requires an evolutionary leap outside the comfortable confines of one's self, family, church and nation. To make such a leap we need God's Spirit, since ultimately to be a true escapee we must evacuate the most precious of all boundaries: our own skin. With a skinless body you can encompass within yourself all of humanity and all creation, including our small blue planet and all the cosmos, as you become one with the Cosmic Body of Christ.

Yet the thought of being a courageous lone ranger — a lone religious and civil outlaw escapee — can be too frightening a vocation to embrace. However, fear not; you are not alone. Even if you have no companions to share your lust for liberty, you have the same Spirit of Liberty who accompanied Jesus in his passage across his religious and legal fences. The Ever-Free Spirit is eager and enthusiastic to be your prayerful partner in reaching toward the fullness of life. Our human brain, regardless of how evolved it is, is still too primitive and undeveloped to be able to comprehend all it means to be fully alive. With all of our highly sophisticated technology we are still aborigines when it comes to our capacity to live fully. Yet it is possible to be more alive than we are. Remember the criterion that we receive from God through Jesus: "I have come among you so that you might have life, and have it in great abundance."[19]

The Republic of God

Jesus used the political language of his day when he spoke of the "Kingdom of God." What he proclaimed had arrived was the evolutionary reality of an elevated society, a regime of justice and equality, of peace and love. His term "kingdom" is cemented into our consciousness and religious language. Unfortunately, over the centuries the connotation of a kingdom has become that of a royal pyramid with an absolute monarch at the top ruling over well-defined descending ranks of nobles, clerics, merchants and peasant classes. If Jesus were speaking today, might he say, "The Republic of God has arrived"? Unlike a kingdom, a republic is a political structure in which all members are equal and determine their laws and leaders by vote. A republic's social order is equated with freedom and liberty. The earliest communities of disciples of the Risen Jesus were just such groups, in which equality existed among all and decisions were reached by spiritual consensus. As Paul tells us, early Christians boasted that in their communities, "there was neither male nor female, Jew or Gentile, slave or free, for they were all one in Christ."[20]

The motto of the Republic of God might even be the same as that of the American Republic: "One nation under God." As in our republics today, leaders in the early Christian church were chosen by those whom they would lead. Even four hundred years into the history of the church, the selection of a bishop or spiritual leader was decided by the entire community. Pope Leo the Great (440-461) affirmed this practice when he decreed, "He who is in charge of all should be chosen by all." Gradually over the next centuries Christianity developed another style of organization, known as holy orders, which was based on the hierarchical feudalism of the Middle Ages. This holy pyramid church lacked the family equality of the early Christian community. Religion, a bedmate with kings and noble houses for centuries, was shocked by the American and French Revolutions. This was true especially of the Roman Catholic Church, which denounced and condemned these infant republics and their democracies as the enemies of God and religion.[21] Many Reform churches, being themselves revolutionary in nature, fused many elements of the new democracies into their structures and were able to influence these social movements. The tragedy for the Roman Catholic Church was in its failure to remember the equality of the early church. By condemning democracy, which emphasized human rights, freedom of the press and rejection of an exclusive state religion, the Church lost an opportunity to influence and be involved in these evolutionary human movements.

The good news about the equality of God's People along with freedom from the "heavy burden"[22] of religious law, was expressed in the very flesh of Jesus by his inclusive, liberating lifestyle. In the second half of the twentieth century this good news was once again announced in the Vatican Council's Dogmatic Constitution of the Church, *Lumen Gentium,* which proclaimed, "All share a true equality with regard to the dignity and to the activity common to all the faithful for the building up of the Body of Christ."[23] While our Reform sister churches have sometimes witnessed beautifully to this original Christian equality, among some of them there also still exists a pyramid-tiered hierarchy and a clerical caste system. True equality in "dignity and activity," especially in ministerial activity, is rare to find in churches that continue to employ the hierarchical model of church formulated in the Middle Ages.

THE MUDDLED AGES

Church historians of the twenty-second century may well describe our own historical period as the Muddled Ages. This is an age of tension, disorder and confusion as an old age ends and a new one begins. Historical eras rarely ease smoothly into the next era. So tension exists today between those promoting a democratic ideal of equality for their churches and those who still support a hierarchical, feudal model of church. The predicament of women, the divorced and gays being prevented from full and active participation in their churches is another significant element in this muddled early millennium spiritual struggle. The Evangelical churches experience a similar religious tug-of-war between those staunchly holding to a strict interpretation of the Bible and those favoring a contemporary understanding of the symbolism of Scripture.

Regardless of which end of the rope you are pulling on, we are all called to "Rejoice always and in all situations to give thanks."[24] These Muddled Ages of conflict provide us with one of those prime situations in which to rejoice and be thankful. Be joyful that the Holy Spirit is not the exclusive property of bishops and those in religious leadership, of vision-visited individuals or of the laity. The Creative Spirit of God delights in working creatively within the tug-of-war between the old and new, between the reformers and the restorationists, between liberals and conservatives, in order to bring something holy and mystical out of these Muddled Ages.

RECONCILIATION OF RELIGION WITH SPIRITUALITY

Is anyone religiously naked? While some native peoples still practice their pre-religious spiritualities, they are not free of religion. For better or worse, in various ways, we all have been influenced by some religion. Just as none of us is without a nationality, even if one lives outside one's country of origin and considers oneself to be a global citizen, so it is with religion. This being the reality at this historical moment, what should be our relationship with religion? As we have seen, Jesus did not establish a religion but rather offered to his disciples a way of life, an invitation to adopt his lifestyle. How do we who live in this third millennium after his birth balance being a member of the Christian religion with being the nonreligious disciple of a nonreligious Master?

Spirituality and religion can be mutually beneficial. Religion can give to spirituality a structure, a language of prayer and rituals to express mysteries that resist being housed in words. On the other hand, because by its nature religion tends to be a preserver of dried yesterdays and the guardian of past customs, a good spirituality can fertilize religion by making it vigorously alive in the midst of daily life. While religion can save spirituality from being an ungrounded or false experience, spirituality can rescue religion from arid irrelevance. A spirituality can "freedomize" religion by giving creative expression to the love of God outside of church-space and by consecrating as sacred all ordinary actions. Religion furnishes sacraments, and a spirituality makes life sacramental. Religion provides a structured sense of home and tradition, while a spirituality transforms religion into a floating aircraft carrier from which we can fly off in quest of unexplored divine places and experiences. We can then return to the carrier both to share the fruits of that quest and to experience the divine in community.

A religion recalls how God has spoken to us in times past; a spirituality attends to how God speaks to us today. Our spiritual ancestors who heard God speaking to them thousands of years ago lived when there were no spiritual directors or long lists of religious rules. For them spirituality simply meant being faithful to God's designs. It can be the same for us as we balance religion and spirituality. The early eighteenth century spiritual writer Jean-Pierre de Caussade wrote of the people of the pre-religious period: "Then it was enough for those who led a spiritual life to see that each moment brought its duty to be faithfully fulfilled. On that duty the whole of their attention was fixed at each successive moment.... Under God's unceasing guidance their spirit turned with conscious effort to each new duty as it was presented to them by God each hour of the day."[25] If his words sound familiar, it's because the Spirit is a holy underground river springing up spontaneously in each age with the same fresh, life-giving water. Caussade echoes our now-familiar wisdom of the German mystic Meister Eckhart that becoming holy simply requires doing the next task before us with all our heart and soul and with delight.

SIMPLE RELIGION

Simple living is encouraged by Christianity, and a liberation spirituality encourages a simple religion. Religion tends to require the completion of countless obligations and duties, while the Way of Jesus is simple. It is a way of love, and it can be contained in his words, "thy will be done," which simply means following God's designs for us moment by moment in each duty of our day. God's will can sound mysteriously unknowable, especially in actual moment by moment situations. Yet God's will is revealed precisely in our daily moments. God's design is for each of us to do the works of God as we go about our daily tasks: answering the telephone or a knock at the door, responding to one interruption in our agenda after another, or suffering from some physical pain or frustration with dignity and grace. The lifestyle of the Galilean Liberator reveals how such "unholy" occasions can become the work of the Holy One. God enfleshed in Jesus is at work in every moment, transforming death into life, converting darkness into light, setting free the enslaved and imprisoned, and granting forgiveness for injury. Such is God's will for us. Each moment in our life brings its own duty to which we are to respond with a fullness of loving attention, and in the process we become Godlike. This is the essence of a simple religion, a religion reduced to the essentials.

The most magnificent truths are the most easily forgotten. God is as enfleshed in our bodies as the Divine Mystery was in the human flesh of Jesus. Jesus believed in that mystery of incarnation and gave God free reign in his life. That reality is at the core of Christian faith. Place your hand over your heart and you will hear a soft pounding: It is God trying to get out. God is pulsing in your heart, softly pleading, "Let me out so I can love in your loving. Release me so my compassion can be present in each of your acts of kindness." Place your hand on your wrist and feel God tapping out in code, crying with a velvet velocity, "Let me use your arms and hands so I can touch those who are lonely and lost. Let me use your hands to carry food to the poor who pray for my help. Let me be your legs so I can perform deeds of humble service. Please let me out!"

Unconscious Holiness

Jesus the Simplifier of Religion told a parable about the spiritual life and the Reign of God in the Gospel of Mark. In this simple story about a farmer who planted seeds in his land, Jesus hides the secret of holiness. Day after day as the farmer rose and went to bed, the seeds sprouted and grew. The farmer didn't know how the seeds did this, they just did. Of its own accord, Jesus says, the land began to yield its fruit, first with the tiny blade, then the ear and finally the full grain in the ear. When the grain was ripe, the farmer harvested his crop.[26] End of story — and the secret? Both we and the Reign of God grow the same effortless way when we unite ourselves completely with the divine design. When we eagerly cooperate with God moment by moment, even on an unconscious level, our souls grow, secretly developing without our even knowing how. God passionately desires our holiness and goodness; we have only to cooperate by making everything in our day the soil from which the God-seed can grow naturally. This is more than good news; it is the marvelous tidings of the spirituality of Jesus: Simply let God use whatever happens next in the soil of your life as fertilizer for your becoming Godlike and growing in God-unity.

Sacraments and ritual actions, Bible reading and meditation, vocal prayers and interior silence can be very useful, and they can also be hindrances. They can inhibit our growth in holiness when they are performed halfheartedly or merely as religious duties, and especially when they lead us to ignore the practical tasks of each moment or to regard them as merely secular activities. The Reign of God is in our midst as we go about the tasks of our life. Jesus tells his disciples, "Stop being anxious about where you will get your food or what you will wear. Unbelievers are obsessed about these things. Be believers — seek before anything else God's reign in your lives, God's way of holiness, and all these things will be given to you."[27] Believers who live the reality of God's Reign know that "God's way of holiness" of which Jesus spoke is not the way usually found in a religious manual. We become Godlike not at the feet of some guru or spiritual master, nor by attending the classes of some great theologian. We find it by being faithful to God's designs unfolding in each moment of our lives.

God's way of holiness involves living out a simple spirituality in which we make use of all things as tools for our transformation. And we are called to use them with a sense of holy indifference, which leaves their productive fate in God's hands. The Divine Mystery may will to use some act of formal religious worship for our growth. God may just as well productively use an emotional pain or physical suffering to transfigure us into mirrors of the divine image. Holy indifference does not mean stoic apathy. On the contrary, we must passionately care and, paradoxically, also passionately not care. Holy indifference is related more to the final outcome than to how I respond to things. Indeed, I can act passionately and still leave the fruits of my actions to God. Holy indifference also implies a willingness to embrace whatever comes my way, to embrace each second of life with all my heart and soul, allowing the Holy Spirit Converter to secretly use each moment to draw me closer to God whatever the task that comes to me. Those of us eager to rush our spiritual development by a diligent religious practice should frequently read Jesus' parable of the farmer whose crop grew without his efforts or any personal intervention.

Jesus and his closest disciples were able to integrate a spirituality of liberation into their Judaic religion. They employed the traditions and Scriptures of their religion for their growth yet without doing so in the typically religious way. Jesus and his spiritual community retained their Jewish identity while radically returning to the spirit of the earliest desert days of their religion and even to the ancient pre-religious days that were devoid of temples and priesthoods. They lived a simple religion that led to a "secret," unconscious holiness. By following in their footsteps, we of the twenty-first century can find hope and a spiritual way of life.

THE DANGERS OF BEING SPIRITUAL

The apostles enjoyed freedom from the slavery of their religion, a freedom the Great Liberator offered them in his first proclamation in their hometown synagogue. Indeed, he had "come to set the prisoners free,"[28] and had done so for them. Yet they were not completely free! Look, for example, at the ongoing process of Peter's freedom in the Acts of the Apostles: Even after Jesus' resurrection and the Pentecost experience, Peter is still gradually letting go of some of the restrictions of his religion and realizing that God accepts all people who are right-spirited.[29] The same need for postgraduate work may be true for us. It can be dangerous to believe that being committed to the simple religion of the Master makes us fully free from the Prison of Religion. Constant vigilance is required for freedom, even after successfully reconciling our religion with a good spirituality. So, to the famous Thessalonian trinity of praying always, rejoicing always and always giving thanks, a liberation spirituality adds a fourth core practice: Stay awake always!

SLUMBERING BACK INTO THE PRISON OF SLEEP

Surrendering to spiritual sleep is an effortless sliding back into slavery. This sleep is not the usual repose but, rather, is an imprisoning lethargy induced by the hypnotic powers of church and state. The Exodus is a liberation story of the great escape of the Israelites from their Egyptian slavery, which fused them together as one nation, one people, under God. Yet their shouts of victory were soon replaced by snores as they abandoned their Exodus freedom to became subjects of a king and the temple priesthood. As the old Irish expression goes, "From clog to clog takes only three generations" — clogs being the heavy wooden-soled shoes worn by indentured peasants. St. Paul, writing to the early Christians of Rome, warned of this danger of losing the Spirit's gift of liberty they had gained at their Baptism into Christ: "...you did not receive a spirit of slavery to fall back into fear."[30] Indeed, freedom from both political and religious enslavement requires constant vigilance, so Jesus admonished his disciples, then and now, to stay awake, "to watch and pray."[31]

PRISONERS OF SLEEP

The dozing disciples in the Garden of Gethsemane can so easily be us. At that moment they are unholy icons not simply of tired disciples; rather, they are prisoners of inertia, drowsy images of the subjugated, victims of the power web of Rome and the Sanhedrin. Authoritarian structures, especially religious authorities, by their absolute power as vicars of God, easily cast spells of fear-stimulated apathy and impotency over their subjects. In the garden Jesus chides Peter, "Simon, why do you keep falling asleep? Do you not have the strength to stay awake one hour? Stay awake and pray, so that you will not enter into temptation."[32] The inability of the closest disciples and friends of Jesus to stay awake was not due to the late night hour or because they had eaten a large meal with several cups of wine. Their continuous lapsing back into sleep at this critical hour is consistent with much of their waking lives, for they had been lethargically slumbering since childhood. Jesus warns of "the temptation" of being possessed by the hypnotizing powers of the demonic forces of the Anti-Kingdom. The ongoing apocalyptic battle for each disciple in each age begins when we're children.

Ched Myers, peace organizer and Scripture scholar, links this inability to stay awake in Gethsemane with the disciples' earlier impotence to perform an exorcism.[33] A father comes to Jesus with his son who has been possessed by a mute and deaf evil spirit. This demon torments the boy by throwing him down to the ground and causing his body to become stone rigid. The father complains to Jesus that his disciples had been unable to expel the evil spirit from his son. As the father is speaking, the boy is suddenly seized by his demon and goes into convulsions. Jesus looks with compassion on the afflicted boy and asks, "How long has he been held captive like this?" The father replies, "Since childhood." Then, effortlessly, Jesus releases the boy from his bondage to the spirit. Some time later when they are alone with Jesus, the embarrassed, impotent disciples ask Jesus why they were not able to cure the boy. Jesus tells them, "This kind of demon is expelled only by prayer."[34]

Myers believes the account of the sleeping disciples of Gethsemane was recorded in order to provide a mirror-image for future disciples. When Jesus refers to *prayer* as the power source for healing, Myers says he is speaking of the intense personal struggle within each disciple to resist the temptation to abandon the Way, the radical lifestyle of Jesus.

He says we are tempted by the demon "embedded in our imperial culture," a culture that is both political and religious. It has kept us impotent, docile subjects of the *status quo,* the way things have been since we were small children. While the word *embedded* means being fixed firmly in a surrounding majority, it carries an additional forceful visual image of being *in bed*, of being locked in a permanent place of sleep.

At Gethsemane, it is Peter, James and John who are possessed. Jesus attempts to call them to a self-exorcism, to use that powerful means he had proposed earlier: prayer. But they fail to sustain their conscious prayer and so remain impotent and limp before the demonic grip of the temple powers that are about to arrest and kill Jesus. Like those three disciples, we have been asleep since childhood, in a perpetual coma caused by the enchantment cast by the Anti-Kingdom's religious and regal powers. When we pray, "Lead us not into temptation," the great temptation we must resist is not adultery or stealing or transgressing other social, moral or religious boundaries. The greatest temptation from which we must escape is remaining asleep and apathetic, being mutely silent before the intimidation of those twin powers. The evil spirit that possessed the boy was mute and deaf. When we are in the Anti-Kingdom's grip, we are deaf to the good news of the Liberator's invitation to live a lifestyle of liberty. That evil spirit also steals away our tongues, making us mute servants, voiceless disciples afraid to publicly object or complain about injustices and oppression. A child is a natural coward. We can easily remain cowards our entire lives.

STAY AWAKE AND PRAY TO BE HEROIC

Ernest Becker wrote, "Our central calling, our main task on this planet, is the heroic." He quotes William James, who said the world was "...essentially a theater for heroism."[35] The first Passion Play was truly a theater for heroism. Jesus' entire public life after his baptism by John was heroic; his heroism wasn't restricted simply to the third act with its trial, humiliation and crucifixion. The Liberator-Savior's daily life was passionately heroic and compassionately redeeming. Jesus' invitation to, "Come and follow me," is a most frightening challenge. As Becker says, "...each system cuts out roles for performances of various degrees of heroism: from the high heroism of a Churchill, a

Mao, or a Buddha, to the 'low' heroism of the coal miner, the peasant, the simple priest; the plain everyday, earthy heroism wrought by gnarled working hands guiding a family through hunger and disease."[36]

The Holy Hero of Galilee elevated that so-called "low" heroism to a level as high as the heavens by inviting peasants and princes, parents and paupers to live his lifestyle of dynamic loving and nonviolence. When Jesus made loving the I.D. badge of his followers, he could just as easily have said, "By this will all know that you are my disciples, by your *heroism.*" The love of self, to which Jesus' great law calls us as a pattern for our love of neighbor, contains the passionate desire to remain free of all the imperial and religious demonic powers that so easily can imprison us in the sleep of docility. "Come, follow me.... Stay awake and pray."

The power that energizes us to walk the razor's edge of Jesus' lifestyle of liberation is prayer. As Ched Myers suggests, prayer is essentially resisting the temptation to live only on the surface of life. Prayer is the mystical shield for warding off the hypnotizing bewitchment of the authoritarian rule of church and state. Jesus unites the spiritual Siamese twins of prayer and faith, saying they have the power to move mountains and remove temptations. Praying is not simply saying prayers. To pray is to live as fully as possible, right in our flesh and bone reality. It is an energizing intimacy with the Divine Mystery, who is the prime agent of the transformation of self. We receive from God what we expect, and when we expect that nothing within us, our world or our church will change, then nothing does. If we believe we are impotent before church or state, we surrender ourselves in resignation as an inmate in the prison of the faint and afraid. Jesus tells us to stay awake and pray in order to have the strength to resist the temptation to sell our soul to save our skin. We need to pray to stay as wide awake as Jesus, John the Baptist, Joan of Arc, Dietrich Bonhoeffer and Oscar Romero did. Along with the countless unknown others who refused to be spiritual sleepwalkers by resisting the temptation to surrender to the imperial powers, these heroes were silenced or killed. Death, physical or spiritual, is the great threat of the imperial powers.

Thanatophobia is the capacity to think about and fear our death. We humans, unlike our cousins in creation, can reflect upon our own death. The consequence of this evolutionary ability, however, is that we are constantly faced with dread. Religion is often simply a refuge from thanatophobia. Churchgoers, anxious about their death, tend to remain pew-faithful to their religion even when it fails to nourish them. Moreover, nonpracticing church members, when old age and death begin to breathe down their necks, usually return to their religion. Recalling that spirituality was birthed over thirty millenniums ago, when early humans began to ask the haunting primordial question about death, "Where am I going?" we can appreciate how strong is the force field that binds us to religion.

Chapter Fourteen Inventory of Escape Tools and Unshackling Reflections

ESCAPE TOOL #42
– PRAYER FUMBLER ALLY

Nothing invokes a sense of guilt like the question, "How's your prayer life?" Of those who do pray, I suspect the majority would give themselves a grade of "C" or even "D," feeling they do not know how to pray properly. Those who are honest would likely respond, "I should pray more. My prayer lacks devotion: So often it's routine."

St. Paul echoed our common feeling of failure at prayer in his letter to the Christians in Rome, "We do not know how to pray as we should."[37] However, he followed that confession of being a prayer fumbler with the good news, "The Spirit comes to the aid of our weakness…the Spirit intercedes with inexpressible groanings. And the Searcher of hearts knows what is the desire of the Spirit."[38] The Spirit of Love converts our feeble efforts into songs that delight the heart of God. So, rejoice in being a fumbler at prayer since by acknowledging such a weakness you become strong in the Spirit.

The next time you ache to pray but don't know what to say, consider this prayer:

Spirit of Love,
>   Prayer Wheel of my heart,
>   gather up out of my life
>   all the broken bits and pieces
>   of my doubts and dreams,
>   my groanings and sorrows.
> Then, spin out of them
>   a lover's poem of praise
>   and sing it to my God.
> Amen.

Is a Democratic Religion the Answer?

I don't want the church to become a democracy. I want it to be
something better than a democracy. I want it to be a community.
>   — Brazilian poet-bishop Pedro Casaldaliga

Bingo Religion

Nineteenth century Catholic missionaries to Africa introduced the
teachings of Christian salvation to their converts along with the game
of bingo. The game's name is a verbal corruption of *beano,* a game of
chance patterned on *keno,* from the French *quine,* for "five winning
numbers." These early African converts to Christianity saw clearly
the difficultly of winning heaven since it required keeping countless
laws and avoiding ever-present sin. To obtain heaven, as it was taught
to them, was more a matter of chance than of grace. These African
converts quickly connected the reward of salvation with the shout of
the winner of that game of chance, and their name for heaven was
bingo.

"Eternal rest grant unto them, O Lord, and may they enjoy
perpetual bingo." Not only nineteenth century African converts, but
many Christians today also view winning heaven as a spin of the wheel,

the good fortune to die in a state of grace. For those caught on the perpetually turning wheel, the squirrel cage of doing more and more penance to remove sin and die in a holy state, attaining the freedom of salvation is, indeed, like winning at bingo.

An Eagle Parable

Anthony de Mello tells a parable-story about an eagle's egg that accidentally fell from its mother's nest to the ground. It landed, unbroken, among some chickens, who sat on it as one of their own. When the eagle chick was hatched, it was lovingly raised by the chickens. Thinking it was a chicken, the eaglet behaved like a chicken. But one day a large eagle flew over the chicken yard where the now full-grown eagle was pecking away among the chickens at grain on the ground.

"What are you doing?" shouted the eagle as it circled overhead. "You are an eagle; why are you pecking around on the ground like some chicken?" The young eagle looked up and said, "That's what I learned from my parents." After circling around again, the large eagle cried, "You are no chicken; you're an eagle. Act like one. Stop pecking around on the ground and fly!" After a couple of failed attempts to use its wings, the young eagle slowly rose up into the air and flew away. The young eagle's heart was filled with awe and joy as it magnificently soared high on the winds.

A Parable P.S. to de Mello's Story

The young eagle rejoiced to find out who he truly was and flew back to share the good news with his foster parents in the chicken yard. It was almost night when he arrived, and all the chickens were in the Chicken Coop. He entered the coop and proudly announced, "I've discovered that I'm an eagle! Thank you for feeding and caring for me when I was a little chick. Now I must fly away and be who I really am." The Chicken Coop was filled with shouts of angry outrage. The High Rooster solemnly declared, "You will not! No one leaves the Chicken Coop! Regardless of who you *think* you are, you are one of us, and here you will stay. Anyone who leaves the Chicken Coop sins gravely and will go to hell!"

The thought of being condemned to hell filled the young eagle with panic, so he never again left the Chicken Coop. Upon learning of the young eagle's decision, the large eagle flew low over the Chicken Coop and shouted down at him, "Chicken!"

A MEDITATION ON "SEE, I MAKE ALL THINGS NEW"[39]

These words of the Cosmic One who is seated upon the throne in the Book of Revelation echo the words of God in Isaiah, "See, I am doing something new."[40] It's paradoxical that organized religions and institutionalized churches — even those that honor these Scripture passages — typically disdain whatever is new in favor of the very old. Church members often seem more moved to worship in old-style Gothic churches fragrant with embalmed medieval surroundings and rituals. The rule of thumb for church buildings is *the older, the better*. While these grand stone structures demand constant repair at great expense, the costs are gladly borne by the faithful since these great religious shrines are a source of church pride and also of great financial profit because of all the tourist-pilgrims. Yet what if the overriding principle was not restoration but renewal?

While great medieval Gothic cathedrals in Europe or in America are inspirational, are they true to the Scriptures? To find a worship space in harmony with those inspired words of Revelation, perhaps the best place to go is Japan, to visit the shrines of Ise. These shrines are always new — or at least never more than twenty years old. Since about 690 C.E. (A.D.), both the *Naiku*, or Inner Shrine to the supreme goddess Amaterasu-Omikami, and the *Geku*, or Outer Shrine to Toyouke-no-Omikami, the goddess of food, clothing and life necessities, have been rebuilt from the ground up every twenty years.

Over the centuries a ceremony of reconstructing a new shrine has been repeated at Ise with great devotion. Every care is taken to ensure that the new structure will be as beautiful and elegant as the one replaced. In *The Creators,* Daniel J. Boorstin writes, "In the Ise tradition, the

Japanese do not waste their energies repairing the great works of the past. Instead, they do the same work over and over again themselves. They build their Chartres [medieval French cathedral] anew in each generation."[41]

Think of the profound spiritual ramifications if every twenty years we would completely rebuild our parish churches from the ground up! We could even go a step beyond the Ise tradition of repeating their previous design and make our churches completely new. Would not such a radical rebuilding also have a significant effect upon making our faith expression new? Architecture shapes attitudes. Old architecture reinforces old ideas. New architecture forms new ideas. We might thus consider building only in wood rather than in stone or brick so that our ideas don't become set in stone, so that our ways of understanding truth and our ways of relating to each other can more easily be refashioned by the Creative Spirit's hand.

If you have already been "bricked in" by the structure of your church, you can still find creative ways every twenty years or so to become a completely new church community. Even if you can't change the architecture of your church building, you can reform the architecture of your community's soul. While this is easier to do in the Japanese Ise way of harmony with nature's rise and decline, remember that nothing is impossible with the help of God.

Churches and shrines are symbols of each one of us. Continuously freshen up your daily prayers by making them new. Experiment with saying new prayers, with different ways to be grateful, with exhilarating new ways to be joyful. While keeping some ritual observances as anchors, you might view your personal church as being made not of stone, or even wood, but of cloth! Allow the Holy Wind to gently twist and turn you in ever new ways of prayer and spiritual practice. Then you can say, "See, Lord, like you, I am making all things new."

ESCAPE TOOL #43 – BE NAUGHTY AND PRAY OUTDOORS

Pre-religious spiritualities were intimately connected with nature. Creation itself was the cathedral that deeply nourished the spirituality of these peoples. Although the scenes of the greatest occasions in Christian experience — the Incarnation, the Paschal Mystery, the Ascension and Pentecost — are all set outdoors, Christianity has become an indoor religion. Christianity is an urban dweller, and when it functions outside a building it tends to be awkward. From early on, Christianity has been suspicious of nature's potential religious charisma. A thousand years ago, according to the Franciscan priest William Short, those coming to confession were asked by the priest, "Did you pray elsewhere than in church, that is, near a spring, near stones, near trees or at a crossroads?"[42] If the answer was yes, it was followed by condemnation and dire warnings. A millennium later, today's clergy still often malign and belittle those who prefer to worship under the stars or among the trees instead of praying inside God's house.

For your soul to expand and your spirit to be set free, however, you may need to be naughty and pray outside as often as possible. Escape into the Great Temple in which Christ the Liberator performed all his religious deeds, that Cosmic Cathedral of the Universe, in all its ten billion galaxies. That wall-less, ceiling-less church is ever being created anew as the universe expands at the speed of light racing to follow the Creator's tracks.

BE HOPEFUL – WHAT A DIFFERENCE FIFTY YEARS CAN MAKE

Early in this twenty-first century, religious fundamentalism in Christian churches and other world religions appears to be escalating rapidly. Yet, be hopeful. Things can change dramatically in a relatively short time. The Second Vatican Council's statement that, "...all share in true equality with regard to dignity and activity...for the building up of the Body of Christ"[24] came only fifty-two years after a declaration by Pope Pius X. Early in the last century Pius stated, "The church is essentially an unequal society. That is, it is a society formed by pastors and flock...as far as the multitude is concerned they have no other duty than to let themselves be led."

Sunset Splendor

As this new century unfolds, remember history when you evaluate the drive of religious restorationists to return to former times and hold various positions of religious fundamentalism. Remember too that as the sun is at its most spectacular at sunset, so it is with societies and institutions. In *The Time Falling Bodies Take to Light*, William Thompson says that when some established way of life is ending there is inevitably a struggle by people to hold on to that way of life by giving to it a more intense expression.[5] When knighthood was about to disappear in the declining years of the Middle Ages, the knights' body armor became very elaborate. It was similar with the Native American Indians when they were overwhelmed by the immigrant Europeans' rapid expansion into their lands. As their way of life was about to be destroyed, they created the Ghost Dance. This ritual recalled the former splendor of their culture and affirmed their ultimate victory over their white oppressors. The past century's explosion of small independent ethnic nations — each proudly waving its flag and ethnic identity — was a glorious finale to an earlier era. This happened as the world was being fused together by technology and business to create a global reality.

So, view the present state of the world with abounding hope. See the frantic armed combat between members of different religions, the disguised and blatant religious prejudice and the declarations of orthodox superiority as expressions of a holy Ghost Dance of a dying age.

Chapter Fifteen
Old Age Prison

Many a reader of this book will consider this chapter a "skipper" or perhaps a "saver" to be read when they are old. Yet regardless of your age, you're already on your way to this predestined prison. So, there's no better time than now to begin to plan your escape route.

The only crime of which those incarcerated in this prison are guilty is growing old. Aging is not a criminal activity, yet how easily it turns one's body and mind into a prison. Moreover, aging is that fearful penitentiary whose inmates, in time, all become Death Row residents.

> Aging is dreaded.
> Aging is denied.
> Aging is imprisoning.
> Aging is ugly.

ANTIQUES ARE BEAUTIFUL; BEING ONE ISN'T

So unattractive is aging that annually billions of dollars are spent attempting to camouflage it with hair dyes and hairpieces, facial creams and skin tucks. While these provide a temporary cover-up, they do not assist your escape from old age; in fact, they can hinder you! Society's idolatry of youth is incarcerating, jailing in jealousy those no longer youthful as they envy their slim-bodied, youthful and godlike juniors.

The youthful, hearty, supple Adonis and Venus are the deities worshipped in the Temple of Physical Fitness. Indeed, ancient is the quest to escape being ancient: the exploration to find the fabled Fountain of Youth. Today's Ponce de Leon chemists search for the elixir of youth not in the swamps of Florida but in their test tubes and gene cell reformations. Live longer and look younger: This is the promise of twenty-first century chemistry.

No one has yet escaped — or ever can escape — Eden's curse of physical aging. The wise, however, can find freedom by truly growing as they grow old, regardless of how much their bodies age and decline. While life appears to be lived by the young and only observed by the old, for those who attain wisdom it is in reality the other way around. For who can truly know how to live until having tasted the vintage of many seasons? Do not envy the young; admire and appreciate their physical beauty while seeking an ever deeper inner beauty. Seek liberation from the deterioration of old age by germinating an ever more youthful mind and spirit. Seek your senior liberty by consciously and wisely emigrating to the next stage of life.

THE FIRST WAVE OF IMMIGRATION

Deported prisoners were among the first immigrant settlers to arrive in the American English colonies. They were later followed by thousands of escaping prisoners. These latter immigrants had successfully broken out of the prisons of poverty and oppression in their homelands. They were eagerly migrating in search of liberty and a better life. In 1869 alone, over 352,000 immigrants arrived in America. History records that the transcontinental railroad could not have been built without the backbreaking labor of these Chinese, Irish and other foreign immigrants. Fifteen years later, in 1884, over one and a half million immigrants specially recruited from Europe arrived to homestead farms and towns along the new railroad lines that spanned the vast empty prairies. Between the years 1881 and 1890, over five million immigrants arrived in America, and these new foreign residents were essential for the development and expansion of our country.

THE NEW WAVE OF IMMIGRANTS

A new, vastly larger wave of immigrants than the millions who came in the nineteenth century is presently approaching America's shores. Unlike previous immigrants, they are not foreigners. They are Americans born between 1946 and 1964, and their numbers have been estimated at over 78 million![1] This great new wave, of course, is comprised of those on the threshold of immigration into the land of old age. As Malcolm Cowley said, "To enter the country of old age is a new experience, different from what you suppose it to be. Nobody, man or woman, knows the country until he has lived in it and has taken out his citizenship papers."[2]

While the actual year of entering old age is ambiguous and indefinite, two things are clear. Not only is the number of immigrants increasing, so too are the borders of the country of old age. Among the 273 million Americans, there are now 70,000 centenarians — those over one hundred years of age. Once newsworthy, that advanced age will soon become commonplace. The U.S. Census Bureau estimates that by the middle of the twenty-first century the number of centenarians will reach 834,000! Like nineteenth century immigrants to America, these immigrants on their way to 100, or at least to an advanced age, will also greatly contribute to our culture and nation. Yet as we can see, old age will become an extended period of life that will require advance preparation if it is to be rich and fruitful.

Prudent are those who prepare for each new stage of life, and even more critical is the preparation required for migration to the last twenty to thirty years. While the majority of this new wave of immigrants is not packing their bags, being in communal denial of their aging, entering into your senior years can be an adventure of freely emigrating — or it can make you a victim of deportation. Blessed are those who in their forties or early fifties begin to pack their bags and make plans to freely enter their senior years. Typically, preparations are focused only on medical care plans and financial security. While these realities certainly need attention, they are only one aspect of the strategic anticipation of old age.

Reflect on Malcolm Cowley's image of seniors taking out citizenship papers in the Country of Old Age. Our immigrant ancestors, seeking to fully enjoy all the benefits of citizenship in their new homeland of the United States, attended naturalization classes. To become a liberated senior citizen who can enjoy all the benefits of the Country of Old Age requires similar preparation.

SENIOR CITIZENSHIP CLASS

Liberation and immigration are parallel processes. May the following imaginary immigrant citizenship class provide opportunities for you to explore ways to escape from *geriatricphobia,* the fear of old age. That haunting terror contains horrible images of being incarcerated in a nursing home, spending your last years as a captive of a rocking chair, sentenced to unproductive, empty hours and being victimized by physical pain and incapacity.

Welcome students, regardless of your age, to the Country of Old Age, where you will soon become citizens with full rights and benefits. You say you're not old? Regardless of your age, one day you will live in the Land of Seniors, and it is essential that you do not immigrate as some prisoner of fate or as an aged-alien, a stranger in a strange land. For your thoughtful reflection a variety of presenters will offer their liberating thoughts and personal histories of aging to assist you. Each of these presenters is an escapee from the prison of old age and is a good role model for those who wish to be liberated seniors. So students,

> Pay attention.
> Do not sleep in class.
> Take notes.
> Ask questions.
> And there *will* be an examination.

I have the pleasure to introduce our first presenter, Jesus the teacher of Galilee. Indeed, while refusing various titles of honor such as Messiah and Lord, he never objected to the title of *teacher.*

"Thank you. Well, students of aging, it is a privilege to share with you some of my thoughts on life and death. If you wish to live to a good old age and die a happy death, 'Do not be afraid of those who can kill the body, but cannot destroy the soul; rather be afraid of the one who can kill both the body and soul.'[3] The Spirit is the soul of youthfulness, wonder and curiosity. Take heed, my friends, in your middle age, 'avoid greed in all forms, for though one may be rich, one's life does not consist of possessions.'[4] Consider the wealthy farmer who built larger barns to hoard his great harvest. 'God said to him, "You fool, this night your life will be demanded of you, and the things you have prepared, to whom will they belong?"

Thus will it be for the one who stores up treasures for himself but is not rich in what matters to God.'[5] Or take the case of old Cardinal Mazarin, who would drag himself through the crowded galleries of his art collection mumbling, 'We shall have to leave all this behind.' Poor man, he failed to learn the secret of life that anything capable of being grasped in your hand is also capable of slipping like sand through your fingers. If only Cardinal Mazarin had sought after what cannot be possessed, then his last days would have been full of life and joy. Students of old age, if you have not yet learned that lesson, begin today to enjoy with all your heart what cannot be held in your hands.

"You may ask, what can be had without it being possessed? Love, for one thing, and life, for another. The very reason I came into this world was to offer a wondrous gift: '...that you might have life and have it in great abundance.'[6] I must have spoken about life a hundred times — it is at the heart of my good news. Whenever I spoke about having life in great abundance, I never understood why people thought I was just speaking about something beyond the grave — what religion refers to as eternal life. All life is eternal; it is an endless river of infinity. I am Life — because I am one with God, who is Life. If you live in God, and God lives in you, then your life today, tomorrow and into endless tomorrows is infinite. I like what Michael Talbot said, 'We are, as the aborigines say, just learning how to survive in infinity.'[7]

"An important part of aging is striving be like those Australian Aborigines by learning today how to live in infinity. To do so has tremendous implications for your ability to love one another and your enjoyment of life. Be awake to the fact that each day of your life you are making your infinity. Not only you senior citizens, everyone at any age should be consciously building their infinity. Use the precious little time allowed each of you in your life span to make a beautifully rich infinity. I am infinitely alive, and you will be too if you accept my challenge of life in great abundance. My lifestyle included living with gusto, zeal and great intensity. I was able to do so because I constantly had my approaching death in view. If you wish to taste the fullness of life, frame your life within the reality of your death. Come to terms with your death; speak about it often, as I did. Speaking to others about your death is actually life-giving since it confronts the great lie, the denial of death. If you strive to live today in infinity, in the real mystery of my life, you will never be taken a prisoner of aging or death.

"Thank you for listening. It has been a pleasure sharing these thoughts with you."

Our next teacher is the Spanish mystic, Saint John of the Cross.

"Students of aging, what do you expect to experience in your elder years? That is a critical question since what we receive from God is what we expect from God. Think about that. If you expect little, then you will receive little. Jesus said, 'Ask, and you shall receive.'[8] That saying is packed with the unspoken wisdom, 'Don't ask, and you won't receive.' God, your Beloved, longs to lavish upon you all that you need and desire from life. So have faith in your expectations of life's gifts. Recall that in some villages Jesus could not work any miracles because the people didn't believe; they didn't expect anything. Many are those who expect their elder years to be unproductive, sad and lonely, and unfortunately their expectations are realized."

Next, students, we will hear from the author of *Tropic of Cancer*, Henry Miller, who will speak from his personal experience of aging.

"I'm eighty-one years old... The whole society from time immemorial has always worshipped youth...(yet) we all know who've been through youth that it's far from being a glorious period in one's life.... Youth has to do with spirit, not age. Men of seventy and eighty are often more youthful than the young. Theirs is real youth...it's the youth of mind and spirit, which is everlasting...."[9] "As you near the end, your sense of wonder increases.... If you were to ask me on my deathbed, What is your last word? I'd probably say, 'Mystery.' Everything understandable becomes more and more mysterious to me. Not more and more familiar, but more and more mysterious.... So what is the most important thing in life? It is Spirit, with a capital S. Without it you are nobody, nothing...."[10]

Our next presenter is Maurice Goudeket, the author of "The Delights of Growing Old." He was married for thirty years to the famous French novelist, Colette. A few years after her death he remarried, and at age seventy-one became the father of his first child, a son. He shares with our citizenship class some of his thoughts about being age 75.

"And now every fresh day finds me more filled with wonder and better qualified to draw the last drop of delight from it.... Is it indeed this that they call growing old, this continued surge of memories that comes breaking in on my inner silence, this contained and sober joy, this lighthearted music that bears me up, this wider window on the world, this spreading kinder feeling and this gentleness? 'I have nothing to do today.' That is a remark that no longer has any sort of meaning to me...so many activities open before me that my only difficulty is choosing between them.... I get up before anyone else in my household, not because sleep has deserted me in my advancing years, but because an intense eagerness to live draws me from my bed. In the same way I drop off every night with a kind of secret satisfaction as I think of the day to come.... Every morning my breakfast coffee has a fresh taste, and this comes from me as much as it does from the pot."[11]

Here, students, is our final guide into senior years.

"Future citizens of Old Age, allow me to introduce myself. I am the playwright Paul Zindel. I encourage you not to be anxious as you age, for you are only going through another evolution in life. The central component of what makes you who you are cannot die! I would like to present to you the opening lines of my play *The Effects of Gamma Rays on Man-in-the-Moon Marigolds*. As the house lights go down and the curtain opens upon on a darkened stage, the voice of Tillie is heard:

'He told me to look at my hand, for a part of it came from a star that exploded too long ago to imagine. This part of me was formed from a tongue of fire that screamed through the heavens until there was our sun. And this part of me — this tiny part of me — was on the sun when it itself exploded and whirled in a great storm until the planets came to be. And this small part of me was then a whisper of the earth. When there was life, perhaps this part of me got lost in a fern that was crushed and covered until it was coal. And then it was a diamond millions of years later — it must have been a diamond as beautiful as the star from which it had first come. Or perhaps this part of me became lost in a terrible beast, or became part of a huge bird that flew above the primeval swamps.

And he said this thing was so small — this part of me was so small it couldn't be seen — but it was there from the beginning of the world.

And he called this bit of me an atom.

And when he wrote the word, I fell in love with it.

Atom.

Atom.

What a beautiful word.'[12]"

Thank you, Paul. Well, students, that concludes this class. I regret that we lacked time to hear from others who made their last years so productive. I refer to seniors like P.T. Barnum, who at the age of 71 was inspired to join his circus with James Bailey's to create "The Greatest Show on Earth," the famous Barnum and Bailey Circus. Who said senior years have to mean inactivity!

Then there's Frank Lloyd Wright, who at age 91 designed the famous New York Guggenheim Museum. Never say you're too old to leave behind something of great beauty. Moreover, aging doesn't prevent making a difference in society. Mahatma Gandhi was age 77 when he successfully completed negotiations with Great Britain to grant India its independence. And Good Pope John XXIII was 77 when he became pope and began the reformation of the Catholic Church by calling together the Second Vatican Council. He was 80 years old when the Council began — so who says revolutionaries must be young?

At the age of 74 Galileo published his masterpiece, *Dialogue Concerning the Two New Sciences.* Michelangelo was 72 when he began his work as the architect of Saint Peter's Basilica, and Antonio Stradivarius was in his 90s when he fashioned his most famous masterpiece violins, the *Habeneck* and *Muntz.* Political revolutionaries, artists, writers, architects, painters and countless ordinary people have made their last years their most productive. Students about to receive your citizenship in the Country of Old Age, do not retire — graduate!

Old Age Exam

Take a few minutes to review what you learned from this class. These exam questions reflect the ideas presented by our visiting speakers.

1. Do you daily try to find ways to use your creativity?
2. Do you expect from God a long and enjoyable life?
3. Do you believe that real youth is of the spirit, not the body?
4. Do you enjoy it when life seems mysterious, or do you want everything to be explainable?
5. Do you strive always to learn new things and experiment with new ideas? Do you find change refreshing or threatening?
6. Do you question ideas, positions and convictions? Are you curious even about your religious beliefs?
7. Do you make play part of your lifestyle? Do you enjoy the acts of tinkering and dabbling?
8. Do you exercise both your body and mind on a regular basis?
9. Do you seek ways to experience wonder?
10. Do you experience life in great abundance, as Jesus promised, or does the vitality of your life seem to be decreasing?
11. Do you practice how to survive and live in infinity?
12. Do you try to live with zest and enthusiasm?

Surplus Time – a Gift or a Curse

According to Horace Deets, AARP executive director, our life expectancy is almost 30 years longer than it was at the beginning of the twentieth century. The average life span in 1900 was 47 years, and as this new century began the average life duration was 77! In a way, you've been given a bonus of an extra 30 years! So, ask yourself, "For what purpose? What will I do with those bonus years?"

You have two basic choices. The first is to cultivate a lifestyle that includes a good diet, physical exercise and ongoing learning, creativity and prayer. The other choice is a lifestyle of inactivity, disease, overweight, loneliness and depression. Those who choose the first option can echo John J. McNeill; "…as my body grows older, my spirit becomes younger.… I am now 73 years old. I have discovered that every decade of my life has been happier and more peaceful than the last. Each decade has brought with it a greater intimacy with a God of mercy and love and a greater trust in God's love for me."[13]

Aging and Liberty

The loss of freedom is always painful. An apprehension about the loss of personal liberty that usually accompanies old age is a healthy concern. A defensive anticipation would include learning to be disabled — not in the sense of being crippled but, rather, in not being free to come and go as you please. Recall that when you were a teenager one of the precious rewards of growing older was reaching the age when you could get a driver's license. That small piece of paper was your Declaration of Independence. Your giddy freedom of movement was soon taken for granted, until some mechanical failure or a blizzard prevented you from exercising your liberty to come and go as you wished. By contrast, anticipate that your extended senior years will eventually impair your freedom of movement by preventing you from driving an automobile. In the last twenty years of the twentieth century the number of *fatal* crashes involving drivers over the age of 70 had risen 42%!

In the first twenty years of this new century the number of drivers 70 and over will explode to over 30 million! Highway professionals concerned about the implications of this reality are warning that Golden Age drivers will soon kill more motorists than drunk drivers! While many seniors drive safely into their 90s, many other aged drivers suffer from poor vision and hearing, partial paralysis, slower reactions and even dementia. Be prepared, then, for the appearance of an aggressive campaign initiated not by MADD but by MAAD, *Mothers Against Aged Drivers.* The public may well demand new laws forcing senior drivers to take frequent vision, hearing and road tests. Senior driving may also become very expensive as the highway death rate caused by older drivers will cause increasingly escalating auto insurance costs. While science, diet and exercise may allow you to live thirty to forty years longer than those of the last century, you may experience significantly restricted freedom of independent movement. Wise seniors will practice being gracefully dependent as they maintain maximum independence.

Homo Sedens and Play

Sage seniors will also exercise. Resist becoming *Homo sedens* (a sitting human), and daily be an active *Homo erectus,* (upright, walking human). After the age of fifty the inclination is to allow oneself to physically sag and to engage only in sedentary activities. Resist this inclination with determination. Proper physical exercise is essential for the graceful aging of both body and mind. The human body is not designed for inactivity. Minimizing the negative effects of aging requires being more or less as physically active in your 40s and 50s as you were in your 20s.

On the other hand, while bodily activity is essential to healthy aging, it must be done wisely, with healthy accommodation to your age and physical condition. Between 1990 and 1996, according to the U.S. Consumer Product Safety Commission, sports-related injuries in men and women 65 and older increased by 54%. The fifty-year-old weekend athletes in age-denial who attempt to play aggressive sports with their aging, out-of-shape bodies pay for their play with physical injuries. Whatever the exercise, it should be done with common sense.

Recess time! When you were a child in school, recess was an important time in the day. The same is true for seniors, otherwise known as aging children. The function of recess times in elementary school is for children to burn off excess energy so they can quietly resume their studies. For elder-children, it's done for the opposite reason — to create energy! Healthy energized seniors engage in at least thirty minutes of daily play in such forms as walking, gardening, yoga or swimming. Recess-exercise retards anxiety and depression since it increases the brain's feel-good chemicals such as serotonin. It also lowers levels of adrenaline, which can contribute to negative moods. At the minimum, one should exercise at least three times a week. Yet while no normal child would refuse to go out to play at recess, it often takes self-discipline for older adults to go out for recess.

Fred Warshofsky offers good advice when he says, "Live on the second or third floor all your life, and take the stairs. Building muscles directly benefits the heart."[14] Even if you live on the ground level, don't ride elevators, but use the stairs every chance you get. While it takes more time to use the stairs, the health benefits are worth the few lost minutes.

The brain needs oxygen to remain healthy. Exercise promotes an increased flow of oxygenated blood, revitalizing both mind and body. Along with a fresh supply of blood, the mind also needs intellectual exercise. Stimulate your mind with crossword puzzles, do math without a calculator, learn new and different things, read challenging books.

New ideas create a growth in the brain of new dendritic branches, and stimulating activity pumps rejuvenating chemicals into broader areas of the mind, aiding keen thinking and increased memory functioning.

PREVENT DESTRUCTIVE AGING BY BEING GODLIKE

The first thing we learn about God in our Judaic-Christian Scriptures is that God is creative. So be Godlike by using your creativity. If you wish to enjoy those bonus thirty years of life, begin today to find enjoyable outlets for your creativity. You say you're not creative? Quite frankly, that's nonsense! Everyone is creative! After all, each of us is made in the image of God, and God is creative. Jamake Highwater states, "Among the languages of American Indians there is no word for 'art.' For Indians everything is art...therefore it needs no name."[15] It is heresy to believe that creativity is reserved only for artistic people, for everyone began life as a creative person. To produce a painting, a pie, a garden, a beautiful meal or to make love is to be Godlike. As soon as we realize that we are indeed creative, we begin increasingly to reap positive benefits. Creativity grows us. Those who in midlife start to exercise their creativity enjoy increased physical and mental health and find their creative activities even more enriching in their elder years. Expressions of creativity produce a deep sense of well-being and self-esteem. Moreover, positive emotions birthed by creativity encourage the growth of our immune functioning, holding at bay sickness and the negative effects of aging. Remember: Creativity grows us.

CREATIVITY EQUATION

This empowering divine-human activity of creativity is defined by Gene Cohen as, "our innate capacity for growth."[16] He created an equation similar to Einstein's theory of relativity equation, $E = Mc^2$, calling his $C = Me^2$. In Cohen's equation, creativity is C, while the M is the mass of knowledge, which is multiplied by the effects of two dimensions of experience squared: e^2. The first of these dimensions of experience is our psychological and emotional growth over the years, while the second is the accumulated experience of life with its accompanying wisdom. Our years from middle age on into old age can be a most creative period since we have acquired a deep well of experiences on which to draw.

Recent research has shown that in the second half of life creative expression along with ongoing education and new learning not only challenge our brains but also cause further positive biological changes. Studies have shown that brain cells involved in the use of the memory and thinking appear to communicate with one another in two basic ways. Cohen speaks of this interaction, "One way is through branch-like extensions known as dendrites. The other way is through the release of chemical messengers between these branches...sprouting new dendritic branches and an increase in production of acetylcholine, the chemical messenger most involved in memory and thinking functions."[17]

After the age of fifty, each decade provides unique gifts to creative elders. Besides the gift of increased liberation that comes with retirement from the normal business duties of life, there is the state of psychological freedom that could be called the liberty to "fool around" and experiment. Healthy, mature seniors enjoy the novel freedom from the need always to be successful, allowing them to engage in a form of experimenting that is so critical in our society: playing with failure. No longer under pressure to prove themselves as important to anyone, no longer obsessed with "having" always to be right or know the correct answer, they can now enjoy expeditions into uncharted waters. At the age of 86, Pablo Picasso produced a series of 347 novel, daring etchings. He continued painting for the rest of his life before dying one morning at age 92, after having spent the entire previous night painting! Giuseppe Verdi composed his operatic masterpiece *Othello* when he was 74 and *Falstaff* when he was 80. While you may not be making masterpieces like Picasso or Verdi, you do have the creative potential to make beautiful servantpieces.

SERVANTPIECES

Anyone can create servantpieces! These are special yet often commonplace creative artworks that enhance the lives of others: a beautiful and delicious dinner, rearranging your house with an artistic flare, elegantly escorting an elderly person on an outing, creating a lovely flower garden or writing a poem. The first poem I learned by heart was one I discovered as a child on the bathroom wall of the home of my two unmarried elderly aunts. While brief, it deals with the most common obstacle to creativity and an enjoyable life:

Through fear of taking risks in life
I've missed a lot of fun.
But the only things that I regret
Are those I haven't done.

Each person's creativity is imprisoned by that fear of taking risks, of making mistakes and looking silly. Whenever you are held captive by the risking-taking fear, pray to the Enterprising Spirit for the gift of daring and then plunge deeply into whatever precarious venture you fear. As you dive beneath the surface anxiety of risk-taking, be aware that every act of creativity is of God and so is an occasion of prayer. Making a meal can be prayer. Creatively making love can be prayer. Arranging flowers in a vase can be prayer. Being with a grandchild who is drawing a picture and daringly drawing one of your own can be prayer.

Of course, along with ample occasions for creativity, old age is marked by a progressive diminishment of body and mind. Time draws its distinctive declining image on the canvas of our face and physique, its slow strokes wearing down the flesh and bringing accompanying aches and pains. The loss of memory is embarrassing. The piercing pains of arthritis are disabling. For those who have reached an antique age-line, mirrors are avoided: Painful is the distorted image of our methodically deteriorating form. While the magic of self-deception can make mirrors fib for a time, photos don't lie. Photographs usually are unbecomingly revealing; their frozen-still mirror-images of reality are disagreeable and disturbing, twisted images with ugly liver spots, sagging wrinkles and disappearing hair.

Quite likely, the elder Jesus knew from personal experience the physical diminishments that appear with aging. The social-scientist Scripture scholars Malina and Rohrbaugh tell us that at age 33 he would already be an elder in his culture.[18] Perhaps sixty percent of the population would have died by age sixteen, and seventy-five percent would only reach their mid twenties. Fewer lived beyond their thirties, and ninety percent would be dead by their mid forties. Moreover, Jesus' body was certainly not that of today's 30-year-old. It would have shown much more advanced signs of aging caused by the poor diet and harsh living conditions of the average peasant, which further made for a low resistance to disease. He certainly must have recognized these prophetic ominous signs that his days were numbered and, therefore, did not blind himself to the nearness of his death.

THE LAST SUPPER MEMORY MAKING

Among the various fears associated with growing older and dying is the dread of having to leave behind those who depend upon us. Jesus personally knew that anguished feeling of having to leave those who relied upon him in many ways. As he and his friends shared their last meal together, he promised, "If you love me...I will not leave you orphans; I will come to you."[19] Cannot we who are believers in the Communion, and Communication, of Saints also make that promise? Death cannot divide what love has joined together. As the Liberator-Savior prepared for his Passover into the fullness of infinity, he created a bridge between himself and his friends, saying, "Do this in memory of me."[20]

At his Last Supper, he urged them, "Remember me," each time you break bread, share fish and take wine together. At this last of many such meals, during which they had shared food and love, he also promised, "...I will be with you always."[21] Remembrance is the key given to those whom death leaves behind, a key that frees them from the incarcerating grief of loss. Follow his example whether your death seems near or far and imitate the Master's invitation: "Each time you hear that song, remember me. Each time you walk in this garden, remember me. Whenever you drive down this road, remember me. As you elevate your wine glass, remember me." The possibilities of this Holy Presence-by-Remembering are as many and diverse as there are times of shared love and friendship.

THE LAST BREAKFAST

After his resurrection, the Risen Jesus appeared several times to his disciples when they were gathered at table. After a night of fishing in the Sea of Galilee, his disciples also experienced him in a sunrise morning meal on the seashore. At this *Last Breakfast* Eucharist, the Risen One shared a cookout of fish and bread. At this meal he also spoke with them about old age. After asking Peter three times if he loved him, the Risen Jesus quoted a Palestinian proverb about old age: "When you were young, you used to dress yourself and go where you wanted; but when you grow old, you will stretch out your hands and someone else will put on your clothes for you and lead where you do not want to go…. Follow me."[22]

While Jesus used that folk proverb to foretell the fate of Simon Peter, it also has personal implications for each of us. The proverb describes the mandatory surrender that takes place in the last years of old age, like being led away to a nursing home or simply having someone else have to dress us and help us walk. The words of the Risen Liberator advise a graceful compliance in the final disabling stages of aging. "Graceful" means embracing with love, gentleness and dignity what destiny holds for us in our final days. For seniors, the Risen Jesus' words at the Last Breakfast about Simon Peter's approaching death should be as significant as his words at the Last Supper. A paradoxical marriage unites and harmonizes those two discourses. Like a divine duet they sing of love's loyalty to the bitter end and of a faith-saturated surrendering in love. Blessed, then, are those elders who welcome the slow physical and mental losses of old age with such an Islamic love.

SURRENDERING TO MYSTICAL INTIMACY

The very word *Islam* means "surrender." By definition, Muslims are those who have surrendered themselves to the will of God. A holy death is one preceeded by a holy old age, which involves an *Islamic* capitulation to the aches and pains of our elder years. This is not a white-flag surrender of a defeated warrior or the white towel thrown into the ring by a bloody, battered, exhausted boxer lying on the mat. Rather, it is a lover's ecstatic surrender to the beloved's embrace.

Teilhard de Chardin, at the height of his life, composed this prayer: "Lord, grant that I may see, that I may see You, that I may see and feel You present in all things and animating all things."[23] His writings reveal a man who strove to see God in others and in all of creation — indeed, throughout the cosmos. Later, as his body began its natural decline, an aging Chardin realized that this desired mystical eyesight required an ever greater dose of faith and surrender. In *The Divine Milieu*, he wrote,

> …may I recognize you under the species of each alien or hostile force that seems bent upon destroying and uprooting me. When the signs of age begin to mark my body (still more when they

touch my mind); when the ill that is to diminish me or carry me off strikes from without or is born within me; when the painful moment comes in which I suddenly awaken to the fact that I am ill or growing old...in these dark moments, O God, grant that I may understand that it is you...who are painfully parting the fibers of my being in order to penetrate to the very marrow of my substance.[24]

In his old age, Chardin saw that our greatest life-assignment is experiencing the Divine Mystery in the diminishing abilities of our body and mind. What a challenge! The invisible God is readily perceived in the wonders of nature, when "the Glory" is expressed in flesh and flower. It doesn't require great faith to be stunned awake by great beauty. We easily find the presence of God in the glorious radiance of a sunset, in the vast, sweeping majesty of a blue-green ocean or in the wonder of a child's birth. What requires real faith-sight is experiencing God in the agony of arthritis, feeling God's fingers creasing your face into a mass of wrinkles or slowly erasing your fondest memories. The mission of the greatest mystics is to have the ultimate mystical vision of seeing and feeling God in the physical decline that leads to death. The climactic mystical communion involves surrendering to the process of being slowly consumed by God as you shrink and stoop, wrinkle by wrinkle and ache by ache, until in death you and God become fully one.

SURRENDERING TO GLORY

In his poem, "Ode: Intimations of Immortality from the Recollections of Early Childhood," William Wordsworth wrote,

> Our birth is but a sleep and a forgetting,
> (We)...cometh from afar:
> Not in entire forgetfulness,
> And not in utter nakedness,
> But trailing clouds of glory do we come
> From God, who is our home:
> Heaven lies about us in our infancy!
> Shades of the prison-house begin to close
> Upon the growing boy.[25]

"Trailing clouds of glory do we come." What a magnificent description of our birth entry into this world. Wordsworth's beautiful image is radically different from religion's prevailing depiction of us as entering life crippled and permanently disfigured before God by the repulsive reality of original sin. Those who are graced to go through the aging process in a sacred way have usually struggled for a lifetime to escape from the prison-house that seeks to prevent them from basking in heaven's glory present not only at birth but throughout their life. Pray for the graceful gift to depart from this earth for your God-Home in the same way as you entered into it: "trailing clouds of glory." As you pray for that kind of holy death, remember that we usually receive from God what we expect.

Chapter Fifteen Inventory of Escape Tools and Unshackling Reflections

ESCAPE TOOL #44 – VINTAGE MEMORIES

You can escape old age's imprisonment by bottling your memories. In *The Journey's Echo,* Freya Stark compares memories to wine, "Good days are to be gathered like sunshine in grapes, to be trodden and bottled up into wine and kept for age to sip at ease beside his fire. If the traveler [of life] has vintaged well, he need trouble to wander no longer: the ruby moments glow in his glass at will."[26] Even those of us whose physical movements are restricted by aging can still journey backwards in time whenever we remember.

In "The Delights of Growing Old," Maurice Goudeket adds, "All the time there is a humming of the great swarm of memories feeding upon my past years, and the mere throbbing of my arteries makes my head swim like wine."[27]

THE ART OF MAKING WINE

Sage seniors, especially after an enjoyable dinner, a conversation with a good friend or making love, make fine wine by bottling up those memories. The method is simple and takes only a few seconds: First, lovingly squeeze the grapes of the experience into juice. Then, add a splash of the water of wonder. Lastly, add generous amounts of the sugar of gratitude. Thus processed, pour the memorable experience into a wine bottle, cork it and store it away to age in the wine cellar of your heart. Visit your wine cellar frequently and gently remove the cork from a few selected bottles to sip your memories, savoring their life-giving elixir. The rarest vintages grow more delicious as they age. Wine drinking is good for the heart. Enjoying vintage memories also strengthens the immune system. Studies have shown that recalling previous pleasures of lovemaking and other happy times releases chemicals in the brain that heal us, increase our resistance to disease and nourish good health.

ESCAPE TOOL #45 – PRAYING IN BED

Upon awakening, before you get out of bed, pray. You can begin with a brief thank-you for a good night's sleep. Or if it was a restless night, briefly express thanks that you had a good bed in which to be restless. This can be followed by a second expression of gratitude for the gift of another day of life. To enhance this gift, frame the new day by praying, "Today, I am one day closer to my death." As easily as crystal is shattered, so this simple prayer smashes the illusion that we have endless days of life remaining. Nothing fractures wonder more than the fallacy that our death is far off. This false notion leads to one of the most frequently committed sins: taking life for granted. We take for granted not only life but the daily bounty of beauty it contains. We can also say this early morning prayer in its Native American Indian version: "Today is a good day to die." It's considered bad luck to get out of bed on the wrong side, but even more unfortunate for our enjoyment of life is to get out of bed without saying a brief prayer.

Two Prayers for Old Age

Chardin's Prayer

Echoing the words of John the Baptist in relation to Jesus, "I must decease and he must increase,"[28] as he grew old, Teilhard de Chardin prayed:

> [God] must grow greater in my life, in my Reality, and my interior world as I grow less...to accept, to love interior fragility and old age, with its long shadows, and the ever-shrinking days ahead...to love diminishments and decline.[29]

In this prayer Chardin speaks of loving the diminishments that come with old age. Though falling in love is usually considered a youthful adventure, he challenges us to fall in love with the ravages of old age by romancing our ever-dwindling days. The faces of those who are young and in love glow blissfully. The wrinkled faces of elders can also shine with a youthful inner radiance if, instead of only begrudgingly accepting their deterioration, they fall in love with their aging.

Abbe Cimetier's Prayer

Abbe Francisque Cimetier died in Lyons, France, in 1946. He had taken care that all his personal affairs were in order and at his death left behind only a single sheet of paper. That paper, found in a drawer in his desk, contained a prayer written in his own hand:

> O Energy of my Lord, irresistible and living Force, since, of us two, You are infinitely the stronger, it is for you to consume me in the union that shall fuse us together. Give me, then, something even more precious than the grace which all the faithful beg from you. It is not enough that I die in communion. Teach me communion in dying.[30]

Holy Communion is a central ritual of Christian worship, and for many is a weekly practice. Cimetier's prayer elevates each reception of Holy Communion into a holy rehearsal for our death. His prayer is an excellent post-communion reflection for those of any age, since none of us knows the time of our death. His prayer, or a similar prayer of your own composition, is especially suited for seniors. It's image of

God consuming us, instead of us consuming God in Christ, leads us into the reality of "communion in dying."

Escape Tool #46 – Holy Curiosity

While aging involves the natural loss of certain faculties, one quality that should never be lost is wonder. Albert Einstein said, "One cannot but be in awe when [one] contemplates the mysteries of eternity, of life, of the marvelous structure of reality. It is enough if one tries to merely comprehend a little of this mystery each day. Never lose a holy curiosity."

That question-mark-halo recommended by Einstein should be used as a crowbar. Use it to pry open religious beliefs to find in them the hidden wisdom so often clamped shut by dogma. Use it to jimmy open the mystery of the loves you have experienced in your life. Find inside them the mystery of God present in the touch of human flesh, in the exhilaration of passion and in the intimacy of shared hopes and dreams. Be curious, asking questions like, "Why is aging essential in the divine scheme of creation?" Use questions to ponder the wondrous webwork of your unfolding destiny in life. Even if you live to be over 100, never lose your holy curiosity.

Hungrily Waiting
and an Inclusive New York Times Prayer

John McNeill says, "My prayer life consists in being in touch with that hunger and thirst [for God], not letting anything fill it in or block it off, or hide it from me…my prayer life is then very simple. I spend a lot of time just being in touch with the longing, being open to it, and waiting…. I also spend some time everyday 'praying' *The New York Times*, formulating a prayer to every headline and article. In this way I strive to let my prayer reach out to the whole world."[31]

THE TWO GREAT A & A FEARS

Those immigrating to the Country of Old Age dread developing Alzheimers, the disease of dementia, especially when there is a history of it in their families. This affliction is more than the loss of short-term memory, it erases the knowledge of the identity of those you love and even your own identity.

Equally fear Alzheimers' cousin disease of *Alzheimersphere,* an affliction that affects hundreds of millions. This is a disease of the heart rather than the mind and imprisons its victims in only half a world: hence its name from hemisphere, meaning "half-a-globe." Those afflicted only think of the world in terms of the northern hemisphere. *Alzheimersphere* is also a form of dementia, in which its victims forget who they and others are. Its sufferers are unable to recognize their own brothers and sisters in the family of God who live in the other half of the world. They feel no compassion for their family members forced to labor in sweatshop working conditions so they and other *Alzheimersphere* sufferers can buy cheap clothing and appliances. In the name of Free Market Capitalism they bless and condone the exploitation of their very own sisters and brothers in the Third World, unable to recognize them as the exploited.

ESCAPE TOOL #47 – BE A DEFENSIVE WORRIER

Don't be an optimist when it comes to the anxieties of old age. Be defensive about your concerns over health or losing your freedom of movement or whether you'll have sufficient money to maintain yourself. If you're realistic about your approaching elder years, you'll worry, but do so as a defensive pessimist. Dr. Julie Norem of Wellesley College encourages using anxiety as a motivational energy. Defensive anxiety is a unique type of worrying in which you make contingency plans to deal with possible future difficulties. She says that those who tend to be optimistic and who are unable to creatively imagine possible problems often find themselves less prepared to respond to difficulties when they do arise.

Old Age Lusts and Carnal Pleasures

Bernard Berenson, a scholar and art historian, said of his 90s:

[Ninety is] a year in which Old Age has increasingly got hold of me, making me timid about going downstairs, increasing every natural deficiency...on the other hand I have never enjoyed work more than now. Indeed, it is almost the "only carnal pleasure" left me.

My thoughts at 92 were, I still want to learn, I still want to understand, and I still want to write. How shall I get rid of these lusts?... How I still enjoy sunlight, nature, and stormy skies, and sunsets, and trees and flowers, and animals including well-shaped humans, and reading and conversing....

At 93 my life with all my disabilities is anything but a picnic. So why cling to it? Partly out of mere animal instinct. Partly out of curiosity about tomorrow and the day after tomorrow.[32]

Escape Tool #48 – Be Gentle and Yielding

Rigor mortis, as we all know, is a rigid stiffness of the body that occurs shortly after death. Years before death, however, it is common for a *rigor mortis* rigidity to appear with a hardening of attitudes. Unless precautions are taken in midlife, old age spawns a cranky negativism and a sour outlook toward the modern world, society and young people. This common pre-death *rigor mortis* of the mind is the flowering of a cynical and critical attitude about life and people that its victims have cultivated for many years. As soon as the early symptoms of this infectious naysayer disease appear in your forties and fifties, take defensive, preventive action.

When you detect stiffening symptoms in your attitudes, recall the ancient holy wisdom of China from the Tao Te Ching:

We are born gentle and weak.
At death we are hard and stiff...
therefore the stiff and unbending
are the disciples of death.

> The gentle and yielding are
> the disciples of life. [33]

To escape this chronic aging condition of finding fault, practice being flexible toward new things and toward various changes in your life. "Yield" and examine life's changes from all sides; inspect them for positive aspects instead of only the negative. Whenever you are inclined to lament the decline of certain social customs, gently search instead for the beneficial aspects of their loss. Suspend negative judgments, (especially about other people), be flexible and intentionally replace your judgments with positive evaluations about society's evolutionary changes. This is especially true when judging young people, their music, style of dress and attitudes. Life is ever evolving, unceasingly spiraling upward, even if at times it appears to be declining. Regardless of the gradual stiffening of the joints of your body, keep your spirit ever elastic and flexible toward change. Be a disciple of life. Remain such a supple disciple, even when you are placed in your coffin.

SALMON SPIRITUALITY

The Coho, Sockeye and Copper River Salmon are valued for their rich color and high oil content. Since salmon stop eating once they begin their long, demanding spawning journey, their stored oil is a necessary source of reserve energy.

The Copper River of Alaska is fed by glaciers and races through torrents between 400-foot mountain walls on either side. The salmon are born high in the upper reaches of this river and then descend toward the Pacific Ocean. They spend four to eight years traveling thousands of miles, making a giant figure eight, during which they pass near the coastlines of Japan and Russia. They complete their long Pacific journey by returning to the same river that was their place of birth. In the large body of water at the mouth of the Copper River, the salmon prepare to endure the difficult climb up the rapids and back to their original birthplace. Once they reach home, they finish their life by renewing the natural process with their offspring. Of the countless rivers that flow down from the mountains of Alaska to the ocean, how do the salmon know which is the right river? The answer: Each river has a different scent, and the salmon follows its nose.

> Blessed are those who can smell heaven in their approaching death, and so prepare for it.
>
> Blessed are those who can sense the nearness of the river of death that will take them back to the source from which they began.
>
> Blessed are those who have carefully stored up the essential resources required for their final journey home.

Chapter Sixteen

The Prison of Death and the Tomb

Death imprisons when it is feared as painful.
Death imprisons when it is associated with the loss of physical control,
  and the loss of consciousness — and the attending isolation.
Death imprisons when it is incomprehensible or ambiguous.
Death imprisons with guilt when we must abandon
  those who are dependent upon us.
Death imprisons when we judge it as a personal failure.
Death imprisons when regrets over past failures
  and sins are unresolved.
Death imprisons when the dying have only lived half a life,
  and have never really loved or been loved.
Death imprisons when adventuresome opportunities in life
  have been squandered because of fear.[1]

THE GRAVE ROBBER

Why did Jesus of Nazareth die? He had to die — because he was human! Yet while he fully shared in this most human of activities, he did so as a liberator. Since childhood, many of us have understood his death as a requirement to open the gates of heaven closed by the primal sin of Adam and Eve. The sacrificial death of Jesus on the cross was necessary to atone for the sins of humanity. This explanation of his death is viewed today as inadequate if only because it implies a cruel, bloodthirsty God who would demand a ransom in the form of such a terrible death.

Jesus' death was necessary primarily because that is the fate of all created beings, in whose fullness he shared by the incarnation. He did not die of natural causes, however, but was killed because of his way of life, for what he did and said. He was executed because he had bypassed religious rituals and cultural constraints and had challenged the authority of the establishment. He taught a God of love, of infinite pardon and unlimited compassion, not some God who takes delight in bloody sacrifices or wills that any son or daughter should suffer a cruel and terrifying death. As the enfleshment of God, Jesus was the embodiment of God's love, pardon, justice and joy. By his whole life, Jesus revealed that God's will is not death but life. Jesus' destiny was to make visible the divine design that all life is to be infinite and that death is only an evolutionary stage in our human-divine unfolding. As such, Jesus of Galilee was God's great grave robber.

FAITH TO MOVE MOUNTAINS — AND REMOVE DEATH

Jesus spoke with complete conviction about possessing life in great abundance, a fullness that death cannot diminish. Among his religious opponents were the Sadducees, a religious group within Judaism at his time. They were composed of the priestly aristocracy, and their supporters included the conservative classes of merchants and rich landowners, who generally endorsed peaceful collaboration with the Romans. The Sadducees did not believe in the resurrection of the dead or in the existence of angels and spirits. The other major religious group, the Pharisees, did believe in the resurrection of the dead. So Judaism was divided into two opposing religious opinions about death and the afterlife. Regarding life after death, Jesus did not hold an *opinion*. He knew in his heart that life not only existed but actually increased after death. The priestly classes were well educated and could cleverly philosophize and debate about questions of life after death. While a wise man, Jesus was uneducated. When he spoke about life after death, he quoted from the catechism of creation: "As a farmer knows, unless a seed dies and is buried in the rich soil, it remains just a hard seed. If you want a rich harvest, the seed must die and be buried so that it can sprout and produce fruit a hundredfold. So it is with us. Death does not steal life; death is the womb of a more expansive life, for this is how God has designed creation."[2]

By such simple natural logic, he liberates all of us who may lack the philosophical and theological knowledge to be able to debate with intellectuals over the issue of the afterlife. To reaffirm our belief in life beyond death, we only need to look at the catechism of the cosmos and see the divine patterns of life emerging again and again out of death. The finest way to express any belief is simply to live it. Those who strive to make their lifestyle in harmony with the Galilean Grave Robber are not intent on preaching or intellectualizing their beliefs about life and death. Rather, they speak in the loudest language: They live their belief in concrete ways. They live out their faith by the way they experience existence's numerous little deaths, whether in the loss of something or someone precious, the sunset of a beloved cause or institution or the many diminishments that are part of the aging process. They enflesh their faith through the 10,000 minor deaths that fill daily life. A disciple's life pattern is that of the Great Liberator, who dynamically lived his belief in life right up to the moment of his last breath on the cross. Jesus lived life, not the great lie — and invites us to do likewise.

THE GALILEAN WAKER-UPPER

Jesus not only affirmed life beyond the grave, during his lifetime he shared with a few persons the gift he himself would be given at the moment of his death. On one occasion Jesus responds to the plea of the synagogue leader Jairus to come and lay hands on his dying daughter. At once they set out for his home, but on their way there, news comes that she has already died.[3] Disregarding this sad news, Jesus continues on his way to the home of Jairus. Upon arriving, he tells the crowd of weeping and wailing mourners that Jairus' little girl isn't dead, that she's only sleeping. They, of course, know the difference between sleep and death, and they splatter him with laughter and ridicule. Calmly shedding their ridicule with a smile, Jesus enters the house and awakens the twelve-year-old girl by simply telling her "to arise." To everyone's astonishment, she does arise and walks about in delight.

The Liberator is a waker-upper. Besides Jairus' daughter, Jesus woke from the dead his friend Lazarus and the widow of Nain's son. Moreover, he awakens those asleep in docility to the imperial powers, as we saw in Chapter 15, and also those deadened in a coma of denial or doubt. Jesus the Waker-Upper calls his followers to arise from their perpetual sleepwalking. Jairus' little girl wasn't the only one in the above account who was asleep, so were her parents and the crowd of mourners. Being twelve is on the edge of being a teenager; by pushing boundaries in search of independence, twelve-year-olds can be very difficult for their parents. This could well have been the case for Jairus and his wife. However, when the shadow of death fell across his beloved daughter, Jairus woke up in a hurry. The probability of death suddenly transforms what we once considered difficult and burdensome, shrinking difficulties into total insignificance. The Great Awakener's primal and ongoing call is to wake up to a new era, a new way of life in the Reign of God.

DEATH IS THE GATEWAY TO THE KINGDOM OF HEAVEN

"The Reign — the Age — of God, has arrived. Die and believe in the Good News."[4] These were the joyful tidings proclaimed by Nazareth's prophet and porter of the gates of heaven here on earth. As we've noted, repentance is the first requirement for entering this Divine Time Zone, and repentance is a form of dying. Every conversion is a death. One must die to one's way of life if one wishes to begin living another way. Death is the toll bridge that we must pay to cross over in the process of escaping from any addiction as we painfully die to whatever holds us captive, whether tobacco, alcohol, drugs, work or power. We must die before we can live. Admission to the Reign of God requires the death of the false person, the inflated ego. This me-absorbed self, always desiring to be honored and respected, always in first place, always right and in control, is what absolutely must die.

If anyone missed that requirement in Jesus' glad tidings about the arrival of the Reign of God, he said it again plainly enough for a child to understand, "If you wish to be my disciple [and reside in the Reign of Heaven] you must deny your very self, take up your cross and follow me."[5] If you wish to have life in great abundance, you must die — today and every day. When embraced with great love and faith, these living deaths make one immortal.

Extravagant Life

"I am among you," said the Emancipator Jesus, "so that you might have life and have it in great abundance."[6] Such extravagantly overflowing life is precisely what Jesus himself lived. His personal magnetic power was a by-product of the pulsating inner life that radiated outward from his core. This bountiful saturation of life in the Galilean Liberator flowed both from his profound lived-belief that God was enfleshed in him as well as from the fact that he permitted the dark shadow of his approaching death to fall upon his daily life. The advancing shadow of death helps us focus on the joy contained in simple things. It impels us to make precious what once was only common and ordinary. For those who believe with conviction in their oneness with God, who is Life, death is only a temporary eclipse and no more threatening than today's approaching twilight. For those who believe as Jesus believed, death has lost its sting.

Death is Pornography

Yet for the majority, as physiologist Rollo May has said, death is pornography. Because the word death is the truly unmentionable dirty word, in polite conversation people do not die, they "pass on." In medical jargon, patients never die, they "expire" — always at a precisely recordable moment in time. This is to say that our typical response is to deny death and to hide from it. However, to experience any kind of liberation requires acknowledgment of our imprisonment; escape is impossible from that which is denied.

Usually, death is not in a hurry. After all, we are all prisoners on Death Row, regardless of our age or state of health. Each of us is born terminally ill. For the first third of life, however, the consequences of our irrevocable illness are not normally visible, and so the disease of death is easier to deny. Terminal cases in their teens through their early thirties appear radiant with vibrant health and vigor. By the end of the thirties, while the symptoms of the death are not necessarily visible to the eye, various organs have begun to come under the sway of death's slow dance. Except when it arrives early in the form of an accident or some incurable disease, death is a slow killer. By midlife, death's fingerprints are more visible in the signs of gradual diminishment in physical stamina, sexual drive and the body's ability to heal itself quickly. With each additional decade of life our physical and mental diminishments increase. Yet even when faced with all this compounded evidence, the mind incredibly but steadfastly is able to deny that death is approaching.

Creeping death is painful. Dr. Willem Berger, the eminent Dutch priest-psychologist, gives voice to the aged person's pain at his or her increasing bodily weakness: "How I hate the thought of turning into a corpse. It's so hard to accept I'm becoming more and more of a burden to everyone." Then Dr. Berger places upon the lips of the dying a critical question about death: "For me the big question is how I'm going to die with any dignity when every day I lose more dignity."[7] Our body is the primary image we have of ourselves, how we appear to others. Our body communicates who we are and what we can and cannot do. Dr. Berger underscores this central importance of our body: "The dying man is likely to find his body steadily becoming less and less an instrument and more and more a wreck, a prison which renders him helpless and puts him into the hands of others."[8] Significant for us is his use of the word prison to describe these end days when death can no longer be denied and begins to threaten the dying person's love relationships and friendships. Liberation from this Last Days Prison must begin decades before one starts to see the face of death in the mirror.

WAR AND PEACE WITH DEATH

The advancing stages of death begin as midlife ends, marked by the growing fear of experiencing increased diminishments of one's body, mind and memory. Escape from these imprisoning limitations is possible by consecrating them, by making divine the diminishments of aging. The prophetic Jesuit Teilhard de Chardin encourages us to strive to find the Sacred One in these last stages of life, to experience God even in our disintegration. In his classic book *The Divine Milieu*, he writes, "Humanly speaking, the internal passivities of diminishment form the darkest element and most despairingly useless years of our lives...old age little by little robbing us of ourselves and pushing us on towards the end.... Death is the sum and consummation of all our diminishments: it is evil itself.... We must overcome death by finding God in it."[9] So, the struggle with the evil of death requires two hands:

As we saw in the last chapter, with one hand Chardin encourages us to surrender to the process of aging. Surprisingly, with the other hand, he encourages us to rage and rebel against these evil diminishments and do all in our power to delay and avoid them. He encourages us to make war against the decline of aging, even though there is no hope for victory, since Death always prevails. At least, Death is the victor in the next-to-last round. In the end, Life is victorious.

To revolt against death seems like insurrection against God! For how can we rage against the divine plan for all living beings? Religious training calls its members to an acceptance of death, not rebellion. We are piously told to embrace death docilely as the will of God, not to rage against it. By his example, the Great Liberator gives us permission to express frustration and resentment at the end of our lives. In his dying moments he cried out, "My beloved Father, my God, why have you abandoned me? I have become the adopted son of Pain and Death, while panic and terror claim me. My God, my God, why have you abandoned me?"[10] Freud, along with many other masters of the mind, dealt with the angry feelings of those facing death, and much has been written about the enormous effort required to work patiently through this anger and the other profound emotions that accompany dying. Blessed are those helpers with love-sealed lips, who do not endeavor to put out the fires of anger with the holy water of pious words. Those who attempt to have the dying perform sanctimonious somersaults would likely have stood at Calvary's cross, pleading, "O Jesus, do not say that God has abandoned you. God is here, surrounding you with love at this moment. Let us pray, Jesus, for your acceptance of God's holy will." Rather, blessed are the dying persons' bedside companions who allow them to freely vent their angry rage at death, at fate — and at God. Blessed are those with gifted caregivers who allow them to die without being made to feel guilty for their natural feelings of resentment and even for their doubts about the existence of God.

AFTER THE FIRE STORM

Allow these natural flames of anger to blaze freely, waiting patiently for them to decline. When you hear the Spirit's voice of intuition whisper that it is an appropriate time, begin to transform the last lingering flames of anger into the fuel for a healthy acceptance of death. At this point, the hope-filled words of promise contained in Scripture and the lived example of the dying Redeemer-Rescuer can nourish and inspire the dying.

To grapple with death by yourself is dreadful, perhaps the most painful of all experiences of loneliness. Jesus knew that pain of dying alone. When the companion criminal crucified alongside him was able to rise above his own pain and show compassion to the dying Jesus, he was gifted that very day with Paradise. Combating the enemy of life is easier when shared. Those who wrestle death at some point usually reach out for assistance. The approaching termination of life causes long and deeply submerged conflicts to rise to the surface. Those who are dying often grapple with old, unresolved conflicts, with lingering fears and with not fully resolved sexual issues. These past unhealed anxieties can come as thieves to rob the dying of a peaceful conclusion to their lives.

Often deathbeds are visited by regrets about unfulfilled dreams and unhealed interpersonal resentments. Caregivers of the dying do them a disservice when, with the best of intentions, they attempt to minimize these feelings, especially feelings of guilt. Companions of the dying need to be good confessors, able to listen with understanding and silent compassion. Instead of applying some sanctimonious salve by saying, "God loves you" or "It's God's will," the dying should be gifted with what they truly need: holy and understanding ears. These non-ritualized deathbed confessions are escape tunnels from the prison of guilt. Those who lovingly listen with complete acceptance, devoid of moral judgment, can liberate the dying from that which prevents them from a peaceful departure. Absolution of sin is not a clerical copyright. Remember the Master's words: "Come, follow me."[11] Notice also that to those in need of forgiveness he did not say, "I forgive you" but rather, "Your sins are forgiven."[12] Consider the healing and cleansing power of those four simple words. After listening to the outpouring of regrets, mistakes and guilty feelings, the companions of those who are dying should listen for the guidance of the Holy Spirit. When they "feel" the commissioning voice of the Spirit, they can silently trace the sign of the cross on the forehead of the dying person, kiss the person on the cheek and consider saying, "'Your sins are forgiven' — be at peace."

DEATH FRIENDLY

Those who wish to care wholesomely for the dying must first have faced and come to terms with their own death. The fear of death is potent. Those who are dying can smell the fear of death in their doctors, nurses, hospice workers and clergy. Dr. Berger quotes Henri Nouwen, who described such a situation involving a young soldier who had been badly wounded, "When he spoke of priests who visited him in the military hospital, he saw how ill at ease and uncertain they were, and how they tried to hide this by forced joviality and superficial chat."[13] The clergy who came to help liberate the dying man were unable to do so because they themselves were still prisoners of death. Dr. Berger continues, "One important element in the contacts between healthy and dying people is the powerlessness which seizes them both when they want to express their love and care...and their grief at the impending separation."[14]

The fear of our own sense of powerlessness when confronting death imprisons us, especially when linked with an inability to express affection and gratitude to the dying person. Family or friends, especially men, often wait for the right moment and for the courage to say, "Good-bye" or "I love you." Some families seek to correct this failure to express genuine emotion by concluding every telephone conservation with "Love you." While praiseworthy, such expressions easily become as common as "Good-bye" unless care is taken to ensure that those sentiments remain meaningful. Consider, in special circumstances, telling the dying person why you love him/her, giving examples of what makes him/her lovable and precious. A happy death is one where we die loving and being loved. A sad death is one where we depart from life with an unfulfilled longing to know we were of value to those around us, without knowing we were loved. Poet Vachel Lindsay speaks of this lonely longing in his poem entitled *Rain*.

> Each storm-soaked flower has a beautiful eye.
> And this is the voice of the stone-cold sky:
> "Only boys keep their cheeks dry.
> Only boys are afraid to cry.
> Men thank God for tears,
> Alone with the memory of their dead,
> Alone with lost years."[15]

Anointing the dying is an ancient sacrament of the church. The finest last anointing is with the extravagant oil of expressed affection and gratitude. To be able to anoint with this oil requires that we escape two prisons. First, we must be released from that prison of the fear of death that we ourselves must face in our personal departures. Second, we must escape our tongue-tied fear at expressing our deepest feelings of love and affection for friends and family. While love is natural, paradoxically, frequently expressing it often does not seem to be. What once was so natural for small children often becomes very difficult for adults.

THE BURIED SECRET FEAR

Alongside our dread of death there is another surprising fear. Ernest Becker said, "The two great fears are the fear of death and the fear of life."[16] Surprise! Life itself is feared, even if it never appears on any top ten list! As with death, we typically hide from life by using the strategies of denial and repression. Becker goes on to say, "...most of us by the time we have left childhood we have repressed our vision of the primary miraculousness of creation. We have closed it off, changed it, and no longer perceive the world as it is to raw experience."[17]

Survival requires that each child be a magician. At an early age, in order to survive, each of us magically changed the reality of awe-inspiring creation into a nonthreatening scenery backdrop for life. We tamed raw, primal life and domesticated creation into something manageable and drably normal. This preschool abandonment of awe was our way to avoid the terror of life. "So one of the first things a child has to do," says Becker, "is to learn how to abandon ecstasy, to do without awe, to leave fear and trembling behind...."[18] The paradox of life is that mysticism and artistry require a radical return to pre-denial childhood. Creativity and mystical intimacy are personal experiences of momentarily manageable pieces of primal raw creation that suspend the conventional laws of society and religion.

To be engaged in life without fear requires dying, and it requires doing so more than once. Becker continues, "...poets and religious geniuses have long known: that the armor of character was so vital to us that to shed it meant to risk death and madness.... That is why from earliest times sages have insisted that to see reality one must die and be reborn…yet to suffer one's death to be reborn is not easy. And it is not easy precisely because so much of one has to die."[19]

God is everywhere. There's nothing dangerous about believing that, correct? This earliest learned catechism belief appears harmless and even reassuring, yet when believed and perceived, it's not only a comforting reality but one that fills us with terror. A God-filled world is so overwhelming, so jam-packed with stunning beauty, that its majesty and terror can paralyze those who view it. Blessed are the self-blinded! Perhaps the primal beatitude is to be held spellbound by life, by God-filled reality. Yet it's also a primal fear. Indeed, without the defense of denial we would lay perpetually prostrate on the ground in adoration.

To escape this great fear of God's overwhelming presence, we construct a four-leveled fortification. The first two phases are composed of the tactics learned as a child for how to get along in society, what words to use to win approval and how to appease others. The defenses of these two phases contain pleasant, empty talk about the weather, politics or sports, as well as the ability to play whatever roles the various occasions of our life might require. Just as houseowners who install security iron bars on their windows and doors to keep thieves out, and in the process create their own iron barred prison, so our tiered fortresses created to protect us from life also imprison us.

THE ANTI-LIFE UNDERGROUND BUNKERS

The third and fourth levels of this self-fortress are more like underground bunkers. While the first two tiers seem to be logical shields, the lower two are baffling defenses. The third tier, an endless winding passageway with no exit, is created by our attempt to hide from feelings of being empty and lost. The paradox of this defense is that it leads to a place of ever greater isolation and loss, reinforcing the very fear we are trying to escape. The fourth level is a dungeon at the bottom of our heart that we create to contain our denial of death. The great masters of psychology agree that until we descend into that pit and destroy the beast of our denial we can never be fully alive. Until that final defense of denial is conquered, we will never live naked of defensive disguises.

"Hypocrites! The truth will set you free,"[20] cries Jesus the Liberator to any of us wearing anti-death disguises that also help us avoid abundant life. Look honestly at yourself: Be truthful and acknowledge that what you call your "personality" is in reality your defense system. It is there primarily to protect you from being fully alive as an absolutely unique God-enfleshed person. As with all national military defense systems, you have invested vast resources in the building and maintaining of your personality structure in order to protect you from the strangest of enemies — God, who is Life. To "deny your very self,"[5] is to choose to walk out of that complex stronghold of the self and to live instead in a pulsing and alive yet vulnerable "weakhold," naked of your disguise defenses. To deny your camouflage, to stand self-stripped of the armor of the Lie, is threatening — and it is also divinely liberating.

"I am among you," the Emancipator says, "so you can have life, and have it in great abundance."[6] Is that a promise for some future reward, or is it a pledge intended for now and every day? Inevitably in life, some gifts are never used; they are stored away in closets and attics. Have you hidden away that gift of life because it would be too threatening even to attempt to experience extravagant life? Such an incarcerating fear is reinforced by the social taboo requiring that we avoid anyone living at the maddening intensity of top speed, full-throttle forward with joyful enthusiasm. After all, when everyone else in society is comfortable with life at the domestic low current of 110 volts, why should anyone attempt to live at the dangerous, even deadly, high voltage of 220 — or even 2,220?

HORIZONLESS INFINITY

Just as a carpenter can build his own coffin, each of us has a personal workshop where we are to construct our own death. This workshop is "a room with a view," a view that's horizonless. The absence of a defined vista can be frightening because our horizons ground us. Only recently have we been able to view pictures of horizonless space taken by cameras mounted on telescopes orbiting in space far above our finite earth. Although frightening, the lack of something to ground us can free us to think about infinity.

This ability to image infinity is an evolutionary aptitude in its infancy. As the Australian Aborigines say, "We are just beginning to learn how to survive in infinity." We can't grasp a God who is infinite, and it's even more of a challenge to perceive ourselves as also being boundless. Moreover, infinity does not begin after death; we are living in it right at this moment. The implications of such a mind-boggling realization can be profound. The great global spiritual teachings agree that at this moment each of us in the workshops of our bodies is constructing our personal infinities. Death closes our workshop: Who and what we have constructed from our birth to the moment of our departure becomes who we are into infinity. When a small girl was given a class assignment to describe eternity, she wrote, "Eternity is if you are eating a sandwich when you die, you go on eating it for all eternity." Jesus strongly emphasized the necessity to be busy earnestly constructing our infinity while still in the skin-covered workshops of our bodies. His words indicate many of the tools and strategies available for this life work:

> "Watch constantly. Stay awake! You do not know when the appointed time will come."[21]
> "Be on guard lest your spirits become bloated."[22]
> "Do not be caught asleep, be on guard."[23]
> "Night is coming when no one can work."[24]
> "I'm among you so you can live in great abundance."[6]
> "Is not life more important than food?"[25]
> "How narrow is the gate that leads to life."[26]
> "Whoever loses his or her life for me will find it."[27]
> "What can you offer in exchange for your life?"[28]
> "Your possessions do not guarantee you life."[29]
> "I myself am the bread of life."[30]
> "My words are spirit and life."[31]
> "It is the spirit that gives life."[32]
> "I am the way, the truth and the life."[33]
> "I say to you, today you will be with me in Paradise."[34]

This reflection gives rise to one of the mysteries that has long haunted spiritual masters: Does God at the microsecond of our death compensate for our lazy negligence and permit us to taste the abundance of life? Does God fill with the fullness of abundant life those who in their lifetimes have disregarded, ignored or never attempted to experience that gift promised by Jesus?

A LIFESTYLE AND A DEATHSTYLE

Jesus' lifestyle, his spirituality, was also a deathstyle. Life and death were the constant themes of Nazareth's Liberator, who said he had come to set the prisoners free. The way he lived and died confronted head-on the two great imprisoning fears of life and death. Karl Graf Durckheim describes a framework that suggests how he integrated death into his life:

> Three kinds of death can be died:
> Death of old age and disease;
> Death in service of a cause;
> Death as the bridge-toll to the further shore.

> All die the first;
> Many are prepared to die the second;
> But the third is open only to those few
> In whom death of this life already lives
> As experience, promise, and inner law.[35]

Our Deliverer daily experienced this third type of death as a promise of, and an inner law of, life. To cross to the further shore, he generously paid the bridge-toll required by his life work. He paid the toll brazenly assured that a further shore existed. Perhaps the reason so few are willing to pay the cost of crossing that bridge is that they only *hope* there is a further shore. Rather than mere hope, or even faith, did Jesus *know* there was a further shore? If so, was his knowing not because of divine foreknowledge but rather from a source that is also available to you and me? If his certainty of life after death was by some gift of divine knowledge, then the scene in the Garden of Gethsemane was only playacting. His tearful agony and sweating blood in the olive garden — his prayer for God to remove the chalice of suffering — wasn't real. Perhaps the source of his knowing is a profound conviction based on his intimate unity with a God who loved him with great passion. Since such a love is beyond death, it holds the knowledge of the further shore. But, then, why the sweat and blood? On this side of the bridge, all convictions are tainted by the shadow of doubt. Such a doubt can be healthy, for it impels us into the womb of faith and loving trust. The movement through doubt to trust, however, inevitably involves a passionate struggle expressed in sweat, blood and tears.

THE SHADOW OF DEATH

Whenever the shadow of approaching death falls across someone dear to us, we suddenly awaken to how much we love and value that person. The nearer death comes to us personally, the more we enjoy and appreciate the ordinary things of life: a hot cup of coffee, watching children play, the sound of friends laughing. In fact, the creeping eclipse of death's shadow falling across daily life is essential for experiencing life. Graf Durckheim speaks about how the daylight of this world blinds us to the starlight of the world beyond this one. Durckheim says the light from our one day-star blinds us to the millions of stars in the sky that are present both day and night. The darkness of night cures our sight, allowing us to experience even a microscopic percentage of that vastly wider and greater cosmos in which we live. The few star specks we can see are part of over 200 billion stars in our galaxy alone — among the more than 100 billion galaxies! By day the light from our sun is so powerful that our workaday world is all we experience. One of life's paradoxes is that we are asleep to that larger reality during the day, and awake during the night.

The blinding brightness of this world makes us prisoners of sleep in a dying world — prisoners of death, decay, aging and fear. "I have come to set the prisoners free,"[36] Jesus said, and once free they shall have life in great abundance. For centuries those seeking that kind of animated, abundant life have searched for the Fountain of Youth. Search no longer.

DEATH AS THE FOUNTAIN OF YOUTH

The sooner you can awaken to living with your death, the sooner you can become drunk on the joy of being alive. The awareness of the approaching end of this life creates a special twilight time. In everyday life a twilight moment comes twice a day: as night is dying and the sky is slowly enlightened by the appearance of our morning day-star and again as day is slowly dying and the sky is darkened by approaching night. Twilight is the time when the brightest stars are visible. Similarly, when life is lived in a continuous sacred twilight zone, we can glimpse the otherworld of the universe that exists alongside this world. That other dimension is one of unsurpassed freedom and limitless love, a world without sunsets and sunrises, the mystical marriage of darkness and light. The life of this otherworld throbbed in the veins of Jesus with such intensity that he knew death could never still its life pulse. As you read this text, that same life throbs within you. Taking your pulse can be prayer: It marks the heartbeat of God saying, "I am Life. I am the Life of the world and of the otherworld."

BELIEVE

The Galilean Rescuer believed what the Spirit whispered in the inner-ear of the scribe of the Book of Wisdom:

> God did not make death,
> nor does God rejoice in the destruction of the living.
> For God created all things to have being and life...
> and the creatures of the world are wholesome.
> God formed humans to be imperishable,
> making them in the image of the divine nature....[37]

That ancient Divine Declaration of Independence from the tyranny of death contains four glorious freedoms:

Freedom from the false theological notion that God created death as a punishment.

Freedom from the preposterous concept that God rejoices in the death of anyone — the perverse and wicked or the innocent.

Freedom from the haunting terror that we are perishable, destined from birth for termination.

Freedom from the concept that we're birthed blemished by sin instead of wholesomely created in God's likeness.

Daily live out your independence scribed originally in the Book of Wisdom and know you were created for life. Live those words of wisdom and you can go about your life under the kind of umbrella-shadow of death that radiates with joyful, abundant and endless life. Yet like a boomerang, the question returns: If we are created for life and infinity, designed in the image of the Imperishable One, what is the meaning and purpose of death?

DEATH HOLLOWS US OUT FOR COMMUNION

Teilhard de Chardin sees death as God's way of hollowing us out and emptying us so that the Divine Mystery can fill us to the full. He speaks of death's depleting work when he writes, "the function of death is to provide necessary entrance into our inmost selves."[38] Then he makes these thoughts into a prayer:

It was a joy to me, O God, in the midst of the struggle to feel...the hold you have upon me;...grant that when my hour comes, I may recognize you under the species of each alien or hostile force that seems bent upon destroying or uprooting me. When the signs of age begin to mark my body (and still more when they touch my mind)...when I suddenly awaken to the fact that I am ill or growing old; and above all at that last moment when I feel I am losing hold of myself..., O God, grant that I may understand that it is you...consuming me in the union which should weld us together...teach me to treat my death as an act of communion.[39]

The dying last words of the Great Liberator on the cross are those of Holy Communion: "'Father, into your hands I hand over my very self, my spirit.' When he had said this, he breathed his last."[40] In this life, Holy Communion is the ritual of receiving the Divine Mystery into our hands, while in death it is we who are received as Holy Communion into God's hands. Death is the Ultimate Holy Communion. We prayerfully prepare for this Holy Absorption by frequent, commonplace communions in which we reverently release our very selves into the hands of God:

> O God, into your hands I place my dilapidated body.
> O God, into your hands I place my faltering memory.
> O God, into your hands I place my creeping cancer.
> O God, into your hands I place my despair.

And on the other hand:

> O God, into your hands I place my daily enjoyments.
> O God, into your hands I place my delight in dining.
> O God, into your hands I place my accomplishments.
> O God, into your hands I place my love affairs.

A spirituality that includes such frequent inclusive holy communions rehearses heart and tongue for the Final Holy Communion.

DEATH, THE GREAT LIBERATOR

While the fear of death imprisons so many, it also holds the key to liberation. Death is no thief in the night; death is Heaven's midwife. Death liberates all those who depart into a benevolent eternity.

Death liberates those who seize its suffering as an opportunity for courage and heroism.

Death liberates those who accept it as the final realization of their highest values.

Death liberates those who enter it as a natural process that is cosmically transformative.

Death liberates those who have been able to find God in their diminishments of advancing old age.

Death liberates those who have tasted death a thousand times before they die.

Death liberates those who can die still abounding in life and gratitude without regrets.

Death liberates those who have loved greatly, since such love allows them to love in infinity.

THE PRISON OF LIFE – HERE AND NOW

Any authentic spirituality cannot honestly avoid the question raised early in this chapter about dying with dignity. Recall how Dr. Willem Berger placed upon the dying person's lips this concern: "For me the big question is how I'm going to die with any dignity when every day I lose more dignity."[8] The rapid advancements in medical technology over the last thirty or forty years have made it possible to be incarcerated in the prison of the medical system. The terminally ill become captives of various apparatuses and serpentine tubes linked to life-support machines and feeding tubes. Whenever death is viewed as a personal failure of the physician, especially a death for which he can be judged legally responsible, the terminally ill are held hostage. The necessary freedom to choose life or death then ceases to be the choice of the terminally ill and becomes a decision of others. "Death is a personal event. It belongs to the dying. It doesn't belong to the doctor,"[41] says Dr. Sherwin Nuland, M.D., author of the book, *How We Die.* He goes on to propose that today's physician is almost entirely focused on fighting disease and death. In our society, which is obsessed with always winning, it is natural that doctors do not want to lose. Regardless of the financial cost, medicine, focused on winning, will attempt to keep a patient alive as long as possible. Those incarcerated by the fixation of medical science long to have the Galilean Healer and

Deliverer by their bedside and to hear the words, "I have come to set you free."

DEATH IS NOT FAILURE

The good news of the death of Jesus thunders loudly, "Death is not a failure; death is the victory of life." Jesus never told the sick and suffering that their plight was God's will. As God enfleshed, his work was relieving pain and suffering, thus revealing that alleviating pain was the work and will of God. This good news not only communicates God's love, it also liberates us from the prison of modern medicine's philosophy of simply prolonging life. Jesus' death and resurrection proclaim that even when dying in the direst of conditions the God of life is present. Jesus freely accepted his own death and endured it with great dignity. In this pattern, do not the terminally ill have the right to freely choose their death so as to die with dignity instead of being imprisoned in unconscious vegetation or caged in the shell of a body unable to perform human functions? At Gethsemane Jesus remained awake as he faced into the specter of the death that awaited him. Then, on the cross he refused the hyssop, the painkilling drug, that was offered him. If our deaths are to be expressions of the victory of life, we too must have the capacity to be lucid and conscious. We must be at least spiritually awake during the final stages of dying in order to do the inner work that leads to self-transcendence and liberation. Moreover, those approaching the threshold of death should have the freedom to say farewell while they are conscious. At the end of his life Jesus shows us the wholesome necessity of this parting sacrament of love. In John's Gospel account we see Jesus taking leave of his friends at his last supper. Then we're given his brief farewells at the cross, one to his mother and the other to his beloved disciple John. To his aged mother he says, "Woman, behold your son." Then turning to John, he adds, "Behold, your mother." Only moments later he dies.[42]

JESUS DIES WITH DIGNITY

Jesus died an honorable death, even though he died nailed to an instrument of shame and torture, the Roman cross. He did not whimper or whine; he didn't proclaim his innocence or plead that his life be spared. Moreover, he was not consumed with hate for his crucifiers; he did not curse or condemn them. Jesus died as was expected of a

Palestinian man, bearing his pain and suffering in stoic silence, crying out only at the final moment of his death. While surrounded by the shame of being nailed naked to a cross and by the ridicule of his opponents, Jesus died not only with honor but in a heroic way. The ultimate Greek and Roman hero was one who could enter into the spirit world, the world of the dead, and return alive. The classic religions of antiquity all address as a central issue of existence how to endure the end of life. They speak of embracing death without shame, of meeting death with dignity, nobility and grace, regardless of how sad the appearance of the one who is dying. They value departing without guilt, self-hatred and — the greatest challenge — without fear. In the dignified dying of Jesus this is modeled to the ultimate degree. In the Liberator's passion is revealed the ability to rise above his society's greatest shame of being naked — physically, emotionally, psychologically and spiritually — of appearing to be a failure.

One thing that we see throughout Jesus' life was that ability to die a heroic death. The most significant and greatest death in all of Western culture was the result of having undergone the pains of many previous deaths, and the even greater pains of rebirth. Certainly one of the deaths the Galilean Master had been forced to experience was the painful incongruity of having a body in which God was enfleshed yet which was subject to the physical needs of all creatures. As his followers, we too are faced with this seeming contradiction, which involves the acceptance of being a Godlike person who also hungers for food, feels the urges to procreate and experiences being powerless. It requires bearing the incongruity of being Godlike yet suffering shame and indignities, perhaps the most un-Godlike being the necessity to relieve ourselves of bodily waste. To balance these requires heroism and faith. We need heroic persons who can call us out of all the various fears that diminish us and dwarf our growth. As teenagers, many of us are stirred by a passion and dream to become heroic. Yet culture weaves a mesmerizing spell over us, under which we allow our society to define for us the appropriate paths for our heroism, including our vocations. We usually conform ourselves in order to please others, and so become what is expected of us. Because long before his death he had died to social expectations, Jesus frees us to chose our own heroic way to die, regardless of whether or not our choice is socially unacceptable.

JESUS CHOOSES HIS TIME TO DIE

The Gospels hold out a profoundly puzzling question: Why did Jesus of Galilee allow himself to be arrested, tried and condemned to death in Jerusalem? We have already reflected that this death was not willed by God, yet it clearly appears to have been willed by Jesus. Prior to those last days that culminated in the cross, several serious attempts had been made to kill him. In fact, they began the moment he chose to live publicly his enfleshment of God in a heroic lifestyle. Raging resentment filled the hearts of those in his hometown synagogue when they heard his Spirit-torched announcement: "The Spirit of the Lord is upon me, to proclaim the good news to the poor...and to set the prisoners free."[36] The lynch mob rushed forward to hurl him to his death from the brow of the hill upon which the village was built. Yet he easily eluded his would-be murderers then, and again and again when his enemies attempted to stone him to death. Jesus never promoted sacrificing one's own life for any cause, and he even instructed his followers not to seek martyrdom: "If they persecute you in one town, take refuge in the next; and if they persecute you there, take refuge in another town."[43]

Why, then, did he himself not seek refuge as his enemies plotted to arrest and kill him? After the Seder Last Supper, why did he not slip secretly out of Jerusalem and flee to safety in Galilee or beyond, where the Temple authorities had no power to seize him? Like John the Baptist, Jesus denounced the Sadducees and Pharisees to their faces as a nest of vipers. Why then did he remain in their nest in Jerusalem and expose himself to their deadly poisonous power? The fact that Jesus freely chose his death, its place and time, must seriously be pondered to explore the implications for those who are his followers.

The answer to these questions may be Jesus' desire for, and his call to, the ultimate prison escape. Pulitzer Prize winner and Ph.D. in cultural anthropology, Ernest Becker, writes, "The 'healthy' person, the true individual, the self-realized soul, the 'real' man, is the one who has transcended himself. How does one transcend himself; how does he open himself to new possibility? By realizing the truth of his situation, by dispelling the lie of his character, by breaking his spirit out of its conditioned prison."[44] Did Jesus, in the process of his self-realization and spiritual growth, come to recognize that dying was the last great escape? Not a flight from pain or the struggles of life, death was rather the final stage of "repentance," the conclusive conversion. He had called his followers to self-denial; was the death with which he was entrusted the ultimate self-denial essential in fully opening the doors to the Reign of God? Was it in this light that he freely embraced the way in which he would die? Not leaving this act to fate, accident, disease or even old age, did he choose his death so as to transcend himself by releasing his spirit?

As the population explodes with elderly and dying people and as the final stages of death can be prolonged for years, these are not idle, speculative questions. Just as our religious beliefs shape our life choices, they should also frame our death choice. It was once customary among Roman Catholics to pray for a strange blessing, "to die a happy death." Such a happy death involved dying reconciled with God and the church, anointed by a priest in the Last Rites. Given a fuller meaning and a new name, that "Happy Death" prayer could be among the daily prayers of a liberational spirituality. A natural new name for this brief prayer would be the Greek *euthanasia,* which means "a happy, beautiful death." A graceful, happy death is a worthy aspiration. When you daily pray for any such desired future event, you are like a navigator as you set your course and constantly readjust your compass to reach your desired destination. It's wise to further explore this notion of euthanasia so we can keep our bearings as we progress toward our own death.

EUTHANASIA — A HAPPY DEATH

A "Happy Death" wish is, indeed, a death wish. Since it is traditional to wish others a Happy Birthday, why could we not also wish them a Happy Deathday? Happy and beautiful are the deaths of those who die without regrets for how they lived. Happy are the deaths of those who die in communion with God, with life, with their families and friends — and with their enemies. Happy is the departure from this life of those anointed with perfumed ointments of affection and gratitude, able to die with dignity, consciously and graciously accepting death as the release of their spirit. Be careful, however, when you acknowledge to others that you are praying for euthanasia, for such a revelation can expose you to strange looks, if not reprimands. The majority might consider such a prayer to be asking for mercy killing, assisted suicide, or aid-in-dying, which is condemned as sinful by the church. While passive euthanasia is a subject open to question, active, or direct, euthanasia — death intentionally induced by outside intervention — is condemned. By contrast, a truly happy death is not necessarily painless. True euthanasia is not an escape from suffering or a premature release into death. It involves the "hollowing out" struggle that Teilhard de Chardin spoke about as well as dying in contentment, peace and grace.

In the moral debate around euthanasia, a distinction is made between ordinary and extraordinary means of maintaining the life of someone terminally ill. It includes questions about whether to continue or to cease life-support systems when they are futile and there is no reasonable hope of recovery. Also weighed are factors like the dying person's age and physical and emotional state, and the financial burdens that prolonging life will place on the family. Indeed, the costs of artificially maintaining life for a few days or weeks can completely deplete a family's savings. When this effort to extend life is clearly identified as extraordinary, it is generally an acceptable measure to "allow" a person to die by withdrawing life-support systems. While a proactive step, this is regarded as passive euthanasia since death is not directly induced but comes naturally.

The prayer for a happy death can include active preparation for that desired end by ensuring that your family and those closest to you know precisely the circumstances under which you wish to die as well as your burial plans. Resist being a victim of the denial of death and prepare a signed legal document stating your wishes, such as your desire not to use extraordinary means. Also give someone the power of attorney in regard to your health and death arrangements so that person can act on your behalf should you become incapable of making decisions. You have the right and the freedom to exercise some control over your final and most significant act in life.

THE FREEDOM OF CHOICE TO DIE

One measure of human dignity is the degree of our freedom of choice, including choices over our bodies and our lives. That such freedom should include the issue of how one wishes to die is hotly contested. Indeed, logically, the scope of human freedom is limited.

The taking of one's own life has a long history of being considered morally wrong, even though suicide is not directly condemned by name anywhere in the Bible. Even in the suicide deaths of Judas and King Saul, the Scriptures simply state that the way of death was self-determined.[45] Morality evolves, and today when someone takes his or her own life, we say the person has *committed* suicide. The very use of the term *committed*, casts it as a criminal and immoral act. Yet because of great advances in psychology in the twentieth century, religious thinking on suicide has moved from one of condemnation to one of compassion for those so emotionally afflicted as to choose death. Since we are social beings, no individual's freedom to choose is absolute. Important life decisions must be carefully made so that they are free of purely selfish motives and always with regard to their effect upon the good of others.

The distinguished theologian Hans Kung asks, "In the Christian view, do human beings have the right to control whether or not they shall live? It should be noted that I am not putting this question in connection with psychologically or physically healthy people, but in connection with the seriously ill who are ready to die...whether older or younger, are at the end of their lives...for instance with inoperable cancer or the last stages of AIDS.... Is there a right to self-determination — which is responsible in a Christian way — in dying as in living?"[46] Kung states that all of Christian life involves making personal choices and asks why one cannot freely choose to die with dignity instead of in some vegetative condition. Over the last half century, parents have increasingly made explicit choices about when and how many children they shall conceive, decisions about giving life. Should they not in their senior years also make choices about taking life? While parents' choices about family planning have sometimes been less than fully mature — particularly when they have been made simply on the basis of emotional or economic convenience — that does not preclude us from the responsibility of making our own life and death choices. Indeed, we need to continue to grow in our capacity to make discerning decisions. Yes, soul-searching prayer, reflection, spiritual guidance and the wise use of our freedom of conscience will be necessary ingredients in our choices on how we wish to die. But those choices belong to us.

Kung asks, "Would it not be consistent to assume that…God (has) made the end of human life a human responsibility? This God does not want us to foist responsibility on him that we ourselves should bear. With freedom God has also given human beings the right to utter self-determination…. Self-determination also always includes responsibility for oneself."[47] We now understand this God-given freedom of choice to include the determination of one's profession or vocation, whereas in previous ages it was considered obligatory to follow in the footsteps of one's father or mother. There is also much greater freedom to choose one's religion, instead of feeling obliged to retain the same beliefs as one's parents. And certainly, we consider it only natural to have the freedom to choose our life partner in marriage, instead of this choice being made for us by our parents (as it still is in parts of the world). Again and again throughout our life, God expects that we be morally responsible, that we prayerfully inform our consciences and then follow our inner compasses to make personal choices.

LIFE IS CHOICES

From the age of reason onward, young Christians are expected to make moral decisions and life choices, initially based on observing the Ten Commandments and obedience to parents. Life choices become more challenging in our teenage years as we are faced with making personal decisions regarding sexuality and drugs. As young adults, we must decide about our education and training for a life work or profession, and the significant choice of a spouse, a lifelong partner. After marriage come critical choices regarding family planning and the education and discipline of our children. These choices parallel our decisions about religious practice. This includes more than membership or attendance at worship and more than just whether or not we will observe the Ten Commandments. As mature adults we are increasingly challenged to make our life choices in light of Jesus' high moral code of the Law of Love. Many of us find it too difficult to base our choices on the call to pardon those who injure us, never to return violence for violence, to care for the poor and needy and other elements of Jesus' way listed in chapters five through seven of Matthew's Gospel. We excuse ourselves from the choice of such a Christian lifestyle by ignoring those principles or by assuming they apply only to monks, nuns and those with religious vows. If, however, we have lived a lifetime of high moral choices, why should not the end of life also be a moral choice?

The Final Choice

While the medical profession, and those lacking any belief in life beyond death, attempt to deny death's reality until the bitter end, at the heart of our Christian and other Scriptures is a belief that death is a second birth and a great homecoming. Should not those who live out such a belief, after a long and productive life, be entitled to the freedom to return to God? Since the moment of our conception in our mother's womb we have been on that homeward journey back again to the womb of God. When one's death is freely chosen not as an escape from the pain and the weariness of life but rather passionately sought as the ultimate and most intimate communion, can it not be a holy death? Hans Kung quotes this prayer of Brother Klaus von Flue, a wonderful prayer for all of life and for any deathbed.

> My Lord and my God, take from me all
>   that keeps me from you.
> My Lord and my God, give me all that
>   helps me towards you.
> My Lord and my God, take me from myself
>   and give me wholly to you.[48]

When a dying person prays, "give me *all that helps me towards you,*" to what extent is that person free to make use of all the possibilities for such help that God has made available in today's world? On the other hand, to consider exercising any choice over your own death might seem heretical, since God said, "You shall not kill!" Indeed, respect for life involves doing all within our power to protect and promote life as a great gift from God which should be reverenced. The traditional religious understanding is that life must be endured to its ordained end, and so any premature termination of it would be a sin, a violation of divine law.

To Be or Not To Be: To Sin or To Grace

To sin is to violate God's laws, to act contrary to God's will. "To grace" is to act in accordance with God's will. For Christians, the understanding of what is a sin and what is a grace has evolved over the past two thousand years. For example, war and any taking of the lives of others was judged as sinful by early Christians. In time, however, that sin became a grace — even a crusader grace — if those killed were non-Christian. For centuries the owning and selling of human slaves was viewed as part of God's will, and so a grace. It was not judged as sinful until recent history. Segregation of the races was also viewed as a morally appropriate way to maintain proper social order until very recent times. Loaning money at interest — usury — began as a sin for Christians but was eventually baptized as a business grace, and even became a profitable activity of the church itself. This moral shift from sin to grace includes the practice of performing autopsies and proceeds to an acceptance of the Copernican theory and the theory of evolution. Our moral development will continue to evolve with each century and will increasingly address the issue of dying with dignity and grace.

HOMO SAPIENS BECOMES HOMO EVOLVUTUS

Homo sapiens, the thinking human, is becoming *Homo evolvutus*, the evolving or unfolding human. While presently we are not substantially changing on a physical level, we are constantly evolving spiritually. Daily we make new moral choices that in former ages would have been thought immoral. Two millenniums ago Jesus announced, "This is the time of fulfillment. The Reign of God is at hand. Repent and believe in the good news."[4] He also taught us both to pray and to live by the statement, "Your kingdom come, your will be done...."[49] To live his prayer involves the daily unfolding of the Reign of God in the context of our age and place. Personal moral choices cannot be conveniently placed in the hands of others. As we grow up, we cannot allow our parents or other authority figures to make our important life choices for us. These choices require painful soul-searching, the duty of following a prayerfully formed conscience about what is a sin and what is a grace. To be led by the Spirit, in communion with the guidance of Scripture and the moral teaching of past ages, can be threatening. While perilous, this personal unfolding of God's Reign in our lives is essential in the playing out of God's evolutionary design. At each stage in life, for something new to evolve, the death and transformation of something old is required. Thus, in the divine design, dying is enlivening.

The Finale of Freedom — The Overture to Life

Christ is *L'Ovuverture*. This book of reflections on a spirituality of liberation has used many different titles to describe Jesus of Galilee. *L'Ovuverture* may contain all of the others since it means "the Opener." Pierre Francois Dominique Toussaint, the eighteenth century liberator of Haiti, was given this name to describe how he delivered his people. *L'Ovuverture Christ* leads all of us on the way to freedom from our slavery by showing us how to open door after door of prison after prison until we finally open the dreaded door of the last and greatest prison: death.

Jesus, the Galilean Opener, has opened, and still
opens hearts closed by countless fears,
opens eyes blinded by prejudice and work,
opens ears to the whispering inspirations of the Spirit,
opens lives to unlimited possibilities and new beginnings,
opens minds to unexplored truths and new moral choices,
opens tombs of the living dead to an abundance of life,
opens spirits to ever-evolving concepts of God,
opens religion, revealing how to live in a way not bound by law,
    but abounding in love.

Christ, the Risen Liberator, continues this work in our time and, in fact, is more dynamically alive now than he ever was in his own lifetime. He opens closed doors not by magic or miracles but by providing a pattern for a liberating lifestyle. His was a lived spirituality based on his enfleshment of God; in his work and life he expressed what he believed in his heart. Those brave enough to allow God enfleshed in every atom of their bodies to work, love, pardon and create through their lives share in Christ's totally open-ended, ongoing life in infinity. For these followers of the inner-compass of the same Holy Spirit who led Jesus, death is not a final life event. Death is rather a process of becoming, of dying and rising that's undergone numerous times in a lifetime. Dying opens doors, and *L'Ovuverture Christ's* followers experience a life of perpetually opening doors as they escape from one captivity after another. His disciples are known to the world by their love, and also by their free spirit and their inner commitment to assist others in opening their tightly locked doors.

Easter is, indeed, an evolutionary event. Jesus' escape from the tomb was the overture of a new Genesis for all of humanity and all creation. The evolutionary nature of Christ's resurrection, we understand now with greater clarity, includes the liberation, not only of all creation but of the whole cosmos, which as St. Paul told us, aches and yearns for freedom. Jesus' resurrection and his entire life of rising offers a liberation to those who follow him. His life of rising included a resurrection from the restraints of a human life defined by the cramped confines of religious law and outmoded social customs and taboos. His lifelong rising was an overture of a cosmic revolution-evolution in which each person is invited to participate. His very flesh and bone, passions and emotions, human joys and struggles are the Book of the Good News containing God's design for our human evolution. The Gospels themselves thus become Great Escape Manuals for those with open eyes and open hearts.

Jesus' evolutionary invitation, "Come, follow me,"[11] is the greatest vocation possible on this earth. Spurred on by the Spirit, cultivate a thirst to follow him through every open door toward an Easter Evolution, and strive to live daily in the glorious freedom of the children of God.

"Go in peace, and be free."

Chapter Sixteen Inventory of Escape Tools and Unshackling Reflections

ESCAPE TOOL #49 – TALK OBSCENELY

A good escape tool from the imprisonment caused by the denial of death is to defy convention and use those obscene words: *death* and *dying*. Like other four-letter words that are forbidden in proper society, *dead* and *died* are considered vulgar and naughty. But use them anyway. Sprinkle your conversation with them. Bring them into everyday discussions.

Whenever some appliance breaks down, you might say, "Our toaster is dead" or "Dear, the washing machine died this morning."

As twilight lingers after sunset, you might say, "Look, another beautiful day is dying." Use d..d when speaking of the future, "When I'm dead, remember this…" or "When I'm dead, being upset and angry over this misfortune will seem silly" or "Dear, when you're dead, I will always treasure the memory of this trip."

Escape death's denial by discussing with your family your desires for the way in which you wish to die as well as your funeral and burial rites. Prepare legal documents that clearly state your desires around death. While still in good health, put into writing your wishes to die with dignity, the privilege of dying free of having to be plastic-tubed to artificially life-sustaining machines.

THE ZEN SECRET

Once, long ago, in the Land of the Rising Sun, a young man came to Tajimanokami, the great Japanese Zen teacher of swordsmanship. The young man asked to become a student of the master, saying that he desired to become a great swordsman. The master was surprised and said, "Why do you wish to become my student? It is clear that you are already a master of the art." The young man answered, "Sir, I am ashamed to confess that I have never learned this art." The master was confused, for his instincts clearly told him this young man was already a master. He encouraged the would-be student to speak about himself. The young man said, "When I was a boy, I dreamed of becoming a great samurai warrior, yet I knew that to realize my dream I must never have any fear of death. Since my youth I have grappled with death, until now it is no longer an issue for me. Death ceases to worry me." Tajimanokami jumped to his feet, proclaiming, "I knew I was not wrong in my judgment of you! The ultimate secret of samurai swordsmanship is to be free from the fear of death. I have trained hundreds of warrior students, and so far none of them really deserves the title of master swordsman, since they still fear death. Young man, you have no need of technical training, you are already a master!"

Escape Tool #50 – Be a Pother

The excruciating prison of helplessness that often occurs near the end of old age is one from which you can escape by practicing being a pother. That vocation is better known today by its cousin word "bother." But the original word, pother, referred to someone who was a cause of trouble, a nuisance and annoyance. Emotionally healthy people hate being a nuisance. They strive never to be a bother to anyone and always excuse themselves saying, "Please, don't let me bother you, but...." After liberation from the prison of childhood dependence, adults pride themselves on being self-reliant and despise the thought of being pests to others. Today's nursing homes are pest houses. In olden times, a pest house was the name given to hospitals that cared for those dying of some pestilence. Nursing homes are places for aged residents who are unable to care for themselves — and who easily can feel like pests to their families.

The fear of being a pest to others is among the primary pains of the last stages of dying, which often include the loss of a personal ability to care for oneself. The terrible impotency of this helplessness is particularly painful for the once proud and self-reliant. Prepare for your graduation to gracious pesthood by allowing others to do things for you while you are still capable of doing them yourself. Learn to receive graciously as well as to give. Learn the graceful practice of being waited on by others at the same time as you exercise at every opportunity the fine art of assisting others in need, especially the elderly.

The Teacher from Nazareth calls us to be humble servants to one another. His life reveals how he also allowed others to serve him, to support his ministry, wait upon his needs, bring him food and anoint him for death. A true servant also knows how to be graciously served — by God and by others. A dual life of going out of your way to assist others and going out of your way to be assisted contains one the nature's core secrets about communion. There is a paradoxical magic in the gift of doing favors, in which the giver receives the greater reward. When we ask others to go out of their way to do a favor for us, they feel more connected to us than if we had done something kind for them. So, ask others for a helping hand, ask for support, aid and directions — in other words, become a pother. Pothering today prepares you for that future day when you will need assistance in bathing, being dressed, getting in and out of bed, being fed and even going to the toilet.

HAVE A CROWDED FUNERAL

If you don't go to their funerals,
they won't go to yours.

— Yogi Berra

Untangle Yogi Berra's typical twisted logic and you have a wonderful insight into who will attend your funeral. Usually, we think only of the living being present as mourners at a funeral, yet what if there are also invisible guests? These unseen ones who do not sign the guest book are the dead family, parents, grandparents, friends and lovers of the deceased who have come to celebrate their beloved's birth as a new creation. For them this loved one is not so much "deceased" as "increased"! The narrow, confining borders of their beloved's dead body have been shattered, and they are now increased by sharing in the fullness of God. The "deceased" are really the "expanded," now fully one with the Risen Christ, whom Ephesians spoke of as "…filling the universe in all its parts."[50] The fullness of the universe at the publication of this book includes over 200 billion galaxies! Such are the cosmic dimensions of those who have died one with the Risen One.

ESCAPE TOOL #51 — UNBLINDFOLD YOUR EYES

Each time you pass a cemetery, take off your denial blindfold. Make every cemetery a visible reminder of the reality of your death. Drive into the cemetery and get out and walk for a few minutes among the graves. Cemeteries can be great places to walk and pray. You might even use cemeteries as parks and as places to jog. As you jog among the tombstone-lined lanes, think of yourself as running to heaven.

Visit those cemeteries where your family and friends are buried on occasions like Memorial Day and their death day anniversaries.

Use such visits to these entombment parks as spiritual exercises to remind yourself of the most valuable pieces of real estate that you will own — or, rather, that will own you. If you already have purchased that significant narrow plot of land, consider visiting it as well and spending time pondering your future repose there.

Escape Tool #52 — Deathday Fiestas

To escape the solitary confinement of death's seeming physical separation between you and your beloved dead it can be helpful to celebrate a feast, a fiesta of life, in their honor. Each January as you begin to use your new year calendar, record on it the various death dates of spouses, family members, ancestors, lovers, friends, teachers and other significant people in your life. On a special death day, place a photograph, a personal possession or a reminder of your loved one in an important place in your home so as to be in communion with that person. Recall memories of past enjoyable times with him/her and feel the presence of the person from whom you are separated only by a tissue-thin yet shrouded layer of reality. Celebrate a festive meal on the death day and toast your loved one. Purchase some gift for yourself in his/her honor. Treat these death days as little Easters. Those who have loved you and whom you have loved in life are not gone; they can be as close to you as your belief system allows.

The Communion of Saints is real. Christians profess a belief in that reality in their creed. Allow that belief to translate into a divine communion with your personal holy dead, your unhaloed saints. Consider it a Communication of Saints, a Companionship of Saints, as you walk hand in hand, heart in heart, with your beloved dead in times of joy and trouble. And as a Corporation of Saints, let this faith reality inspire you to live in the *Corpus*, the Body, of Christ, which includes all the living and all those now living fully in God.

Prayers and Poems

The following anonymous poem expresses the holy "increase" of those we mistakenly called "deceased." Those who can embrace this poem's liberating message can never be separated from a dead one whom they have loved greatly.

Do Not Stand at My Grave and Weep

I am not there, I am not asleep.
I am a thousand winds that blow.
I am the diamond glint on snow.
I am the sunlight on ripened grain.
I am the gentle autumn rain.
When you wake in the morning rush,
I am the swift, uplifting rush
    of quiet birds in circling flight.
I am the soft starlight at night.
Do not stand at my grave and weep.
I am not there.
I do not sleep.

We are born asleep, and at death we wake up.
— Prophet Mohammed

How to Get Ready for Death

The master gives himself up
to whatever each moment brings.
He knows that he is going to die,
and has nothing left to hold on to:
No illusions visit his mind,
relaxed, his body does not resist.
He doesn't think about his actions
since they flow from inside his being.

He doesn't hold back anything from life;
and so he is ready for death,
as one is ready for sleep
after a good day's work.[51]
    — *Tao Te Ching,* Chapter 50

A Reflection on Chapter 50 of the *Tao*

Lao Tsu, the holy sage of China, paints a poetic picture of the person who has resolved his/her rebellion at having to die and is now at peace. This state is achieved only after dying many times; dying to illusions of control or power, dying to selfishness, dying to anger, dying to resistance at being stripped by old age. To be as ready for death as one is for rest after a good day of hard work is achieved by the final stage of accepting one's own death.

God is Not a Thief

In Susan Trott's *The Holy Man* is a story about a grieving man who comes to the holy man lamenting,

"I have lost my wife. She was taken from me. She's gone, and I loved her so much."

The holy man asked, "Did she die?"

"Yes, she died; that's what I'm saying. She's been taken from me."

"Well, she could have left you," replied the holy man, "and that would have been worse. You would never see her again, plus you would have to bear the pain of rejection. It's sad, yes, and I'm sorry that you had to give her back before she had to give you back."

Confused, he asked, "What do you mean, give her back?"

"You're only adding to your grief by seeing yourself as a victim. Give her back, you'll feel better. She was never yours from the beginning. Nothing is yours — your life, your possessions, your children. They are only loaned to you. Some day you have to give them all back."[52]

A Reflection on God's Pawnshop

The possessives *my* and *mine* are both illusory words. For those who understand how the universe works, these two words are always off-key and inappropriate. Those who live in reality rather than some self-constructed mirage know that everyone and everything in life is only loaned to us. Indeed, we need to treat what is leased to us with the greatest care and love since we are responsible for these gifts-on-loan: our talents, lovers, spouses, children, health, possessions and natural abilities. It is not easy to live with the terms and implications of the Divine Mysterious Pawn Shop because we do not know the precise termination date of our leases. This fact of life makes us perpetual borrowers, for whom daily reality is both disconcertingly unpredictable and delightfully exhilarating. For we never know if this might be the day any of our gifts have to be returned. Yet loaners enjoy life much more than owners. So possess nothing. Rejoice and be grateful daily for whatever God has loaned to you. Whenever you are required to return something special or someone dear, allow yourself to mourn — but not for long. Rejoice and do not be afraid, for we shall all meet again in God's Great Loan Shop.

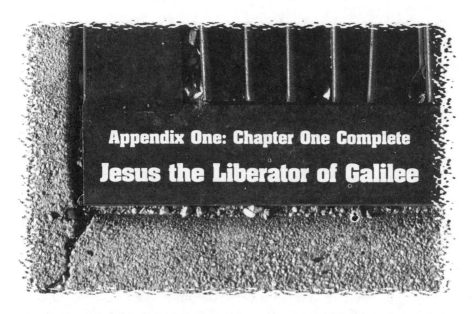

Appendix One: Chapter One Complete

Jesus the Liberator of Galilee

JESUS OUR SAVIOR OR JESUS OUR LIBERATOR?

Jesus is our Savior. All Christians agree on that. However, Jesus is more than a savior in the traditional sense. Years of religious development have conditioned us to equate being saved exclusively with getting to heaven. Yet the original Hebrew Old Testament word for salvation was used in a very different sense. It meant freedom: the well-being or security gained by the removal of some constriction or confinement. Isaiah used the term *salvation* to refer to liberation from any evil, personal or communal. Scripture scholar John McKenzie says that while the scriptural term *salvation* is synonymous with liberation, it also includes the broader vista of a new revelation about the nature of God.[1] As such, it implies entering a new world. Those two broader implications of salvation — a new image of God and a new world — are contained within the message of the Great Liberator, Jesus.

The Messiah — or, in Greek, the Anointed One, the Christ — was anticipated as a liberator. In one of Scriptures' most poetic passages, Zechariah, the father of John the Baptist, prophetically sang of the Messiah as the people's long-awaited liberator:

> Blessed be the God of Israel,

who has visited us with *liberation*
and raised up a horn of *freedom*
within the House of David,
as promised by the prophets of old:
liberation from our enemies,
freedom from all who hate us,
rescue from our enemies,
so that we might live without fear —
lives of holiness and freedom —
giving the People of God
the knowledge of *liberation*....[2]

The name *Jesus* literally means *freedom*. His very name declares his primary work. The angel instructed his father Joseph, "You shall name the boy Jesus — or Yeshua — which means 'God is Salvation-Liberation.'"[3] As he rode on a donkey up to Jerusalem, the jubilant crowds greeted Yeshua of Galilee as a long-awaited liberator, shouting, "Hosanna, Hosanna, blessed is he who comes in the name of God."[4] Hosanna isn't Hebrew for "Hurrah!" It's much more than a shout of praise to God. This Hebrew proclamation actually means, "'Free us, save us,' we ask."

A savior delivers salvation. When speaking of Jesus as a savior, the Gospel writers used the Greek word *soter*. The term had been the title of several Greek gods and goddesses, the chief among them being Aesculapius, the god of medicine and healing. What in the Hebrew mindset had been the work of salvation-liberation became in the Greek translation of Scriptures an act of salvation-healing from the sickness of sin. Today salvation seems almost a copyrighted religious term and is seldom used in a political context, where it has some of its strongest roots. Those who are "saved" experience salvation largely as a healing of their sins. We might even think it possible to be "saved" from our sins and yet still be imprisoned. On the other hand, the liberation of Jesus includes both a healing from sin and an escape from other forms of imprisonment.

REDEEMER JESUS OR LIBERATOR JESUS?

You can redeem coupons and stocks, but can you redeem yourself? Psalm 49 tells us:

One cannot redeem oneself
or pay a ransom to God for one's life.
Too high is the price to redeem a soul;
one would never have enough.[5]

Like salvation, redemption is another religious term; it's usually understood as the recovery of something pawned, as in a ransoming. The Hebrew words for redeem or ransom were used primarily to mean the payment of a sum of money for the release of a person held in detention. The Old Testament notion of redemption also included any saving or freeing action of God. For example, God was said to *redeem* the Israelites from their slavery in Egypt. Yet the Exodus from Egyptian slavery was one of history's greatest *liberations* and *emancipations*. While Scripture refers to the Israelites as being ransomed, no payment was made to anyone.

It was, however, in the Passover event that the New Testament notion of redemption has its primary source. The scandalous, brutal death of Jesus forced his first Jewish disciples to search for some meaning in the cross. They naturally turned to their Jewish Scriptures, particularly to their prophets. Their faith taught them that the old God of the Temple required bloody sacrifice for sins, required a sacrificial scapegoat who would bear the sins of the people. They saw in the Passover lamb a prefigurement of Christ. The blood of the lamb spilled onto the lintels and doorposts initiated the great Exodus into the Promised Land. In a like way, Jesus' blood on the cross opened the gates to the Kingdom of God. The death of Jesus, the lamb of God, the divine scapegoat, was understood as the supreme act of atonement for sin, a payment made to ransom the world from sin.

This sense of redemption was explained as *restitution* by the time of the eleventh century theologian, St. Anselm, the Archbishop of Canterbury. His theory of Jesus' death being the source of our salvation was based on the feudal legal concept that satisfaction for a crime is in direct proportion to the great dignity of the one sinned against. Since our primal parents, Adam and Eve, sinned against God, who is perfect, justice demanded that only someone as perfect as God could make satisfaction for the grievous offense of the original sin. Anselm's juridical notion of the Atonement is deeply ingrained in Christian faith and prayers. Unfortunately, this way of understanding redemption has led to perceiving

God as a vengeful, bloodthirsty judge who required the brutal crucifixion of his son as an act of atonement. This Old Covenant God condoned an eye for an eye, especially, it seems, if the eye was divine.

Space exploration requires departing from the known, from our home base of earth, into unexplored space. Spirit exploration requires the same departure. We can begin to explore a new way of understanding redemption by taking to heart Jesus' understanding of God as a tender, compassionate and caring father. Similarly, any new notion of the redemption needs to include the central New Testament insight that God is love.

We've already seen how the redemption of the Exodus from Egypt was primarily an act of liberation. One of the main places in Scripture where we find the word *redeem* used is in the book of Leviticus. It says that if a person "is reduced to such poverty that he sells himself to a wealthy alien...he may be redeemed by one of his own family, or if he acquires the means, he may redeem himself."[6] Or if one had to sell one's animals or one's home or one's land, it could likewise be redeemed for a just price.[7] But "if a person or the person's property is not thus redeemed, the person and his property shall nevertheless be released in the jubilee year."[8] Remember how we saw that Jesus the Liberator began his public ministry by proclaiming Isaiah's words: "The Spirit of God...has sent me to proclaim liberty to captives...to let the oppressed go free, and to proclaim a year of favor [jubilee year] from God."[9] At the heart of Jesus' mission of redemption was incarnating God's gracious, loving liberation — God's desire that we live in jubilee year freedom. Seen in this light, his death on the cross is the supreme act of that love. As Jesus said, "One can have no greater love than to lay down one's life for one's friend."[10]

John McKenzie further invites us to a richer, broader understanding of the Scriptural term *redemption* when he suggests that it refers to the entire saving work and life of Jesus.[11] The problem with St. Anselm's setting the redemptive death of Jesus in the juridical framework of *satisfaction* is that it tends to reduce Christ's redemption to a single act, a single moment in time: his death on the cross. We need to move beyond feudal legalism. We need to allow our faith to mature, to have a fuller, richer understanding and experience. For Jesus, redemption was a lifestyle; it was fully part of the fabric of his life. His *life* was redeeming as well as his death. We are thus redeemed by Jesus' parable stories, by his new code of morality defined by the primacy of love over law, by his delight in eating and drinking with outcasts and sinners, by his praying and his healing of the lame and blind, by his challenging of the religious rituals of his day. Viewing redemption in this way liberates the reality of redemption, exploding it outward beyond those last three hours of dying on the cross. The whole daily lifestyle of Jesus of Galilee says, "Come, follow me, and live a redemptive-freeing life." That pattern of living was marked not only by his loving, sacrificial death but by all of his life and his whole humanity.

JESUS THE PRISONER

The Scriptures tell us that Jesus was like us in all things but sin,[12] which, then, would include being a prisoner. In fact, his imprisonment was essential for the saving-liberating work of God. For how can you show others the way to escape unless you yourself have been a prisoner? Indeed, the same Jesus who began his ministry by announcing that the Spirit of God had anointed him to set the prisoners free began life as an infant prisoner.

How shocking — the idea of an innocent, newborn child being a prisoner! Yet, such was the fate of the son of Mary and Joseph. Mere moments after his birth in Bethlehem, Jesus was imprisoned by being tightly wrapped in swaddling cloth bands. The shepherds were told, "This will be a sign for you: you will find an infant wrapped in swaddling clothes."[13] The infant care custom two thousand years ago was to wrap up every newborn child mummy-like in swaddling bands. While this was the practice for all infants, recall that the angel told the shepherds it would be "a sign." The purpose of a sign is to give information or direction. So, what is the meaning of this *sign* of being bound up in swaddling bands?

One decoding of the sign of the swaddling confinement of this newborn savior might be that as a liberator it was only right that Jesus should begin his life personally knowing the reality of restraint. Infants were usually kept in swaddling bands for as long as two to three years to ensure that they would grow straight and well-formed. Yet even after his parole from being swaddled, Jesus continued to be bound by various rigid bodily, social and religious restrictions. The swaddling bands were a sign of the innumerable restraints that had the power to keep him a prisoner from the moment of his birth until his ultimate liberation.

SOCIAL-SACRED SWADDLING BANDS

From his birth onward Jesus was imprisoned by the hundreds of religious laws and ritual requirements of his Jewish religion. His childhood religious instructions would have imprisoned him under the obligation of shunning sinners, those who failed to observe the numerous laws of Moses. He would have been bound to avoid all contact with hated Samaritans and uncircumcised Gentiles. Jesus would have been incarcerated by his cultural conditioning about the proper place and role of women in Galilean society and by legions of social restrictions and ancient taboos. He would have been taught a patriotic yet restraining hatred for the enemies of his people, especially the Roman military oppressors. Like every youth, he would have been held captive by the expectations of his family and fellow villagers about who he should be, and how he should act and dress. Because of his culture and his very humanity, Jesus would have had to free himself of the swaddling clothes of a desire for security based on social position or political power.

The Gospels are stories of Jesus escaping from prison after prison — and calling others to follow him. Understanding them as stories of liberation acts as a catalyst to energize the Gospels with new personal meaning and challenge. His life is a heroic story of an escapee who was able to break out of society's innumerable prisons until his final great escape from the most secure of all earth's prisons — death and the tomb.

HOW DID JESUS' DEATH LIBERATE US?

How in his death on the cross did Jesus the Prisoner deliver us? That haunting door-question, now opened, remains to be answered. Of course, Jesus could have run away, but instead he freely allowed himself to be arrested, imprisoned and sentenced to capital punishment. Frequently he spoke of the unconditional need for a faith that would allow God to work wonders in us and through us. His profound faith, particularly expressed in his loyalty to his loving God in the face of death, challenges us to believe as he did and to overcome our potent prehistoric fears of pain and dying. Such was his loyalty that he remained steadfast when his closest friends deserted him and even God seemed to have abandoned him. Such a sustaining faith reflects a deep inner commitment and not merely an intellectual belief in religious teachings or dogmas. We need to pray for such a loving loyalty, realizing that such faith is a gift of the Spirit. The image of Jesus nailed to the cross is the ultimate sign of loving fidelity, the price of lifelong union that is willing to endure any pain to remain one with the Beloved. How liberating is such a love-death in a culture like ours where love is usually calculated according to the capitalistic norms of investing only if the profit will be greater than the investment, calibrated by what is comfortable and terminated whenever it is painful.

LIBERATING THE MESSAGE OF LIBERATION

For many people, Scripture no longer barks. Slumberized by deadening repetition, the words of Jesus and the prophets are often voiceless to arouse us to action. The message of the Gospels has been domesticated, especially those words that were once dangerously revolutionary, like the implications of the Sermon on the Mount[14] or the need to become like a child[15] — who in Jesus' day was wholly without power or influence.

Indeed, Jesus' message was radical and life-changing right from the start. After his baptism Jesus ended years of silence and began to proclaim the Gospel of God. The theme of his teaching was, "This is the time of fulfillment. The Kingdom of God is at hand. Repent, and believe the good news."[16] What is the meaning of this message for us personally and for our freedom?

It's a healthy spiritual practice to liberate biblical words from their straightjackets so they can breathe again and can awaken and challenge us. As we have already seen, one way to restore ancient words to life is to return to the root meanings of these words. By tracing the original meaning of salvation back to its connotation as a freeing action expands the notion of "being saved" beyond its present restricted religious meaning.

Conversely, another technique to enliven biblical language is to update Scriptural terms. Exchanging contemporary words for religiously exhausted terms often enfleshes them with new implications. For example, *kingdom* is a restraining, if not extinct, word. In this twenty-first century very few kingdoms still exist other than in fairy tales. Yet Jesus' use of "the Kingdom of God" is an expression whose meaning is rarely ever decoded or revised for today's world.

Perhaps we can experiment with reinterpreting the Kingdom of God as "The New Era" or "The New Time Zone of God." It's not only a new day — a whole new way of being has arrived with the fullness of time of which Jesus spoke. It's a zone in which all clocks moved ahead to God's New Time, a time both radically real and different. What arrived when Jesus first proclaimed his Good News was the continually unfolding reality of God's presence in the world. Unwrapping this mystery as a lived reality is the primary daily duty of his disciples. Faithful disciples, by their living out of the Gospels, make that New Era of God more visible in the world than it was at the time of Jesus. Such an unveiling vocation requires daily effort and determination to keep pushing "the Kingdom" beyond its present acceptable religious and social frontiers. Good disciples are endless expanders of boundary lines.

Another way to sharpen the domesticated Word of God back into a double-edged sword is to add an engaging adjective or two. To give a razor sharp edge to the "Kingdom of God," we might, for example, add in front of it the adjective *peaceable*, echoing back to Isaiah's vision of a peaceable kingdom, in which the lion and the lamb, the bear and the cow could lie together. Similarly, the "United" Kingdom of God would suggest the inclusive implications of the New Era announced by Jesus. Traditional religions are habitually exclusive, whereas God is inclusive. "God's United Kingdom" would express the inclusive attitude and lifestyle of the Redeemer of Nazareth, who time and again included those on the fringe who were hungry for the love of God. He didn't raise barriers that separated him from religious outcasts and social misfits. He didn't require repentance as a prerequisite for them being near him, eating at table with him or experiencing his love. It's no wonder that those excluded by orthodoxy were so eager to join his company. All were part of God's family; all were welcomed by him. This encompassing and incorporating is aptly expressed by a popular new term, the *Kindom* of God. All peoples are kin — our relatives, our family members — since we share a common Holy Parent.

The Enchanted United Universe

American priest-theologian Robert Barron uses another intriguing name for the Kingdom of God: "the Enchanted Universe."[17] This concept expands the Mystery beyond the confines of earth and out into the rest of creation, into the whole cosmos. For Barron, God's United Enchanted Universe is not a mythical construct, it's at the heart of reality. It's an enchanted reality in the sense that it's filled with what Thomas Moore calls a magical "exaltation of existence."[18] This reality of the "Kingdom" did not arrive two thousand years ago with Jesus, it has existed since creation's first explosive microsecond. Fifteen billion years ago the expanding cosmic flaming fireball contained the Enchanted Universe when it screamed ecstatically outward into spacious nothingness. Not only is this the real world, it's a *united* world in which everything is intimately interconnected in a divine cosmic communion — from the atoms circle-dancing inside your skin to circle-dancing Australian Aborigines. Jesus humanly enfleshed this United Enchanted Universe, and he likewise invites each of us to awaken passionately to this reality embodied in our flesh.

The United Enchanted Universe is the passion story of continuously dying and rising anew. All matter is constantly being destroyed and reborn again in the process of recirculating life-energy. This understanding of the nature of the universe brings us back to the haunting question about the meaning of the painful death of Jesus on the cross. Is it simply an atonement, the winning back of our lost divine friendship and obtaining a secure place with God in heaven? Or does that gory gospel of death and resurrection also carry the good news that not even death can separate us from one another, from life and from the love of God? Jesus dies choking on the feeling that God has forgotten him, yet with his last gasping breath he prays, "O beloved Father, into your hands I commend my spirit."[19] Good Friday seems at first glance to celebrate an absent, impotent God who appears to allow evil to triumph over goodness.

When God is felt to be absent and powerless, how easily we can be imprisoned by doubts and fears, even as we profess our creed in an almighty God. A truant God seems to allow the most sordid evil to swagger triumphantly over the innocent, right under the nose of the impotent powers of good. The mysterious message of the cross, however, frees us from our apprehension about such an absent God, announcing instead that God is most present when we most sharply feel devoid of God. The wisdom of the cross should also free us from any notions of a vengeful God who turns away from sinners and is only near to the good and pious.

Living in the Enchanted United Cosmos is joyful, jubilant and exhilarating. Sadly, most of us live our daily existence in another place, as inmates in the Prison of Unreality: We dwell in a fractured, divided world and, unfortunately, in a fragmented church. To escape imprisonment and reside in the United Enchanted Universe requires, as Jesus said, two actions: repenting and believing. The first half of the Great Liberator's equation implies the necessity for escaping. This need "to repent" can be simply expressed in a single statement: *Before you can get in, you have to get out.*

BEFORE YOU CAN GET IN, YOU HAVE TO GET OUT

Jesus told Nicodemus that "no one can enter the Kingdom of God without being born from above."[20] Pierre Teilhard de Chardin echoed that need for continual spiritual rebirth when he likened matter to the "flesh of Christ." In his *Hymn of the Universe* he said, "Blessed be you, mighty matter, irresistible march of evolution, reality ever new-born; you who by constantly shattering our mental categories, force us to go ever further and further in our pursuit of the truth."[21] You must get out of the old divided world before you can enter the new united world, must abandon the old you before you can become a new you. Each of us must be willing to be shattered and to "repent," to undergo a change of heart and mind. That call to constant conversion is the nuclear heart of the Gospel of God. Naturally, Jesus never heard of the Gospels of Mark, Luke, Matthew or John. His was the Gospel of God. After his cousin John the Baptist had been arrested, Mark's Gospel tells us that "Jesus went about Galilee proclaiming the Gospel of God."[22] That first Gospel was written boldly in every cell and organ of his body. Its text was artistically illuminated in the color of his skin and eyes, his face and other bodily features. This original Gospel flowed from him in liquid words as well as in the blood of his veins; it was chanted by his human emotions and fears, his dreams and hopes.

The Gospel of God is inexhaustible, yet it can be the shortest of all Gospels. It can be reduced to only six words: "God is Love. Love is God."

Jesus proclaimed that divine dogma not so much by words as by living it. He had a boundless capacity for expressing love for his friends and for those who were no one's friends: sinners, social outcasts and those exiled to the margins of life. He loved them in public violation of his culture's strict religious codes so that through his flesh he could express God's loving delight in outcasts. He feasted with them not as one who came to "reform" them but as one who lustily enjoyed their company. In the process they were radically re-formed according to the pattern of the Gospel of love.

LOVE KEEPS THE LAW – LOVE BREAKS THE LAW

Jesus came saying he did not want to abolish the law but rather to fulfill it.[23] Yet he was constantly considered to be a lawbreaker, whether he was healing people on the Sabbath or befriending tax collectors, prostitutes or hated foreigners. The law the Liberator lived out in his daily lifestyle was the Spirit of the law, the law that summed up and completed the Law of Israel, the law of the uniting, all-inclusive love of God. He broadened the boundaries of the law and the common conception of God into a God of all peoples, so that all peoples became God's chosen people.

The cross is the sign of Christianity and also the sign of our liberation, since it proclaims the power of liberating love to remain loyal right to the end. The cross is the fulfillment of the law of love. It's a symbol of God in human flesh deeply loving us to the bitter end. To reflect on that kind of love holds the power to free us from shallow "good times and sunny days" loving. It can save us from capitalistic love: I'll love you as long as I get more back on my investment than I put into it. If after investing my love in you I get nothing back, then I shall depart to deposit it elsewhere.

If Love breaks the law, must it not also sometimes break promises and vows? Jesus spoke harsh words about the scribes and Pharisees, the same religious leaders who accused him of being an outlaw. He said, "They bind up heavy loads, hard to carry, to lay on other peoples' shoulders, while they themselves will not lift a finger to budge them."[24] Solemn promises and vows can be such burdens when they are made into hard-and-fast laws. What was intended to liberate love can imprison the soul and even become a life-cross. This isn't to suggest an easy way to get out of lifetime commitments, but one has to address the haunting question facing those crucified on a vow. When is it time for them to come down off the cross? They must struggle with questions like: "When does the suffering cease to be life-giving? When does my vow or promise cease being redemptive? Does God intend that all vows and promises be lifelong, even if the life and love connected to them is dead? The fidelity of loving regardless of the cost can include the painful cross of coming off the cross. As with the call to love our enemies, fidelity to vows for all of life is an *ideal,* not a law. In general, religion has watered down Jesus' sayings about not returning violence for violence. Throughout its history the church has constructed an elaborate moral dodge to allow war and has even sanctioned "holy wars" like the crusades. John McKenzie challenges the nonsense of a Just War Theory when he asks if we hold similar theories about "morally just fornication," "morally just adultery," "morally just rape," and "morally just child abuse."[25]

The Gospel of God is a great evolutionary step forward. Around thirty years old, a very mature age for his day, Jesus began actively living out the Gospel of God in his human flesh. One great step for Jesus produced the next great step for humanity. His announcement that the time of fulfillment had arrived proclaimed that it was time to grow up! The evolution of humanity required following his example of becoming a fully mature human being. In the process, Jesus showed us how to escape the prison of merely being human to become Godlike. That very same Gospel of God he lived out is seeded in your flesh and body! Yet loving *á là Calvary,* faithful regardless of the loss, is only possible for mature lovers. Follow him, and so dare to live as fully as you can God's enfleshment in you. This is truly good news for those daring enough to live out a spirituality of liberation.

CONCLUSION

Chapter Two will be on a Spirituality of Liberation that flows out of a theology of Christ as Liberator. Before you turn to the next chapter, however, spend some time prayerfully pondering what you will find on the next page. At the end of each chapter in this book will be a section called an *Inventory of Escape Tools and Unshackling Reflections*. This section contains various aids, tools and techniques for the art and spirituality of escaping, including quotations about the theme of the chapter, diverse freeing devices and exercises, prayers for escapees, questions for pondering, parables and stories.

Chapter One Inventory of Escape Tools and Unshackling Reflections

(See pages 17-22 for Chapter One Escape Tools.)

Appendix Two: Chapter Two Complete

A Spirituality of Liberation

For many, spirituality implies an activity concerned with the spirit-soul that's separated from the body and material reality. Spirituality is usually defined in terms of exercises for nourishment of the soul: prayer, meditation, acts of asceticism, devotions and religious reading. However, I'd like to propose a definition that liberates and expands that one-dimensional understanding: A spirituality is a lifestyle flowing out of your beliefs.

The content, style and organization of our daily lives are usually the expression of some core belief. And our core, organizing beliefs gravitate around what we consider most important in life, whether money, sex, success, religion or health. If our keynote belief is that money is the center of our universe and the source of happiness and power, then our life will be structured around money. From morning until night your daily life will revolve around thinking about, making, saving and investing money. Our "spiritual" reading will focus on the Dow Jones reports, the *Wall Street Journal* and magazine articles about stocks and the financial markets.

THE CENTER OF OUR UNIVERSE

Everyone has a spirituality or lifestyle that revolves around some core belief. What's yours? Do you desire a truly transforming, liberating spirituality that will inject zest and happiness into your life, one that will enrich you today and create vital, abundant tomorrows into infinity? If you do, consider a spirituality of liberation with this core-organizing belief:

> I believe God is enfleshed in my body
> and is revealed by my every action.
> I believe I live in the midst of
> the unfolding Reign of God,
> which envelops me and all creation.

The consequences of such a core belief would be revolutionary, as is demonstrated by the life of Jesus of Galilee. When he made it an essential requirement to "believe in the good news," he prefaced it with the need to "repent,"[1] to be willing to undergo a radical transformation of heart and mind. Many believe in the good news, but few experience any significant change in their lives. That will be the case even in giving your belief to the United Cosmos of God if you only give intellectual or theological ascent, as if it were simply a dogma. Dogmas such as the perpetual virginity of Mary the Mother of God normally have little if any consequence in peoples' daily lives. Core beliefs, on the other hand, deeply impact the way we organize our day, our money, our time, our choices. Why do so many orient their lives around other things than the one Jesus made his nucleus-belief? Well, it takes courage to live his lifestyle: Only the brave of heart accept his invitation to "Come, follow me"[2] and live out the Gospel of God enfleshed in their hearts, minds, souls and bodies.

GOD WITH SKIN

Ronald Rolheiser writes, "The incarnation is not a thirty-three year experiment by God in history, a one-shot, physical incursion into our lives. The ascension of Jesus did not end, nor fundamentally change, the incarnation. *God's physical body is still among us. God is still present, as physical and as real today as God was in the historical Jesus* (emphasis mine). God has skin, human skin, and physically walks on this earth just as Jesus did."[3]

I'd like to suggest that you read this quotation again. Read it slowly, preferably out loud. Rolheiser's words are worthy of daily reflection since they challenge us to put flesh, our flesh, onto our core creedal belief that the Word of God became flesh in Jesus. Christmas is far too rich for only one day or one season. The feast of the Word becoming flesh should be celebrated throughout the year. Those who daily desire to live that awesome mystery present in their flesh might consider giving a Nativity crib a permanent place in their domestic shrines. Strangely, it seems that the conventional custom of boxing up our Christmas cribs along with other decorations and storing them out of sight until next year makes it easier to be a Christian. Perhaps being freed of having to see that sacred reminder gives us permission to behave as mere humans.

Spirituality and life itself are easier if one is simply a churchgoer. Belonging to a church merely requires performing certain religious practices such as Sunday worship and abstaining from certain actions. Discipleship is different — and difficult. Loyal disciples who believe in the United Enchanted Era of God know how that faith radically changes the orbit of their daily lives. As Ronald Rolheiser suggests, experiencing the wonder, enchantment and liberation of such a Gospel lifestyle requires being a *Carnal* rather than a *Vegetarian* Christian.

VEGETARIAN AND CARNAL CHRISTIANS

By *Vegetarian Christians* I mean those who are anti-flesh. They are Christians who find the enfleshment of God in Jesus and in the world to be too vulgar — to be x-rated — so they "angelize" the Incarnation. They believe God is present in the world, but in some mystical or spiritual sense and not in any really fleshly human, carnal way. These Vegetarian disciples believe that God is present in a transcendental Christ dwelling in the heavens and perhaps in selective places like churches, golden tabernacles and monstrances, but certainly not in beer joints, dance halls or Pizza Huts.

Carnal Christians are those followers who believe in the radical good news that the Incarnation-Embodiment of God began in the full humanness of Jesus of Galilee and that it continues to be enfleshed in us and in all of life. Carnal Christians experience God's presence in sacred places and holy rituals, but also in secular places and in all human activities of life, including the sexual. Believing Carnal Christians cannot imagine *any* place or human act where the Divine Mystery is not fully present.

Following the admonition to "pray always" is thus easier for Carnal Christians. If every dimension of human existence is radioactive with the sacred, then being anywhere and doing anything can lend itself to prayer. A sure principle of the spiritual life is: The God we believe in is the God we will experience. What we believe about the divine mystery is critical to our experience of God. Flatworld prayer looks up when praying to God. The belief that God lives upstairs in heaven has direct consequences for our behavior and prayer. It greatly limits the scope of our spiritual life and makes very difficult the practice of the ceaseless prayer to which the Apostle Paul called all disciples.[4] Carnal Christians thus make better escaped prisoners than the Vegetarian variety since they practice an all-encompassing spirituality.

WATCH AND PRAY

Prayer is not an optional exercise for those longing to be free. Indeed, praying daily is critical for our liberation. The command of our Savior-Liberator, "Watch and pray,"[5] is imperative for recognizing escape routes from what imprisons us. As St. Paul added, we are never to cease using the great escape tool of prayer if we wish to enjoy the "glorious freedom of the children of God."[6]

Paradoxically, however, nonstop liberating prayer requires that we stop praying! At least we need to avoid the practice of G.B.E. Prayers: Golden Book End Prayers. These are the typical prayers that begin and end the day, meetings, meals or religious functions. While these holy bookend prayers are a way to dedicate the activities they initiate and conclude, generally everything in between them is all practical and businesslike. Stop using G.B.E. Prayers if they "excuse" you from staying open to the divine activity in the midst of all your undertakings! Employ them only as rituals of awareness to remind you to fill your tasks and affairs with ceaseless prayer.

Pray ceaselessly, for example, while you eat. Meal prayers are one of the last traditional times in modern life that many people still begin with prayer. Indeed, beginning a meal with a blessing — with grace — is a rich and holy tradition. Liberational spirituality, however, strives to make the entire meal — from soup to nuts, from the blessing to dessert — prayerful. Being prayerful at meal times means being fully present to the food you eat — to its texture and color and taste — with an abiding sense of gratitude. It means remaining attentive to the various needs of those with whom you share the meal and to the presence of the Invisible Guest always present whenever Christians break bread together. Ceaseless meal prayers require constant loving attention to everything connected with the meal, from the preparation to the cleaning of the dishes. At a restaurant, the melody of the meal prayer should play throughout the occcasion in the form of loving attention to those serving the meal and removing the empty dishes as well as to the food and the people at the table. While these attendants are usually strangers, they should not be treated as servant-robots. Such ceaseless meal prayers require the same constant attention to detail as a great acrobat walking a highwire without a net. It's no wonder that being a Carnal Christian at the table is so difficult and that most of us prefer to pray only Golden Book End Meal Prayers. Yet the effort is worth the cost for the freedom it brings. First, it liberates us from greed and gluttony and self-absorption and whatever tends to ensnare us and cut off our connection to God. In the process it keeps us open to the continual flow of divine gifts in the present moment.

We do not just pray *to* God! Whenever we are open-eyed to God's presence, we are praying. So practice being open-eyed: "Watch and pray."[5] This watching is looking for and acknowledging the presence of the divine mystery cleverly camouflaged as the common. Every time we pray silent or spoken prayers, we are ushered into the presence of God. As such, ceaselessly praying is a constant act of consecration since it makes every aspect of life holy, allowing the presence of the Invisible Divine One to be enshrined in our daily world, in others, ourselves and life itself.

Never say "Amen." Consider concluding your spoken prayers with a favorite of those old Saturday afternoon cliff-hanger movie thrillers: "To be continued!" To that cliff-hanger conclusion, Carnal Christians could add, "right now," making their very next action a continuation of their prayer.

THE PRAYER OF LIFELONG LIBERATION

Besides being ceaseless, the prayer of a liberating spirituality is lifelong. No one is birthed fully grown. Life is a continual process of maturing, growing toward the glorious freedom of the people of God. A frequently recycled heresy says that salvation-liberation can be achieved by a single act. For some it is the act of accepting the saving death of Jesus; for others it is the reception of baptism. As significant as those initial experiences are, they only begin the process. Salvation-Liberation, like your finger- and toe-nails, grows continuously. Unlike your fingernails, however, it does not grow effortlessly. Liberation requires focused attention and personal work to mature. And it extends to life's very last chapters, when one attempts to escape from the wrinkled prisons of declining age and finally from the dungeon of death.

THE FREEDOM OF SOLITUDE

One of Jesus' most repeated Gospel messages is "Follow me, if you wish to be free."[2] We are given a window into the Liberator's lifestyle by the frequency of his retreating to be alone and to pray. After his baptism and its mystical experience of the Holy, Jesus is led by the Holy Spirit into the desert and into prayer.[7] In the predawn morning before beginning his preaching ministry in Capernanum, he seeks to be refueled by time alone with God.[8] After feeding the thousands in the wilderness, as the crowds begin to press upon him to make him their king, Jesus slips away to ponder the next step in his life.[9] Then, finally, he retreats to the Garden of Gethsemane as he struggles with betrayal and the approaching passion of his death.[10]

It's no accident that Jesus chooses those times of challenge and crisis for concentrated, solitary prayer. For private prayer is the nuclear power source for evolution into Godliness. The prayer of solitude is recommended by nearly all the great spiritual masters and is an essential component of a liberation lifestyle. While complete isolation is the worst punishment employed in most prisons, solitude is actually the very opposite of isolation. Getting away in solitude from the busyness and business of daily life creates space for intimacy with the Beloved. Secretly sweet is this lover's rendezvous with the Beloved. This love time alone with God and with oneself is healthy and good for the soul-body, and it helps us access and consolidate the inner resources we need to meet the ongoing developmental challenges of life. Moreover, secret prayer is a commanded duty of a good disciple. The Great Teacher of Prayer taught, "When you pray, go into your inner room and pray *in secret* to God."[11]

DESERT APART OR GETAWAY PRAYER

You don't need a desert to pray Desert Apart Prayer. According to Belden Lane, to enter the primal place of solitary prayer requires only an easy two-part escape tool: "Stay in one place and be still."[12] These two simple aspects of desert solitude are no more difficult today — and no less challenging — than they were two thousand years ago. While we may experience more stress factors and more crunch time, the average middle class person today probably has greater opportunities to create such quiet places to be still. We can be alone in the bathroom, a bedroom, a corner in the basement or even outside while taking a walk. And even though it's in motion, our automobile can provide a rolling desert retreat for quiet and reflection.

Like skin, solitude prayer grows on us. Spending time apart from others often seems unnatural and uncomfortable at first. Practice not only makes it more comfortable and natural, but also helps us develop an appetite for self-quarantine. Thus cultivated, solitude holds a key to liberation. This is especially true for those of us living in a noisy society addicted to constant talking, our television sets perpetually turned on, our souls assaulted by the drone of uninterrupted background music and now by the demand for incessant computer communication. Silent solitude is a teacher that frees us from feeling guilty when we don't engage in conversation while riding with a loved one in a car or sitting together in a living room. Silent solitude with God, who doesn't talk, liberates us from shallow chatter and opens us to a fullness of communication. Such prayer liberates us from the need to be always talking in order to feel in contact with another person. Good communication between friends and spouses is an absolute necessity. Good silent communication between spouses and friends may be even more necessary. The ability to be lovingly speechless expresses the contentment and the joy, the confidence and the comfort of a deeply committed companionship. It frees our energies to be truly present to the other and increases our capacity for deeper, more essential communication.

Similarly, just sitting and doing nothing is freeing. Empty and unproductive God-time liberates us from another contemporary addiction: Being Useful. Addicts of the powerful social drug BU get hooked very early in life. Being Useful is a narcotic given to children at an early age when they are praised and valued for being helpful around the house. Along with parents, BU drug pushers include teachers, coaches, pastors and, indeed, all of society. As the great grandchildren of the industrial revolution, all of us seem to be addicted to the need to feel valuable by being productive and useful. Social critic Ivan Illich said, "The emptiness of the desert makes it possible to learn the almost impossible: The joyful acceptance of our uselessness."[13]

Useless Prayer is basic training in a spirituality of liberation. Even if we are able to engage in this joyful, unproductive prayer for only a few minutes, an hour or, wonder of wonders, an entire day, it is critical training for our elder years. This will be particularly true if the last of those elder years involve an extended stay in a nursing home. Many BU drug addicts find retirement intolerable. They suffer painfully from withdrawal when they are no longer needed at work or "useful" to society. Perhaps the worst marriage is not wedding the wrong partner but marrying our identity to our work or profession. When we see ourselves in terms of our work, retirement becomes the torture chamber of no-identity. Blessed are those who in their middle years find enjoyment in periods of being useless, for they shall find delight in their idle elder years.

Rabbi Nachman and Rabbi Jesus agreed. The saintly Rabbi Nachman of Bratzlva wrote a prayer that can inspire us to seek solitude in the way that Rabbi Jesus did. His prayer would make a good agenda planner prayer for each of us. He prayed:

> Grant me the aptitude to be alone:
> each day to be outdoors
> a little while alone
> among the trees and grasses,
> among all that grows,
> and to stay there alone
> and enter into prayer,
> to talk with the one
> to whom I belong.

THE DANGER OF PRIVATE PRAYER

Yet we might wonder, "Is not secret-private prayer egoistically dangerous?" Especially in this contemporary age that encourages prayer groups, shared prayer and public prayer, we might easily suspect that praying alone — whether outdoors or in the secret of our inner rooms — can lead to a self-centered God-and-me attitude. We might fear that private prayer can imprison us.

Yet, at the same time, truly private prayer is impossible! Even if we're in complete solitude, hidden away in a prayer closet, we can't pray privately if we strive to live in God's United Kindom, a kin to the other members of the Body of the Risen One. There is no such thing as purely individual prayer if we pray consciously as a living branch on the Vine of Christ. When Jesus' disciples begged, "Teach us how to pray," he gave them a recipe for interconnected prayer. The Lord's Prayer repeats the small neon-flashing word "us" four times.[14] "Give *us* our daily bread," not *me*. "Forgive *us*," "lead *us*" and "deliver *us*." It's no accident that Jesus used that small two-letter word. It repeatedly reminds us of his United Kingdom. In fact, in Matthew's Gospel Jesus presents us with the Lord's Prayer right after instructing us to pray in private, indicating that even our most solitary prayer is to have a communal breadth.

JESUS EXCOMMUNICATES HIMSELF

Though Jesus was frequently excommunicated by the scribes and Pharisees and ultimately, at the time of his death, by the whole Sanhedrin, we've seen how often Jesus excommunicated himself. In fact, freedom requires excommunication — a unique self-excommunication from normal communication with others. Holy Excommunication involves freely being cut off from physical or electrical contact with others. While Jesus did this repeatedly, separating himself from his community, going alone to deserted places, he did not need to do so to find God. The Gospels show how he found God embodied in his friends, in sinners, in social outcasts and those society and religion had exiled to the margins of life. He whose very person is Holy Communion enjoyed holy companionship with God while eating and drinking with those banished by others, in the process of telling them stories about God's New Era. In this way he appears to have practiced magic. He lived in the Enchanted Kingdom when he saw God not only in the beautifully shaped, the handsome and charming but also in the ugly, misshapen and unpleasant.

Did Jesus' secret prayer times sharpen his ability to see beneath appearances to the Glory hidden within? In his experiences of solitude the Liberator provides for us that kind of pattern of prayer. Perhaps the main ingredient of a successful liberating spirituality is the awareness that solitude experiences are essential endeavors. They are needed if we are to be present to God in ourselves so that we might be more present to God in others and in our work and daily life. Those who get away in a healthy manner ultimately return to their families more truly themselves, more lovable and more loving. Good getaway prayer recyles us, making us more committed to our spiritual evolution, to works of justice and compassion.

HOLINESS

A saint is another name for an escaped prisoner. Multi-millionaires and billionaires are products of a lifestyle revolving around the core belief that money is the most important thing in life. When lived with passion and dedication that belief often produces a very wealthy person. A saint is the product of a lifestyle lived with passion around a core belief in the Enchanted Kin/Kingdom of God. *Saint* is one of those words that sticks in our throats. Most people would be too embarrassed to designate sainthood as their destination in life. Yet Leon Bloy, a French author of the twentieth century, said, "The greatest sadness is not to become a saint."[15] The purpose of any spirituality is to create a saint, a Godlike person, one who is holy. Indeed, God, in the book of Leviticus, commands us to be holy as God is holy.[16]

As with prayer, becoming a saint is not an option. Holiness is not some elite state reserved for a select few. Because it has a long history of being identified with renunciation of this world, of marriage and sexual love, holiness usually feels out of reach for the ordinary layman or woman. If you question this statement, scan the list of the saints of the church and you will find it almost exclusively composed of religious men and women who have taken vows impossible for the married layperson. The root of the Hebrew word for "holy" means *set apart* or *separate*. It is used to describe God as well as those places, persons and things that have been set apart, dedicated to God. The "Holy" signifies that which is tremendous, fearful and absolutely other than created reality — and thus unattainable by normal humans.

The work of holiness is acting in a Godlike way. Indeed, that sounds totally out of reach — or at least like a long and difficult process.

Over the centuries spiritual writers and leaders have made it hard work by prescribing a long list of renunciations from the pleasures of the world as well as requiring long years of penitential purification and prayer and the guidance of spiritual teachers. As a result, few of us seriously consider striving for such an inaccessible goal. Holiness, we conclude, is best left to the religious aristocracy, while simply getting to heaven is the goal for common folk.

Yet God tells us, "Be holy as I your God am holy,"[16] and that command is neither impossible nor optional. The Holy was embodied in the full humanity of Jesus to show to us what is expected in each of us and what is possible with enough grace and desire. If holiness requires separation from the world, then God would have made the world one big monastery. The word *monk* comes originally from the Greek *monakhos*, meaning *solitary*. But the good news of the Gospel tells us it is not necessary to separate ourselves from the world, marriage, sexual love and the marketplace to be holy. If this is not true, then the Gospel is not the Good News.

If God is enfleshed in our bodies and our world, then the widest path to holiness is to be found in our daily duties and the ordinary activities of our lives. Often these common activities seem so mundane and unprayerful it's no wonder we would question how they can be ways to grow in holiness. Moreover, those who live as daily inhabitants of God's Enchanted Cosmos are graced with a gift of inner eyesight by which they glimpse God invisibly hidden in everything. Like those who are sight-impaired, they must see by the use of other senses, by touching God with a braille-like faith.

Those Christians whose belief includes the Presence of Christ in the Holy Eucharist, in the Communion of the Lord's Supper, already practice such inner vision. They see beyond the bread and wine to what is embodied beneath their appearance and taste. As citizens of God's Enchanted and United World, they need only expand this faith capability beyond the table of the Eucharist, out into the world and ultimately into the whole cosmos. If we do in life what we do in Holy Communion, we will be living the Gospel of God.

Another way for holiness to be able to move from the invisible to the touchable was offered by the fourteenth century German mystic Meister Eckhart. His simple prescription for becoming holy was: "Do the next thing you have to do with your whole heart and find delight in doing it."[17] This way is easy to remember but extremely difficult to practice. Yet following Eckhart's simple formula is another way to pray ceaselessly. Doing everything with all our heart and soul and enjoying it as much as we can is an effective way for the desire for holiness to saturate the very fabric of our lives.

CONCLUSION

Saints are those who open themselves fully to the Divine Reality and then fill every task with all of themselves. Saints strive to enjoy — to have fun — doing everything. Saints do everything with passion. Ultimately, saints are escaped prisoners freed from a whole range of vain and shallow pursuits, from greed, gluttony, self-preoccupation, idle chatter, busyness and even the need to be useful. Saints are freed to live the abundant, fruitful, enchanting life of the Kindom of God.

Perhaps a lifestyle of the Gospel of God requires only the courage to organize our daily life around the belief that the Time of God has arrived at our doorstep. A liberation spirituality not only promotes an attitude of ceaseless prayer, it may also carefully cultivate organized times and forms of prayer till they become more and more frequent, if not ceaseless. By such daily structured times of prayer and spiritual nourishment, we can evolve into holiness; we can grow naturally toward a fully developed prayer life. In any case, holiness is not a supernatural state, it is the natural state of everyone created by the Holy One.

Chapter Two Inventory of Escape Tools and Unshackling Reflections

(See pages 26-31 for Chapter Two Escape Tools.)

Notes

The Beginning: Are You Free?

1. See Luke 4: 18.
2. Matthew 4: 19.
3. Matthew 11: 28.
4. See Matthew 16: 24.
5. John L. McKenzie, *Dictionary of the Bible* (Milwaukee: Bruce Publishing Co., 1965), p. 761.

Chapter One Condensed: Jesus the Liberator-Prisoner

1. See Hebrews 4: 15.
2. Mark 1: 15.
3. Robert Barron, *And Now I See: A Theology of Transformation* (New York: Crossroad, 1998), p. 132.
4. Matthew 4: 19.
5. Joseph Cardinal Ratzinger, *Instruction on Certain Aspects of the "Theology of Liberation,"* p. 169, cited in the appendix of Juan Luis Segundo, *Theology and the Church* (Minneapolis: Winston Press, 1985).
6. Ibid., pp. 170-174.

Chapter Two Condensed: A Spirituality of Liberation

1. Belden Lane, *The Solace of Fierce Landscapes: Exploring Desert and Mountain Spirituality* (New York: Oxford University Press, 1998).
2. Mark 14: 38.
3. Romans 8: 21.
4. Leon Bloy, as cited in Donald Nicholl, *Holiness,* (New York: Paulist Press, 1987).
5. Leviticus 11: 45.
6. Meister Eckhart, cited in Donald Nicholl, *Holiness,* p. 106.
7. Isaiah 43: 18-19.
8. Matthew 13: 52.
9. Juan Luis Segundo, *Theology and the Church, A Response to Cardinal Ratzinger and a Warning to the Whole Church* (San Francisco: Harper & Row, 1987), p. 53.
10. Henri Cardinal de Lubac, ibid., p. 156.
11. See Matthew 26: 26.

Chapter Three: Timelock Prison

1. Mark 1: 15.
2. Donald Nicholl, *Holiness,* p. 76.
3. Psalm 46: 11.
4. Matthew 5: 8.
5. Romans 8: 21.
6. See, for example, Matthew 13: 57; Matthew 14: 5; Luke 7: 16; Luke 24: 19; John 9: 17.

Chapter Four: The Great Primal Prison

1. The dates used are taken from Diarmuid O'Murchu, *Reclaiming Spirituality* (New York: Crossroad, 1997). In his book *Thread of Life,* Roger Lewin proposes that upright walking humans first appeared four million years ago and thinking humans two million years ago.
2. Anne Foerst, "In the Beginning Is the Brain," *Spirituality & Health*, Spring 2000, p. 22.
3. *The Dhammapada: The Sayings of the Buddha*, trans. Thomas Byrom (New York: Vintage Books, 1976), p. 3.
4. Hebrews 4: 12.
5. Romans 10: 6.
6. Mark 7: 15, 21-23.
7. Matthew 5: 21-22.
8. Luke 4: 18.

Chapter Five: Wounded Heart Prison

1. Luke 6: 28.
2. *The Dhammapada: The Sayings of the Buddha*, p. 50.
3. 1 Thessalonians 5: 16-18.
4. Quoted by Elizabeth Lesser in *The New American Spirituality*, cited in *Spirituality & Health*, Winter, 2000, p. 30.
5. 2 Corinthians 5: 18-19.
6. See Luke 23: 34.
7. 1 Corinthians 12: 26.
8. See 1 Peter 4: 13.
9. Matthew 18: 22.
10. Cited in Jeffrey Moses, *Oneness: Great Principles Shared by All Religions* (New York: Fawcett Columbine, 1989), p. 72.

Chapter Six: Angerville Prison

1. Paul Jordon-Smith, "Seven (and More) Deadly Sins," *Parablola*, Vol. X, Number 4, Winter 1985, pp. 34-39.

2. Matthew 5: 22.

3. Psalm 37: 8.

4. Mark 3: 1-6.

5. Mark 11: 12-17.

6. 1 Timothy 2: 8.

7. Ephesians 4: 26.

8. Cited in Jeffrey Moses, *Oneness*, p. 56.

9. Ibid., p. 57.

10. Ibid., p. 57.

11. *The Dhammapada: The Sayings of the Buddha*, p. 4.

12. See Matthew 5: 39-44.

13. Cited in Jeffrey Moses, *Oneness*, p. 73.

14. Sam Horn, *Tongue Fu! How to Deflect, Disarm and Defuse Any Verbal Conflict* (New York: St. Martin's Press, 1996).

15. George Bernard Shaw, cited in *Bartlett's Familiar Quotations*, Justin Kaplan, ed., (Boston: Little, Brown and Company, 1992), p. 570.

16. Ralph Hodgson, cited in *Bartlett's Familiar Quotations*, p. 611.

Chapter Seven: The Jail of Impatience

1. See John 14: 8-9.

2. Matthew 16: 21-23.

3. Ephesians 4: 2.

4. 1 Corinthians13: 4, 5, 7.

5. Galatians 5: 16.

6. Galatians 5: 22.

7. Romans 15: 5.

8. Cited in Jeffrey Moses, *Oneness*, p. 57.

9. Sam Horn, *Tongue Fu!*

10. Thomas De Quincey, from "Murder Considered as One of the Fine Arts," cited in *Bartlett's Familiar Quotations*, p. 454.

11. *The Dhammapada: The Sayings of the Buddha,* p. 59.

Chapter Eight: Blue Dragon Dungeon

1. Matthew 5: 3-12; Luke 6: 20-26.

2. Bruce Malina and Richard Rohrbaugh, *Social Science Commentary on the Synoptic Gospels* (Minneapolis: Fortress Press, 1992), p. 48-49.

3. John McKenzie, *Dictionary of the Bible,* p. 84.

4. Philippians 4: 4-7.

5. 1 Thessalonians 5: 16-18.

6. Richard Lovelace, "To Althea: From Prison," cited in *Bartlett's Familiar Quotations*, p. 267.

7. Matthew 25: 40.

8. Klauser, Henriette Anne, *Write It Down, Make it Happen: Knowing What You Want — and Getting It!* (New York: Scribner, 2000).

Chapter Nine: The Great Escape Keys
of Gratitude and Discipline

1. 1 Thessalonians 5: 16-18.

2. Luke 18: 16-17.

3. David Steindl-Rast, *Gratefulness: The Heart of Prayer* (Mahwah, N.J.: Paulist Press, 1990).

4. Philippians 4: 6.

5. Timothy Miller, *How to Want What You Have: Discovering the Magic and Grandeur of Ordinary Experiences* (New York: Avon Books, 1996).

6. Psalm 104: 30.

7. Katra and Russell Targ, *The Heart of the Mind* (New World Library, 1999).

8. George Soares Prabhu, cited in Janina Gomes' review of Keith D'Souza's "The Dharma of Jesus" in *The National Catholic Reporter*, Vol. 36, No. 37.

9. Luke 1: 28.

10. Luke 1: 46-47.

11. Luke 17: 17.

12. *The Dhammapada: The Sayings of the Buddha*, p. 3.

13. Cited in Jeffrey Moses, *Oneness*, p. 21.

14. Frederic and Mary Ann Brussat, *Spiritual R$_X$,* *(New* York: Hyperion, 2000), pp. 104-106.

15. Cited in Jeffrey Moses, *Oneness*, p. 21.

16. Mark 5: 18-20.

CHAPTER TEN: THE PENITENTIARY OF FEAR

1. See, for example, Matthew 6: 31-34 and Matthew 28: 10.

2. Barron, *And Now I See,* p. 5.

3. Matthew 19: 5.

4. Christian Wertenbaker, "Awakening the Emotions," *Parabola*, Fall 1998.

5. Ibid.

6. John and Claire Whitcomb, *Oh Say Can You See* (New York: William Morrow Co., 1987).

7. See Mark 3: 21. Mark records how the family of Jesus came to "seize him," saying, "He is out of his mind."

8. John 8: 32.

9. See Matthew 24: 34.

10. Matthew 10: 28.

11. Matthew 16: 26.

12. Luke 1: 74.

13. 1 John 4: 16-18.

14. Hebrews 13: 5-6.

15. Hebrews 10: 30-31.

16. Thomas Wolfe, *Look Homeward Angel* (New York: Scribner, 1997), p. 1.

17. Romans 8: 15-16.

18. Romans 8: 21.

19. 2 Corinthians 3: 17.

20. See Matthew 6: 25-34.

21. Psalm 23: 1, 4-6.

22. Luke 12: 25.

23. See Matthew 7: 24-27.

24. See Luke 14: 31.

25. See Matthew 10: 16.

26. Baron, *And Now I See,* pp. 4-5.

27. Henri Nouwen, cited in Bill Dunphy, *In the Mean Time*, an as-yet unpublished manuscript.

28. Cited in Jeffrey Moses, *Oneness*, p. 96.

29. Ibid.

30. *The Dhammapada: The Sayings of the Buddha*, p. 123.

31. Luke 12: 7.

32. Melinda Muse, *I'm Afraid, You're Afraid: 448 Things to Fear and Why* (New York: Hyperion, 2000).

CHAPTER 11: THE PRISON OF PREJUDICE

1. Rodney Collin, *The Mirror of Light* (New York: Random House, 1983).
2. Luke 6: 37.
3. Matthew 25: 33-34, 41.
4. See Matthew 15: 21-28.
5. Edward O. Wilson, "Vanishing Before Our Eyes," *Time* Special Edition, April-May, 2000.
6. Hebrews 13: 2.
7. Matthew 25: 35, 38-40.
8. See Matthew 22: 39-40; Leviticus 19: 18.
9. Matthew 7: 1.
10. Galatians 3: 28.
11. Mark 1: 11.
12. Steward Brand, author of *The Clock of the Long Now, Time* Special Edition, April-May 2000.
13. Romans 13: 11-12.
14. 1 John 4: 18.
15. See Matthew 6: 3.
16. Romans 15: 7.

CHAPTER TWELVE: WORKHOUSE PRISON

1. Robert Hendrickson, *QPB, Encyclopedia of Words and Phrase Origins* (New York: Facts on File, Inc., 1997), p. 575.
2. See Genesis 3: 16-19.
3. See Genesis 2: 15-16.
4. *The Church in the Modern World*, cited in Anthony E. Gilles, *People of God: A History of Catholic Christianity* (Cincinnati: St. Anthony Messenger Press, 1983), p. 184.
5. Ronald Rolheiser, *The Holy Longing,* (New York: Doubleday, 1999), p. 32.
6. Teilhard de Chardin, cited in Henri De Lubac, *Teilhard de Chardin: The Man and His Meaning* (New York: American Library, 1965), p. 78.
7. John 4: 34.
8. John 6: 27-29.
9. See John 13: 12-17.
10. See Donald Nicholl, *Holiness*, p. 106.
11. Diarmuid O'Murchu, *Quantum Theology* (New York: Crossroad, 1998), pp. 28-29.

12. Cited in Donald Nicholl, *Holiness*, pp. 101-102.

13. *Mrs. Bryrne's Dictionary of Unusual, Obscure and Preposterous Words* (Seaucus, N.J.: Citadel Press, 1974), p. 71.

14. See Romans 13: 14; Galatians 2: 20.

15. John 9: 4.

CHAPTER THIRTEEN: THE GREAT ESCAPE KEY OF DELIGHT

1. 1 Thessalonians 5: 16-18.

2. Jon Sobrino, *Jesus the Liberator* (New York: Orbis Books, 1993), p. 24.

3. Francis X. Weiser, *Handbook of Christian Feasts and Customs* (New York: Harcourt, Brace and Company, 1958), p. 69.

4. See John 15: 1-11.

5. Jon Sobrino, *Jesus the Liberator*, pp. 69-72.

6. Romans 14: 17.

7. James: 1: 2-4.

8. 1 Peter 1: 6-8.

9. Cited in Jeffrey Moses, *Oneness*, p. 24.

10. Ibid., p. 25.

11. This story originally appeared in Edward Hays, *The Ladder* (Leavenworth, Kans.: Forest of Peace Publishing, 1999), pp. 85-87.

12. Luke 15: 8-9.

13. Luke 15: 4-6.

14. See Luke 15: 11-32.

CHAPTER FOURTEEN: THE SACRED PENITENTIARY OF RELIGION

1. Anne Foerst, "In the Beginning Is the Brain," *Spirituality & Health*, Spring 2000, p. 22.

2. Diarmuid O'Murchu, *Reclaiming Spirituality*, pp. 53-55.

3. Ibid., pp. 39-40, 46-51.

4. Ibid., p. 57.

5. William I. Thompson, *The Time Falling Bodies Take to Light* (New York: St. Martin's Press, 1981), pp. 124-197. I have telescoped Thompson's treatment of corralling cattle with the walled city of civilization and acknowledge his insights in my material.

6. Teilhard de Chardin, cited in Henri De Lubac, *Teilhard de Chardin: The Man and His Meaning*, p. 33.

7. See John 2: 19.

8. See Judges 16: 23-30.

9. See Matthew 23: 23-27.

10. Mark 7: 6-7.

11. James 1: 27.

12. See, for example, Mark 2: 5.

13. See Luke 15: 20-22.

14. Matthew 6: 12.

15. St. Augustine, *Sermo 272, In die Pentecostes Postremus; Ad Infantes, de Sacramento, vol. 38,* cited in Ronald Rolheiser, *The Holy Longing,* p. 88.

16. See Matthew 18: 22.

17. *The Church in the Modern World*, No. 17.

18. *Declaration on Religious Freedom*, No. 22.

19. John 10: 10.

20. Galatians 3: 28.

21. In 1832, Pope Gregory XVI's encyclical *Miari Vos* condemned democracy and modern thought.

22. Matthew 23: 4.

23. *Lumen Gentium*, cited in Anthony E. Gilles, *People of God*, pp. 201-202.

24. 1 Thessalonians 5: 16-18.

25. Jean-Pierre de Caussade, *Self Abandonment to Divine Providence,* translated by Algar Thorold (London: Burns, Oates & Washbourne, Ltd., 1952).

26. See Mark 4: 26-29.

27. Matthew 6: 31-34.

28. Luke 4: 19.

29. See Acts, chapter 10, particularly 10: 34-35.

30. Romans 8: 15.

31. Mark 14: 38.

32. Mark 14: 37.

33. Ched Myers, *Binding the Strong Man* (Maryknoll, NY: Orbis, 1988), pp. 253-255, 365.

34. Mark 9: 29.

35. Ernest Becker, *The Denial of Death,* (New York: Macmillian, 1973), p. 1.

36. Ibid., p. 5.

37. Romans 8: 26.

38. Romans 8: 26-27.

39. Revelation 21: 5.

40. Isaiah 43: 19.

41. Daniel J. Boorstin, *The Creators* (New York: Vintage Books, 1992), pp. 140-141, 146.

42. William Short, O.F.M., *Chicago Studies*, December 1998, Vol. 37. #43, p. 278.

CHAPTER FIFTEEN: OLD AGE PRISON

1. Barbara Kantrowitz, "The Road Ahead, A Boomer's Guide to Happiness," *Newsweek*, April 3, 2000. pp. 56-60.

2. Malcolm Cowley, "The View From 80," *Songs of Experience: An Anthology of Literature on Growing Old,* edited by Margaret Fowler and Priscilla McCutcheon (New York: Ballantine Books, 1991), p. 3.

3. Matthew 10: 28.

4. Luke 12: 15.

5. Luke 12: 20-21.

6. John 10: 10.

7. Michael Talbot, cited in Diarmuid O'Murchu, *Quantum Theology,* p. 164.

8. Luke 11: 9.

9. Henry Miller, *Supertalk*, an interview with Digby Diehl, cited in Malcolm Cowley, *Songs of Experience*, p. 49.

10. Ibid., p. 51.

11. Maurice Goudeket, "The Delights of Growing Old," cited in Malcolm Cowley, *Songs of Experience*, pp. 95-96.

12. Paul Zindel, *The Effects of Gamma Rays on Man-in-the-Moon Marigolds* (New York: Bantam Books, 1970), pp. 1-2.

13. John J. McNeill, "Both Feet Firmly Planted," *The National Catholic Reporter*, April 14, 2000, pp. 22-23.

14. Fred Warshofsky, "The Methuselah Factor," *Modern Maturity*, November-December 1999.

15. Jamake Highwater, *The Primal Mind,* (New York: Penguin, 1981), p. 13.

16. Gene D. Cohen, "$C = ME^2$, The Creativity Equation That Could Change Your Life," *Modern Maturity*, March-April 2000, pp. 32-36.

17. Ibid., p. 34.

18. Bruce Malina and Richard Rohrbaugh, *Social Science Commentary on the Synoptic Gospels,* p. 41.

19. John 14: 15, 18.

20. Luke 22: 19.

21. Matthew 28: 20.

22. John 21: 18-19.

23. Teilhard de Chardin, cited in Henri De Lubac, *Teilhard de Chardin: The Man and His Meaning*, p. 35.

24. Teilhard de Chardin, *The Divine Milieu* (New York: Harper & Row, 1968), p. 89.

25. William Wordsworth, *The Complete Poetical Works* (New York: Bartleby, 1999).

26. Freyda Stark, *The Journey's Echo* (London: J. Murray, 1963).

27. Maurice Goudeket, "The Delights of Growing Old," cited in Malcolm Cowley, *Songs of Experience*, pp. 95-96.

28. John 3: 30.

29. Teilhard de Chardin, cited in Henri De Lubac, *Teilhard de Chardin: The Man and His Meaning*, p. 88.

30. Abbe Francisque Cimetier, ibid., p. 111.

31. John J. McNeill, "Both Feet Firmly Planted," *The National Catholic Reporter*, April 14, 2000, pp. 22-23.

32. Bernard Berenson, *Sunset and Twilight: Songs of Experience,* Fowler and McCutcheon, eds. (New York: Ballantine, 1991), pp. 121-123.

33. *Tao Te Ching*, Gia-Fu Feng and Jane English, trans. (New York: Vintage Books, 1972), p. Seventy-Six.

CHAPTER SIXTEEN: THE PRISON OF DEATH AND THE TOMB

1. This is an adaptation of the work of Spilka, Stout, Minton and Sizemore in "Death and Personal Faith: A Journal of Scientific Study of Religion," *The Psychology of Religion* (Englewood Cliffs, NJ: Prentice-Hall, 1973), p. 135.

2. See John 12: 24-26.

3. See Mark 5: 21-24, 35-43.

4. Mark 1: 15.

5. Matthew 16: 24.

6. John 10: 10.

7. Willem Berger, *The Last Achievement,* originally published in Dutch under the title *Pastorale Begeleiding,* translated by M. Ederveen (London: Grail, 1974), p. 32.

8. Ibid.

9. Teilhard de Chardin, *The Divine Milieu* (New York: Harper & Row, 1960), p. 82.

10. Mark 15: 34.

11. Matthew 4: 19.

12. See, for example, Mark 2: 5.

13. Henri Nouwen, as quoted in Willem Berger, *The Last Achievement,* p. 22.

14. Willem Berger, *The Last Achievement,* p. 24.

15. Vachel Lindsay, *The Rag and Bone Shop of the Heart: Poems for Men,* R. Bly, J. Hillman and M. Meade eds. (New York: HarperCollins, 1992), p. 102.

16. Ernest Becker, *The Denial of Death*, p. 53.

17. Ibid., p. 57.

18. Ibid., p. 55.

19. Ibid., p. 57.

20. John 8: 32.

21. Mark 13: 33.

22. Luke 21: 34.

23. Mark 13: 36-37.

24. John 9: 4.

25. Matthew 6: 25.

26. Matthew 7: 14.

27. Matthew 16: 25.

28. Matthew 16: 26.

29. Luke 12: 15.

30. John 6: 35.

31. John 6: 63.

32. John 6: 63.

33. John 14: 6.

34. Luke 23: 43.

35. Karl Graf Durckheim, "The Voice of the Master," *Parabola,* Fall, 1990.

36. Luke 4: 18.

37. Wisdom 1: 13-14; 2: 23.

38. Teilhard de Chardin, *The Divine Milieu,* pp. 88-89.

39. Ibid., pp. 89-90.

40. Luke 23: 46.

41. Sherwin Nuland, "Taking Back the End of Life," A.A.R.P. Bulletin, September, 2000, pp. 18-20.

42. See John 14-17; 19: 26-30.

43. Matthew 10: 23.

44. Ernest Becker, *The Denial of Death*, pp. 86-87.

45. See Matthew 27: 3-10; 1 Samuel 31: 1-6.

46. Hans Kung, *Dying with Dignity* (New York: Continuum, 1995), p. 23.

47. Ibid., pp. 30-31.

48. Ibid., p. 128.

49. Matthew 6: 10.

50. Ephesians 1: 23.

51. *Tao Te Ching*, Gia-Fu Feng and Jane English, trans., p. Fifty.

52. Susan Trott, *The Holy Man* (New York: Riverhead Books, 1995), pp. 29-30.

Appendix One: Chapter One Complete — Jesus, the Liberator of Galilee

1. John L. McKenzie, *Dictionary of the Bible* (Milwaukee: Bruce Publishing Co., 1965), p. 761.

2. Luke 1: 68-77.

3. Matthew 1: 23.

4. Matthew 21: 9.

5. Psalm 49: 8-9.

6. Leviticus 25: 47-49.

7. See Leviticus 27: 9-18.

8. Leviticus 25: 54.

9. Luke 4: 18-19.

10. John 15: 13.

11. John L. McKenzie, *Dictionary of the Bible*, p. 725.

12. See Hebrews 4: 15.

13. Luke 2: 12.

14. See Matthew 5-7.

15. See Matthew 18: 3.

16. Mark 1: 15.

17. Robert Barron, *And Now I See: A Theology of Transformation* (New York: Crossroad, 1998), p. 132.

18. Thomas Moore, *The Re-Enchantment of Everyday Life*, cited in James Conlon, *Ponderings from the Precipice* (Leavenworth, Kans., Forest of Peace Publishing, 1998), p. 84.

19. See Luke 23: 46 and Matthew 27: 46.

20. John 3: 5.

21. Pierre Teilhard de Chardin, *Hymn of the Universe* (New York: Harper & Row, 1961), p. 68.

22. Mark 1: 14.

23. See Matthew 5: 17.

24. See Matthew 23: 4.

25. John McKenzie, *The Civilization of Christianity* (Chicago: Thomas More Press, 1986), pp. 125-127.

26. Joseph Cardinal Ratzinger, *Instruction on Certain Aspects of the "Theology of Liberation,"* p. 169, cited in the appendix of Juan Luis Segundo, *Theology and the Church* (Minneapolis: Winston Press, 1985).

27. Ibid., p. 170-174.

APPENDIX TWO: CHAPTER TWO COMPLETE
– A SPIRITUALITY OF LIBERATION

1. Mark 1: 15.

2. See Matthew 4: 19.

3. Ronald Rolheiser, *The Holy Longing: Search for a Christian Spirituality*, p. 79.

4. Thessalonians 5: 17.

5. Mark 14: 38.

6. Romans 8: 21.

7. Mark 1: 12.

8. Mark 1: 35.

9. Mark 6: 46.

10. Mark 14: 32.

11. Matthew 6: 6.

12. Belden Lane, *The Solace of Fierce Landscapes: Exploring Desert and Mountain Spirituality* (New York: Oxford University Press, 1998).

13. Ivan Illich, cited in Belden Lane, *The Solace of Fierce Landscapes*.

14. Matthew 6: 9-13.

15. Leon Bloy, cited in Donald Nicholl, *Holiness,* (New York: Paulist Press, 1987).

16. Leviticus 11: 45.

17. Meister Eckhart, cited in Donald Nicholl, *Holiness,* p. 106.

18. Isaiah 43: 18-19.

19. Matthew 13: 52.

20. Juan Luis Seguno, *Theology and the Church, A Response to Cardinal Ratzinger and a Warning to the Whole Church* (San Francisco: Harper & Row, 1987), p. 53.

21. Henri Cardinal de Lubac, ibid., p. 156.

22. Matthew 26: 26.

Bibliography

BARRON, ROBERT. *And Now I See: A Theology of Transformation.* New York: Crossroad, 1998.

BECKER, ERNEST. *The Denial of Death.* New York: Macmillian, 1973.

BERGER, WILLEM. *The Last Achievement.* London: Grail, 1974.

BLY, ROBERT, JAMES HILLMAN, AND MICHAEL MEADE, eds. *The Rag and Bone Shop of the Heart: Poems for Men.* New York: HarperCollins, 1992.

BOORSTIN, DANIEL. *The Creators: A History of Heroes of Imagination.* New York: Vintage Books, 1992.

BRUSSAT, FREDERIC AND MARY ANN. *Spiritual R_X: Prescriptions for Living a Meaningful Life.* New York: Hyperion, 2000.

BYRNE, JOSEFA HEIFETZ. *Mrs. Byrne's Dictionary of Unusual, Obscure, and Preposterous Words.* Secacus, N.J.: Citadel Press, 1974.

Chicago Studies, December 1998, Vol. 37, No. 3. "The Parish in the Year 1000." Published for continuing theological development by priests of the Archdiocese of Chicago.

Chicago Studies, Summer/Fall 1999, Vol. 38, No. 2. "Jesus Christ for the Twenty-first Century."

Chicago Studies, Spring 2000, Vol. 39, No. 1. "The Mission of the Laity in the World."

DE CHARDIN, TEILHARD. *The Divine Milieu.* New York: Harper & Row, 1960.

DE LUBAC, HENRI. *Teilhard de Chardin: The Man and His Meaning.* New York: New American Library, 1965.

FOWLER, MARGARET AND PRISCILLA MCCUTCHEON, eds. *Songs of Experience: An Anthology of Literature on Growing Old.* New York: Ballantine Books, 1991.

HIGHWATER, JAMAKE. *The Primal Mind: Vision and Reality in Indian America.* New York: Penguin Books, 1982.

KAPLAN, JUSTIN, ed. *Bartlett's Familiar Quotations.* Boston: Little, Brown and Company, 1980.

KUNG, HANS AND WALTER JENS. *Dying with Dignity.* New York: Continuum, 1995.

MCKENZIE, JOHN L. *Dictionary of the Bible.* Milwaukee: Bruce Publishing Co., 1965.

MORWOOD, MICHAEL. *Tomorrow's Catholic: Understanding God and Jesus in a New Millennium.* Mystic, Conn.: Twenty-Third Publications, 1997.

MOSES, JEFFREY. *Oneness: Great Principles Shared by All Religions.* New York: Random House, 1989.

MYERS, CHED. *Binding the Strong Man.* Maryknoll, N.Y.: Orbis Books, 1988.

NICHOLL, DONALD. *Holiness.* New York: Paulist Press, 1987.

O'MURCHU, DIARMUID. *Reclaiming Spirituality.* New York: Crossroad, 1997.

O'MURCHU, DIARMUID. *Quantum Theology: Spiritual Implications of the New Physics.* New York: Crossroad, 1998.

Parabola, Spring 1990. "Time & Presence.

Parabola, Fall 1990. "Liberation."

Parabola, Winter 1991. "The Golden Mean."

Parabola, Fall 1995. "Language and Meaning."

Parabola, Winter 1996. "Play & Work."

Parabola, Summer 1999. "Prayer & Meditation."

Parabola, Fall, 1998. "Fear."

Parabola, Winter 1999. "Evil."

ROLHEISER, RONALD. *The Holy Longing: The Search for a Christian Spirituality.* New York: Doubleday, 1999.

SEGUNDO, JUAN LUIS. *Theology and the Church: A Response to Cardinal Ratzinger and a Warning to the Whole Church.* Minneapolis, Minn.: Winston Press, 1985.

SPILKA, BERNARD. *The Psychology of Religion: An Empirical Approach.* Englewood Cliffs, N.J.: Prentice-Hall, 1985.

SOBRINO, JON. *Jesus the Liberator: A Historical-Theological View.* Maryknoll, N.Y.: Orbis Books, 1993.

SUSUKI, DAVID AND PETER KNUDTSON. *Wisdom of the Elders: Honoring Sacred Native Visions of Nature.* New York: Bantam Books, 1992.

THOMPSON, WILLIAM IRWIN. *The Time Falling Bodies Take to Light: Mythology, Sexuality & the Origins of Culture.* New York: St. Martin's Press, 1981.

WALKER, BRIAN AND HUA HU CHING. *The Unknown Teachings of Lao Tzu.* San Francisco: HarperCollins, 1992.

ZINDEL, PAUL. T*he Effects of Gamma Rays on Man-in-the-Moon Marigolds.* New York: Bantam Books, 1970.

The Graduate Author

Edward Hays graduated in the same year as the publication of *The Great Escape Manual*. In 2001, reaching the ripe age of 70, he *retired* as a Catholic priest; however, he prefers to call it a *graduation*. Retirement implies stepping down or backwards instead of advancing forward into a creative new stage of life.

This senior author continues to practice daily being "an escape artist," with the hope that his efforts at this ancient craft are contagious. His first escape was his birth in Lincoln, Nebraska, in 1931. His second was eighteen years later when his parents moved from Lincoln to Kansas City, a cosmopolitan and racially diverse city. His college and graduate study for the priesthood under the Benedictine monks at Conception Seminary provided him with novel options for escaping from the ordinary. In 1964 as a young priest in Topeka, Kansas, his escape studies were escalated by meeting a gifted Dutch escape artist, Willem Berger, a priest-psychologist studying in the United States. Father Berger became his lifelong mentor and spiritual director, who encouraged him to challenge all the chains that threatened to inhibit his freedom.

Trained to be a parish priest, his next escape came in 1971 when Archbishop Ignatius Strecker invited him to step away from parish ministry and begin a retreat center for contemplative prayer. As a preparation, the archbishop invited him to first depart on an around-the-world pilgrimage and learn about prayer by praying with all kinds of people. This experience became for him a great escape hatch by which to enter into the broader, truly catholic world that included Hindu, Buddhist, Zen and Jewish spiritualities. As a student of that great teacher, Guru Travel, his journeys in the Third World, the Near East and Asia became an escape expedition that liberated him from his provincial, Midwestern, myopic view of the world.

After 23 years as the director of a community of contemplative prayer in Easton, Kansas, the next great escape came when he accepted an invitation to be priest chaplain to the Kansas State Prison in Lansing. Paradoxically, as a priest-in-prison, by his association with the prisoners, the poorest of the poor and the outcasts of society, he escaped from the illusion that he was a free man. In his efforts to liberate his prisoner friends from the numerous prisons holding them captive while they were behind bars, he himself learned some new escape techniques.

Entering his eighth decade, he passionately pursues his escape studies with efforts to break out of the Prisons of Propriety, Convention and Social Expectations. He also home-schools himself in escaping the restrictions of old age and the greatest of all prisons, Death. His prayerful hope is that by the grace of God, Allah willing, when his Dead-Line finally arrives he will be a master escape artist. Meanwhile, he continues to enjoy writing— or, as he prefers to speak of it, *taking dictation from The Voices* — and with being involved in his other favorite art form of creating parable-paintings.

Personal Index Pages

As we said on page 9, these next eight pages have been left blank for you to compile your personal index of subjects and page numbers of passages and reflections in this book that have been meaningful for you.